HUMAN BEHAVIOR
THE ART OF SEWING
THE OLD WEST
THE EMERGENCE OF MAN
THE AMERICAN WILDERNESS
THE TIME-LIFE ENCYCLOPEDIA OF GARDENING
LIFE LIBRARY OF PHOTOGRAPHY
THIS FABULOUS CENTURY
FOODS OF THE WORLD
TIME-LIFE LIBRARY OF AMERICA
TIME-LIFE LIBRARY OF ART
GREAT AGES OF MAN
LIFE SCIENCE LIBRARY
THE LIFE HISTORY OF THE UNITED STATES
TIME READING PROGRAM
LIFE NATURE LIBRARY
LIFE WORLD LIBRARY
FAMILY LIBRARY:

THE TIME-LIFE BOOK OF THE FAMILY CAR
THE TIME-LIFE FAMILY LEGAL GUIDE
THE TIME-LIFE BOOK OF FAMILY FINANCE

THE ART OF SEWING

NOVEL MATERIALS

BY THE EDITORS OF TIME-LIFE BOOKS

TIME-LIFE BOOKS, NEW YORK

THE ART OF SEWING
SERIES EDITOR: Carlotta Kerwin
EDITORIAL STAFF FOR
NOVEL MATERIALS:
Assistant Editor: David L. Harrison
Designer: Virginia Gianakos
Assistant Designer: Robert McKee
Text Editor: Don Earnest
Picture Editor: Kaye Neil
Chief Researchers: Wendy A. Rieder, Gabrielle Smith (planning)
Staff Writers: Sondra R. Albert, Angela D. Goodman, David Johnson, Marilyn Kendig, Wendy Murphy, Sandra Streepey, Reiko Uyeshima
Research Staff: Rhea Finkelstein, Nancy Jacobsen, Laura James, Tom Lashnits, Ginger Seippel, Vivian Stephens, Jean Stratton
Art Staff: Sanae Yamazaki (art coordinator), Angela Alleyne, Penny Burnham, Patricia Byrne, Catherine Caufield, Jean Held, Jill Lossen
Editorial Assistant: Kathleen Beakley

EDITORIAL PRODUCTION
Production Editor: Douglas B. Graham
Assistant Production Editor: Gennaro C. Esposito
Quality Director: Robert L. Young
Assistant Quality Director: James J. Cox
Copy Staff: Rosalind Stubenberg (chief), Ricki Tarlow, Florence Keith, Pearl Sverdlin
Picture Department: Dolores A. Littles, Susan Hearn, Carolyn Turman
Traffic: Feliciano Madrid

THE CONSULTANTS:
Gretel Courtney taught for many years at the French Fashion Academy in New York City. She has studied pattern making and design at the Fashion Institute of Technology in New York and haute couture at the French Fashion Academy.

Annette Feldman is a knitting and crocheting designer, both for clothing and interior decoration. She is the author of several books, including *Knit, Purl and Design, Crochet and Creative Design* and *Beginner's Needlecraft.*

Tracy Kendall has for many years designed sets and costumes for commercial films and advertising. She is currently a fashion stylist.

Julian Tomchin is a textile designer who has been awarded the Vogue Fabric Award and a Coty Award of the American Fashion Critics. A graduate of Syracuse University's Fine Arts College, he has been chairman of the Textile Design Department at the Shenkar College of Fashion and Textile Technology in Tel Aviv and now teaches at the Parsons School of Design in New York.

Special consultants for this book were: Samuel and Jerome Friedman, Fur-Tempo, Ltd., New York; Gerty Gruber, a glove designer with Fownes Brothers & Co., New York; Leo Kepler, Bagatelle Creations, Inc., New York; Louis Rosenberg, Artbag Creations, Inc., New York.

Valuable assistance was provided by these departments and individuals of Time Inc.: Editorial Production, Norman Airey; Library, Benjamin Lightman; Picture Collection, Doris O'Neil; Photographic Laboratory, George Karas; TIME-LIFE News Service, Murray J. Gart; Correspondents Maria Vincenza Aloisi (Paris), Abigail Brett (Houston), Ann Natanson (Rome), Margot Hapgood and Dorothy Bacon (London), Lois Armstrong (Los Angeles), Lucille Larkin (Washington).

Published simultaneously in Canada.
Library of Congress catalogue card number 74-16950.

CONTENTS

1 CLOTHLESS CLOTHES 6

2 THE SKIN GAME 18

3 HIDES TO SEEK 94

4 TEST-TUBE TEXTILES 144

5 WHIMSICAL KNIT AND CROCHET 170

APPENDIX

GLOSSARY 183
BASIC STITCHES 184
CREDITS AND ACKNOWLEDGMENTS 189
INDEX 190

1 CLOTHLESS CLOTHES

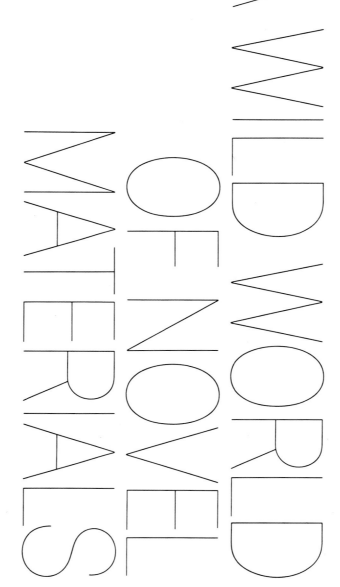

At New York's stylish Waldorf-Astoria Hotel, the ballroom was crowded with hundreds of elegant guests who had gathered to celebrate the 1966 version of The American-French Foundation's posh "April in Paris" charity ball. The blasé crowd, sitting down to a $175-a-plate dinner, had been everywhere and had seen, it thought, everything. But the fashion show that was the feature of the evening turned out to be

A WILD WORLD OF NOVEL MATERIALS

something new and different under the sun.

Each time a model clanked or slithered or jingled up from the darkened ballroom floor onto the spotlighted stage, the guests gaped in astonishment. Even the avant-garde couturier André Courrèges, who by 1964 had put women into pants and mini skirts and vinyl boots, had never dared to flaunt the likes of the weird clothing and wacky materials that four young Parisian designers brought forth that night.

Paco Rabanne, the flashy ringleader of the group, had studied to be an architect, and some of his confections appeared to have been put together with a tool kit rather than a sewing machine. Rabanne showed mini dresses of aluminum squares studded with metallic balls and linked with chains. In addition he brought on a micro-mini dress made from bits of red plastic interspersed with bits of silver; a metallic headdress that a Roman centurion might have worn proudly to a saturnalia; and a cape of ostrich feathers, held in place by Scotch tape, which, Rabanne explained, was easier and cheaper to use than stitching.

Rabanne's young women collaborators in the show were only a trifle more conservative. Emmanuelle Khanh, an iconoclast in the French ready-to-wear industry, showed a short, white quilted silk dress that might have been worn to church—but for the plate-sized magnifying mirror set just above the model's navel. Mme. Khanh herself was adorned in silver breastplates. Christiane Bailly, a former Dior mannequin, presented brown silk dresses with yokes of battered aluminum. And Michèle Rosier, an erstwhile ski fashion designer, summoned forth a model in silver shoes, stockings and hat, to match her silver plastic coatdress.

"Hmmm," said fashion-conscious Rose Kennedy, matriarch of the Kennedy clan, when the lights went on. "Interesting, but I don't believe my generation will follow."

"I hate things that clank," said Mrs. Alfred S. Levitt, the French-born widow of the builder of Levittowns. "I think they look like the tin woodman in the *Wizard of Oz.*"

"They'll rust in Miami," said one skeptic.

But outside the Waldorf, such reactions were less common. These four youthful designers had conceived a countercouture, a rebellion against the Paris Establishment —much as another generation of designers had revolted against Edwardian fashions some 50 years earlier by bringing the exotic look of the Orient to the world of Western fashion. And the newcomers succeeded. The novel materials they brought onstage that night are still enhancing the gaiety and color of life on the streets and the beaches, in homes and cocktail bars and even offices. True, these materials will never displace the classic little black dress. They are not intended to. They are mostly for fashion's fun.

As in the old parlor game, twenty questions, novel materials may be animal, vegetable or mineral—familiar stuffs of nature that have or have not been transformed beyond recognition. Or they may have been bred in laboratories by Ph.D.s who spend their days mating molecules that have never even met before. Basically, however, the novelty of novel materials lies as much in the ways they are used as in the nature of the materials themselves.

While certain materials have been novel since birth, others have been sedately conventional—but became novelties through odd and imaginative new uses. Great-grandmother's beaver coat, for example, reposing in a trunk in the attic, is certainly no novelty. But if it were recut into a swim suit it would be—although the beaver who owned it originally might not think so. The man who first recognized the far-out potential in the stodgy field of fur fashions was the Fifth Avenue entrepreneur, Jacques Kaplan, who introduced what were called fun furs in 1951. To begin with, Kaplan's fun furs were unchic pelts like wolf and hamster; later he dyed them in outrageous colors. Nowadays, even the most sedate and expensive furs, such as mink, have become fun furs. Emeric Partos, furrier for Bergdorf Goodman, has used lightweight mink skins to make pantsuits and jumpsuits. Kaplan himself has created garments in such bizarre furs as wildebeest and Manchurian weasel, and his minks are dyed in medleys of pink, yellow and blue.

Aiding and abetting the notion of novel concepts in fur, the alchemists of synthetic fabrics produce fake furs that are either strikingly realistic or delightfully different. A West German firm, in collaboration with U.S.-based Borg Textiles, has invented a machine that turns out deep-piled pelts of fake leopard, cheetah and six other furs that look as if they had come straight from the jungle—and sell for a mere nine dollars a yard. Other wizards of fakery have produced "furs" that look like nothing ever grown by an animal, and that carry kinky labels such as "Real Live Nothing" and "Critter."

Plain old leather, like conventional fur, could hardly be called a novelty material on the face of it. Men have worn leather on their backs and their hands and feet for thousands of years. But when Paco Rabanne cut it into white patches, linked them together with tiny metal rings, and converted them into jackets for the "April in Paris" ball, leather became a novel material. It became even more novel with the subsequent introduction of the strange skins, such as frog or wallaby, that are being fashioned into both apparel and accessories. And today, subtle, supple synthetic leathers with names like Ultrasuede and Leathersoft are leaders among the novelty fabrics, both for their unique textures and the original ways in which they are being made up.

Another novelty—the use of metal in clothing—actually has a history almost as ancient as that of leather. As far back as the 18th Century B.C., Minoan women wore metal corsets, probably of copper, to accentuate their bare bosoms and slim their waists. During chivalric times, chain-mail armor was *de rigueur* male sportswear—highly utilitarian, but often embellished with ornate chasings, plumes and sometimes precious metals. In 1571, for example, Don John of Austria wore a suit of golden armor to his naval victory over the Turkish fleet at Lepanto.

Today's metal clothing is as showy as Don John's—but strictly for fun. Its principal advocate is a young admirer of Paco Rabanne's with the nickname of Pop-Top Terp. Pop-Top acquired both his nickname and a thriving business when he transformed into clothing material thousands of pop-top rings from aluminum beer and cola cans he picked from the debris in Puerto Rican alleys. Terp ground down their jagged edges, linked them with silver thread, and fashioned them into long coatdresses—2,800 rings to a garment—which sold well at a San Juan department store at $350 apiece. Subsequently Terp's pop-top vests, stoles, belts and hoods caught as many fancies as his coatdresses, and have since become a novelty in Stateside boutiques.

Plastics have been prime candidates for use in the novel-material wardrobe since the end of World War II, when they began to emerge as part of the space-age spectrum of synthetic marvels.

Meanwhile, some other materials born of the space age are showing promise of becoming the most impressive—and one day, the most popular—novel materials of all. Among these is Chromel R., the fabric made of finely woven nickel and chromium fibers used in spacemen's uniforms. Flexible, superstrong and wonderfully light-reflective, it suggests almost limitless possibilities for far-out fashion. Another is Beta cloth, which looks much like new sailcloth and is totally fireproof and six times finer than silk. Its present use is limited to protective clothing for firemen and X-ray patients, but it, too, has a future in fashion. The home sewer will have to be patient for another generation or so though, until retail prices drop a bit from the original levels of more than $1,000 a yard.

Closer at hand is what may well be the very ultimate in novel materials—which Paco Rabanne suggests as appropriate for "today's woman," who, he says, "needs something clean-cut and brilliant."

What fits that formula? "A shining rubber paint that would dry into a second skin."

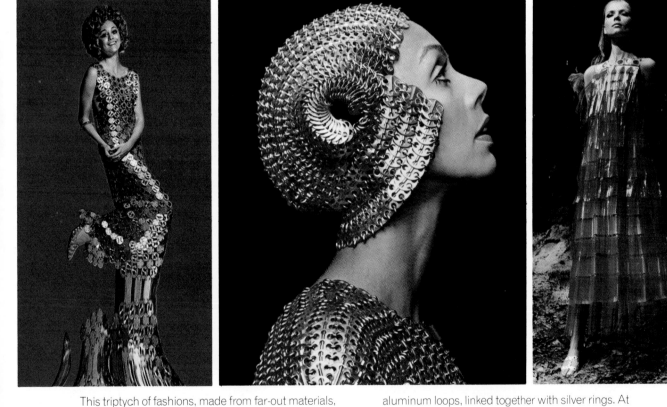

This triptych of fashions, made from far-out materials, was presented by designer Paco Rabanne at the trend-setting "April in Paris" ball of 1966. The metal-clad mermaid at left wears an evening gown made of aluminum loops, linked together with silver rings. At center is a cloche of steel chain mail with matching bolero, and at right squares of pink fluorescent plastic under a shower of shimmering plastic fringing.

New definition for some classic styles

Take a classic style, mate it with fur or leather or some other material with a novel pedigree, and the garment is newly defined. Elegance describes the ensembles here.

At left, pink suede (shown against a ranch lynx coat) adds muted vibrance to a suit; center, a Garbo-esque raincoat makes a dramatic appearance in leather-like ciré; at right, yellow-dyed mink with white trim becomes a theater jacket. Other novel fashions, casual and frankly fun, appear on the following pages.

For fun and games, a rust-red suede poncho and a beige pseudo-suede beret *(right)* are paired up for a stroll in a meadow. A pretty wisp of a monkey-fur jacket is counterpoint *(center)* to a streamlined leather skirt of cabretta. And rabbit fur, combined with faded denim *(left)*, provides mod country wear.

For casual wear, a new synthetic, pseudo suede, is tailored *(far right)* to make a tan weskit and a wine red skirt. A fox collar *(center)* matches its heather cardigan; and metallic yarns work crocheted wonders around metal disks *(above)* in a smart, unorthodox belt.

A lady in fake calfskin leans on pillars of *(from right)* suede, fake cowhide, real cowhide simulating lizard.

2 THE SKIN GAME

Suitcase—to replace leather valise that was eaten by Eskimo during story assignment to Coronation Bay, Arctic Ocean trappers' settlement. Never should have taken leather suitcase north I now know. . . . See attached Hudson's Bay Company's invoice . . . $41.09.

This startling item in a 1965 expense account of a magazine correspondent was duly honored by the publication's business

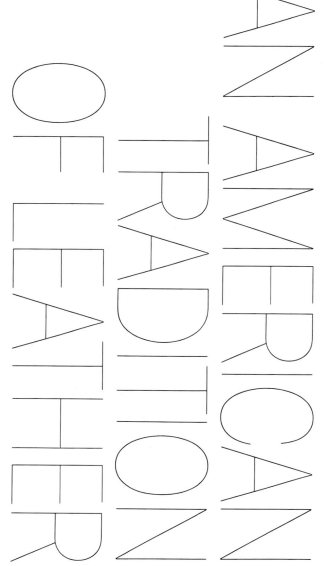

AN AMERICAN TRADITION OF LEATHER

department after the guilty Eskimo sent his confirmation by proxy from Canada's Northwest Territory: "It made marvelous soup, and Udjualuk asked me to tell you that the handle was the best part."

Though designers and the fashion public may not agree that leather is good enough to eat, they have made it a great favorite as a clothing novelty. In dozens of new guises—dyed, stretched, shirred and even simulated, paired with such unlikely partners as metal, plastic and glass, and fashioned into all manner of attire from bikinis to wedding gowns—leather has become a pacesetter in the high-flying world of fashion.

This trend to leather represents a style novelty only in the context of today, for the hide of animals has long been an essential and thoroughly American clothing material. During World War II, leather ranked seventh in the nation's list of critical products. Sixty years before that, Buffalo Bill Cody and Annie Oakley, those two symbols of the frontier, had taken their fringed and beaded buckskins to the East Coast and Europe, where they touched off an instant vogue for the look of "Le Far-Ouest."

The fact is that the real Far-Ouest look had predated Annie and Bill by at least a thousand years. From Alaska to Patagonia, leathercrafting was well known to the American Indians when the first white men arrived. On the Western plains and in the Northern forests, warrior tribes had developed the use of leather, mainly deer and buffalo skins, to a point of pervasive utility and style perhaps unmatched in any other culture. Hunting the hide-bearing game was men's work, but everything else was left to the womenfolk.

Using stone knives, they skinned the animals, scraped the hides, and then rubbed them with their preservatives made of natural fats and animal brains. The Indian woman's other tools and techniques for working the leather were equally primitive. Her rawhide sewing bag contained nothing but a buffalo-bone awl, some sinew for thread and a bone marker for tracing designs.

Yet with these simple implements she made virtually everything worn or otherwise used in the workaday life of her village. Shirts, leggings, moccasins, dresses, lodge covers, drums and a hundred other necessities and niceties of housekeeping and war sprang from her fingers. And the finished work was by no means crude or primitive, even judged by today's standards.

Shields, drums and clothing were painted with intricate designs, festooned with breadwork, and finished with tassels and fringes—all reflected in present-day leather fashions. From wooden frames and dressed skins, Indian mothers fashioned snug cradle boards, whose descendants bounce along on the backs of young women in shopping centers from Boston's Newbury Street to Union Street in San Francisco. And in winter, Indian women and girls slipped into brief underpants fashioned of baby buffalo hide that was in many ways as delicate as the synthetics that make up the most feminine briefs today.

Though pioneer women were slow to pick up either the styles or the crafts of their so-called heathen sisters, frontiersmen quickly saw the utility and comfort of the Indian's leather clothing. For some 250 years men like Meriweather Lewis, Daniel Boone, the voyageurs and other leatherstocking heroes not only wore such clothing but put it into a high place in American tradition.

Inevitably white women found themselves caught up in leathercrafting, especially on the frontier where their own labors were scarcely less demanding than those of the Indians. One such pioneer lady was

Mary Richardson Walker, an early arrival to the Oregon Territory. "This morning rainy," she noted in her diary in September 1838, ". . . Worked some in kitchen, finish making Mr. W. [her husband] lether pantaloons. Ironed." In 1841 she reported that an Indian girl had agreed to make shoes for her baby son, Cyrus. The next year her own craftsmanship had improved so that she wrote with pride: "Cut out eight pairs of shoes."

While the Mary Walkers of the West were learning ways with leather, the empty plains were filling up with herds of cattle—and with that supreme folk hero, the cowboy, whose working paraphernalia was a virtual catalogue of leather goods: chaps, vests, gloves, belts, boots, quirts, saddles, bridles, rifle scabbards, harness, holsters and sometimes even hats. Surprisingly enough, the cowboy, for all his super-American image, was a bird with borrowed feathers. The fact is that most of his leather accouterments were adopted from other men of the saddle from all over the world. The cowboy's chaps, worn to protect his legs in brush country, were introduced by Mexican *vaqueros,* who got them in turn from the old Spanish herdsmens' *chaparreras.* His boots, originally low-heeled and much plainer than the heavily ornamented cowboy boots of today, were first brought to Virginia and the Carolinas by English cavaliers and French Huguenots. His calfskin vest—so durable and comfortable that it was standard issue in the U.S. Army during World War I—dates back to the knight's leather jerkin of the age of chivalry. The same is true of the cowboy's dashing leather gauntlets, which often were handcrafted for the cowhands by Indian women. These women also fashioned other cowboy regalia, adorning garments and bridles with beaded Lone Stars, eagles or designs like swastikas (an Indian motif long before Adolf Hitler discovered it), and adding fringes or tassels.

When a working cowhand got all duded up in such garb for Saturday night, he cut a striking figure. He might wear a hand-carved leather shirt front; a necktie made of snakeskin, or perhaps a neck-encircling leather watch chain, finely plaited and tasseled, with sliding gold ferrules; a calfskin belt with a gold buckle; and a handsomely tooled holster for his gun. Some cowboys made their own finery, for many old cowhands were expert leathercrafters who spent their spare time at such rangeland scrimshaw as whittling fancy designs in their belts, boots and chaps.

With the end of the 19th Century, both the Indian and cowboy workers in leather gradually faded from the American scene. Fine leather was still handcrafted, but as the product became increasingly rare and expensive, leather clothing and accessories became an indulgence of the rich. Efforts to find a cheap and reliable imitation for leather began before the turn of the century and continued, without much success, for more than 60 years. When the synthetics looked enough like natural leather, they tended to tear or puncture easily; the ones that proved sufficiently tough usually did not look like leather. They did not "breathe" like the porous natural articles, and they made the wearer hot and uncomfortable.

At last, in 1964, laboratories began to produce promising substitutes, made from synthetic, nonwoven fibers impregnated with chemical binders. These modern fakes successfully imitated the smooth texture and porous structure of leather, and turned out to be as tough and supple as real leather. In 1972 synthetic suedes also came onto the market. Soft and smooth, these pseudo suedes can be draped and molded as flatteringly as any other high-fashion fabric.

Coincidentally, with the development of such chic synthetics, the public's passion for the leather look was growing; so the versatile substitutes became part of the boom. Honor Blackman, the sinuous "Pussy Galore" of the film *Goldfinger,* gave the trend a sensational boost by wearing a wardrobe made entirely of leather in a British television series in the early '60s. At about the same time, interest in leather clothing gripped such American designers as Bonnie Cashin and Anne Klein.

The renewed enthusiasm for leather came not just from the custom trade. For the stylish new modes in leather and leather imitators were mass-produced on advanced machinery at a price the general public could afford. By 1974 the use of leather as apparel had doubled to represent nearly 20 per cent of U.S. leather production—a signal that American women had taken leather to their hearts and, like that Eskimo, were finding it absolutely delicious.

A century-wide gap in styling accentuates the timeless versatility of leather in adapting to far-out fashions. The two duded-up Western figures are Buffalo Bill Cody and Annie Oakley, wearing costumes that set Paris on its ear in admiration of "Le Far-Ouest" in 1889. Next to Cody, wearing suede cape and snakeskin pants, is a dashing pacemaker in today's trend to leather, while the girl at right wears sleek kidskin pants and tunic.

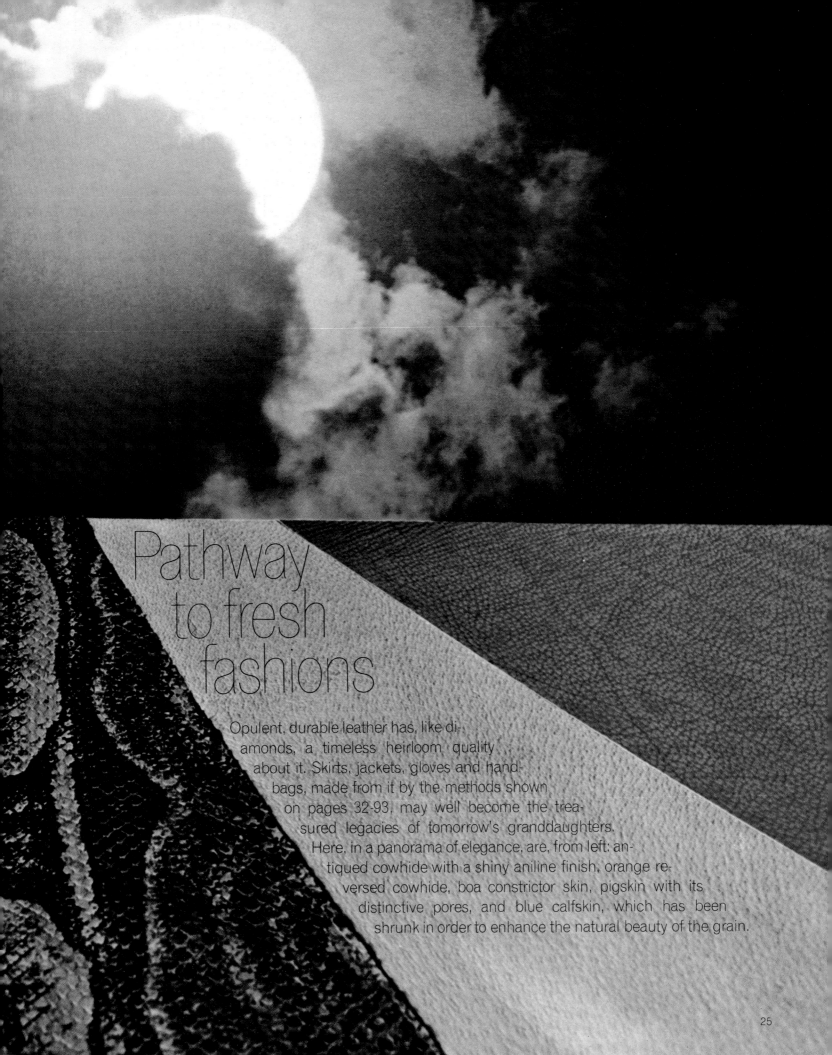

Pathway to fresh fashions

Opulent, durable leather has, like diamonds, a timeless heirloom quality about it. Skirts, jackets, gloves and handbags, made from it by the methods shown on pages 32-93, may well become the treasured legacies of tomorrow's granddaughters.

Here, in a panorama of elegance, are, from left: antiqued cowhide with a shiny aniline finish, orange reversed cowhide, boa constrictor skin, pigskin with its distinctive pores, and blue calfskin, which has been shrunk in order to enhance the natural beauty of the grain.

The new horizon for synthetics

The art of simulating real leather has come a long way from the days of the limp leatherette and brittle acryline of yesteryear. Today's new look-alikes perform like the genuine article and are easier to maintain. Versatile fake skins, like the elegant samples shown here, can be made up into a chic array of garments and accessories. From right: simulated olive green cowhide; light green sueded false lambskin; bogus boa constrictor; turquoise pseudo suede, a very drapable, easily handled synthetic; and sturdy brown imitation cowhide.

A guide to working with leathers

Once you have decided to sew with real leather or fake, there are certain basic things you should know in order to select the right material for your project. The chart on these pages outlines the characteristics of various real and synthetic leathers, and indicates the basic techniques for sewing and caring for them.

While patterns usually designate fabric measured by the yard, most leather—found at leather shops and department stores—is sold by the foot. To calculate the number of square feet of leather needed, multiply the yardage suggested on the back of your pattern for 54-inch-wide fabric by 13 1/2—the number of square feet in a piece of 36-inch by 54-inch fabric. Then add about 15 per cent to allow for wastage. The number of square feet is marked on the back of each skin.

The same rules hold for suede, which is simply the inside layer of a cowhide, pig or lambskin, specially napped and finished.

Synthetic leathers can be a real bargain: they often cost less than half the price of natural leathers. And they are versatile: fakes successfully masquerade as leathers, suedes and reptile skins.

Instructions for turning real leather and synthetics into garments of your choice are shown in the photographs on pages 38-59.

TYPE OF LEATHER	CHARACTERISTICS
COWHIDE	Whole cowhides are available in large sizes measuring from 20 to 25 square feet. From these full hides, garments such as coats, pants and jackets can be made. However, for smaller items such as hats, handbags, belts and trim, a so-called side, or half a hide, can be purchased. The choicest part of a hide is the back, where the thickness is most uniform. Cowhide comes in medium and heavy weights and offers a wide range of colors and finishes—glossy, embossed, antiqued, sueded or disguised as another type of leather or even fabric *(overleaf)*.
LAMBSKIN	Lambskin is somewhat similar in texture to cowhide, though finer. The average lambskin is smaller than cow or calfhide—about 6 to 9 square feet—and more expensive. Skins are available in light and medium weights and many colors. They can be used for a variety of garments including skirts, dresses, coats and jackets—as well as for slippers, handbags and hats. Most suedes are made from the inside skin of lambs.
PIGSKIN	Pigskin is a light- to medium-weight leather available in sueded and nonsueded finishes, and in natural and dyed colors. Most commonly it comes in natural grain, but can be embossed. Because pigskin is usually small —5 to 7 square feet—its use is generally restricted to accessories such as handbags, belts and trims.
SNAKESKIN	The smaller snakeskins, such as whip snake, are more delicate in texture than their larger cousins—boa, cobra and python. The color of the skins varies widely; even skins of the same type may have different shades. (The glossy finish on snakeskin comes from a thin layer of varnish or plastic.) Because many skins are fragile, they are practical to use only for small items such as handbags, belts, collars and appliqués.
SYNTHETIC LEATHER	Synthetic leather is usually produced as a medium-weight fabric, commonly made with a polyurethane face and a knit or woven backing. It has a slight grain, and is readily available in a wide variety of colors, with either a dull or glossy finish. Synthetic leather can be used for any garment in place of real skins—e.g., coats, vests, pants, jackets and accessories. Caution: synthetics are vulnerable to accidental punctures and may sag out of shape.
SYNTHETIC SNAKESKIN	Like synthetic leathers, snake has a fabric backing. This makes it less fragile than real snakeskins. The backing, however, also makes the fabric less pliable; thus synthetic snakeskin is best used for loose outer wear that has few darts or seams.
PSEUDO SUEDES	Synthetic suedes come in light and medium weights, and are available in a wide range of pastel and dark colors—but the fabric is relatively expensive, compared to other synthetic leathers. Lighter weights are ideal for dresses, skirts, shirts, jackets and vests. Heavyweights are good for jackets, pants and coats.

MARKING AND CUTTING	SEWING	PRESSING AND CLEANING
Mark the back of the hide with a felt-tip pen. Hold down the pattern with weights or masking tape. Cut with regular scissors, a razor blade or a mat knife guided by a metal ruler.	Machine sew, using a Size 14 or 16 leather needle and heavy-duty mercerized cotton or polyester thread. Set the machine at 7 to 10 stitches to the inch. Use paper clips to keep garment pieces together, removing them as you stitch. Glue down the seam allowances with rubber cement. For decoration, topstitch with a Size 16 needle and silk buttonhole twist. To create an even more sporty effect, put one raw edge over the other instead of turning the edges under, and make two rows of topstitches. Seams do not require finishing.	Press on the wrong side, using a pressing cloth and a dry iron set for low heat. If the finish is glossy or smooth, you can remove common spots and stains with a damp sponge; but leather with any other kind of finish should be sent to a dry cleaner.
Mark the back of the skin, using a soft, dull pencil or tailor's chalk. Hold down the pattern with masking tape. Cut with regular scissors.	Sew by machine, using a Size 11 to 14 leather needle and mercerized cotton or polyester thread. Set the machine at 7 to 10 stitches to the inch. Use paper clips to keep garment pieces together, removing them as you stitch. Glue down the seam allowances with rubber cement. If you are sewing a seam that curves, cut small Vs into the seam allowance to avoid bunching the material. For decoration, topstitch the seam, using a Size 16 needle and silk buttonhole twist.	Press lightly on the wrong side, using a cool, dry iron and a pressing cloth. With colored suedes, cover the ironing board with brown wrapping paper; otherwise the heat from the iron will cause the coloring matter to soak off onto the board. To remove small spots, use a soft suede brush, gum eraser, dry sponge, terry-cloth towel or soft bristle brush. For major cleaning, send garments made from lambskin to a dry cleaner who specializes in leathers.
Hold down the pattern with weights or masking tape; mark the skin with a felt-tip pen. Regular scissors are perfectly adequate to cut the average pigskin; but for thicker ones, to ensure straight lines, it may be necessary to use a razor blade or mat knife guided by a metal ruler.	Sew by machine with a Size 14 leather needle and polyester or heavy-duty cotton thread. Set the machine at 7 to 10 stitches to the inch. Hold garment pieces together with paper clips, removing them as you stitch. Glue down the seam allowances with rubber cement. Topstitch, using a Size 16 needle and silk buttonhole twist.	Using a pressing cloth and a dry iron set for lowest heat, press lightly on the wrong side. Like other leathers, pigskin should be dry cleaned in most cases. When the finish is smooth, however, the surface can be cleaned with a damp sponge. For dark or heavy spots, add a little mild hand soap to the water.
Reinforce the skin with iron-on interfacing such as fusable Pellon. Mark the interfaced back with a toothless tracing wheel and dressmaker's carbon paper. It is often necessary to piece several skins together to approximate the shape of your pattern. Use silk pins, making sure to insert them only in the seam allowances, as they leave holes in the skin. Cut with regular scissors.	Sew by machine, using a Size 11 to 14 leather needle and mercerized cotton or polyester thread. Set the machine for 7 to 10 stitches to the inch. Hold pieces together with silk pins inserted in the seam allowance. Glue down the seam allowances with rubber cement. The seams require no finishing.	Press on the wrong side of the skin, using a pressing cloth and a dry iron on a low setting. Too much heat removes the finish from the skin. Dry clean. For mild soiling, wipe skins clean with a damp sponge and perhaps a touch of mild hand soap.
Mark the back with a smooth-edged tracing wheel and a dressmaker's carbon. Use silk pins to attach the pattern to the fabric, making sure to insert the pins in the seam allowance. Cut with regular scissors.	Sew by machine, using a Size 14 needle and mercerized cotton or polyester thread. Set the machine for 10 to 12 stitches to the inch. When stitching, keep fabric pieces together with paper clips or silk pins inserted in the seam allowance. Remove the paper clips as you stitch. Glue down the seam allowances with rubber cement, then topstitch to ensure that the seams will stay flat.	Many artificial leathers cannot be pressed. Heat may break down the finish, causing a change in color or texture, and can even cause melting. Before pressing a garment, experiment with a scrap piece of fabric. Press on the wrong side, using a dry iron and a pressing cloth. Apply light pressure and low heat. Some synthetic leathers are machine washable; check the instructions for maintenance on the fabric label. If the fabric is not washable, dry clean.
Mark synthetic snakeskin on the wrong side with a smooth tracing wheel and dressmaker's carbon. Use silk pins to attach the pattern to the fabric, making sure to insert the pins in the seam allowance. Regular scissors are the best tool for cutting.	As with other synthetic leathers, machine sew, using a Size 14 needle and mercerized cotton or polyester thread. Set the machine for 10 to 12 stitches to the inch. Stitch as you would for other synthetic leathers.	Do not press. Some types are machine washable; check the instructions on the fabric label. If the fabric is not washable, have it dry cleaned.
Mark the back of the fabric with a smooth-edged tracing wheel and dressmaker's carbon. Like real suede, the fabric has a nap, so be sure to buy the amount of fabric recommended for a nap layout *(Appendix)* on your pattern envelope. Attach the pattern to the fabric with silk pins—which should be inserted in the seam allowance. Use regular scissors to cut the fabric.	Machine stitch, using a Size 14 or 16 leather needle and polyester thread. Set the machine for 10 to 12 stitches to the inch. Hold fabric pieces together with paper clips or silk pins in the seam allowance. Remove the clips as you stitch. Secure the seam allowances with an iron-on bonding tape. Topstitch, but set the machine for 5 to 8 stitches to the inch.	As with real leather, press on the wrong side, using a pressing cloth, light pressure and a dry iron set for a low temperature. Brush to remove any pressing marks. Pseudo suede is machine washable and can also be dry cleaned.

A many splendored steer

Almost everyone knows what plain cowhide looks like. After all, it is the most plentiful, least expensive and also the most versatile of leathers. But precious few people would recognize the bovine origins of the hide strips at right, masquerading as everything from a lizardskin to a kooky version of Harris tweed. In medium-weight hide, any or all of them would make dressy handbags and belts. In lighter weights, they could be jackets, pants or vests.

The seven strips of cowhide in this steer's profile are finished to resemble, from left: tweed, a tooled floral motif, silver lamé, ostrich, glossy antiqued leather, alligatorskin and lizardskin.

MAKING A HEM ON LEATHER

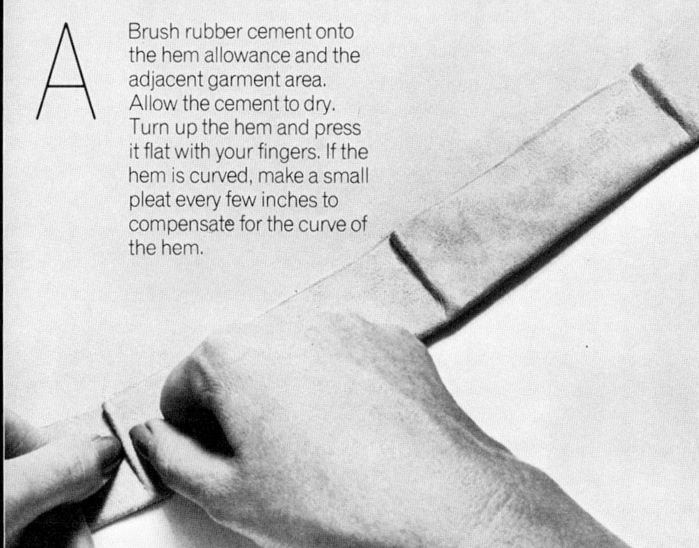

A

Brush rubber cement onto the hem allowance and the adjacent garment area. Allow the cement to dry. Turn up the hem and press it flat with your fingers. If the hem is curved, make a small pleat every few inches to compensate for the curve of the hem.

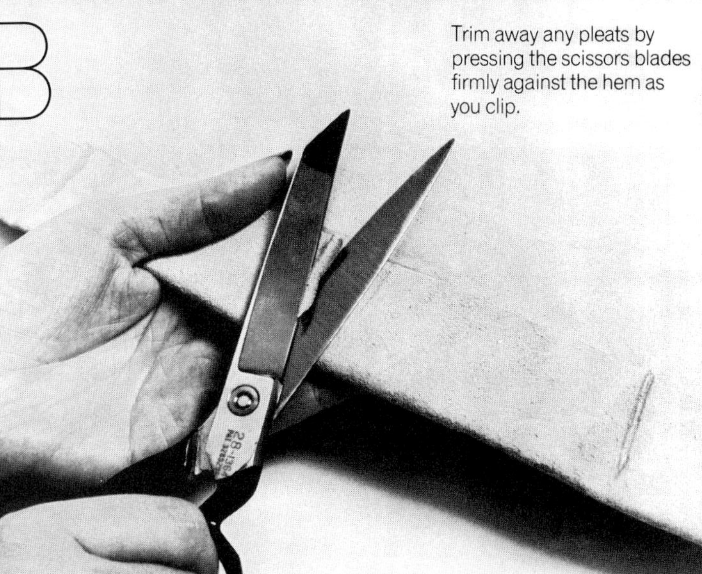

B

Trim away any pleats by pressing the scissors blades firmly against the hem as you clip.

MAKING A HEM ON PSEUDO SUEDE

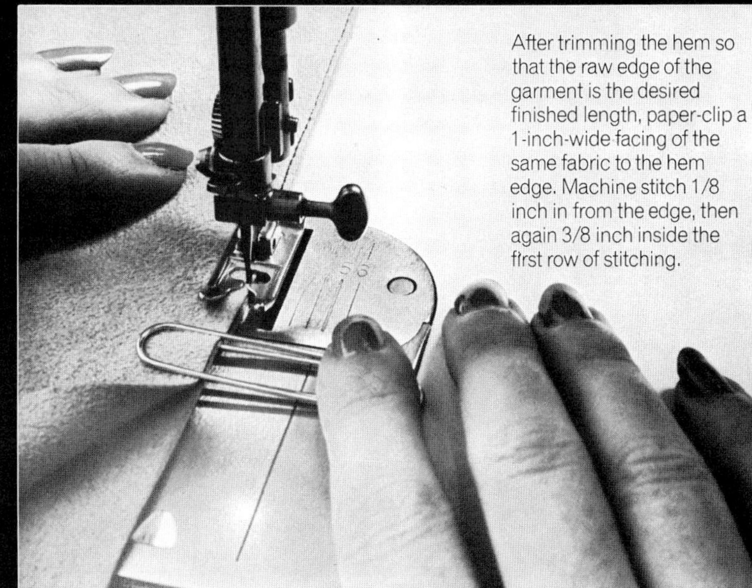

After trimming the hem so that the raw edge of the garment is the desired finished length, paper-clip a 1-inch-wide facing of the same fabric to the hem edge. Machine stitch 1/8 inch in from the edge, then again 3/8 inch inside the first row of stitching.

MAKING A HEM ON SYNTHETICS

After trimming the garment edge so that the hem is 5/8 inch deep, glue the hem up with rubber cement along the hemline marking and topstitch close to the fold. Run another row of stitching 3/8 inch from the first row to catch the raw edge.

LINING LEATHER JACKETS

Since linings must be sewed in by hand and it is difficult to work on real leather by hand, first machine stitch 1/2-inch-wide grosgrain ribbon to the raw edges of the facing inside the garment. Sew the lining to this ribbon using a slip stitch.

Techniques zippers and buttonholes

Applying zippers and buttonhole bindings to leather, synthetic skins and pseudo suedes is much easier than putting these closures onto regular fabric, because with novel materials closures are always simply glued or taped on. (Conventional basting would create needle holes.) Moreover, natural leathers and the pseudo suedes need not be turned under and hemmed; their exposed raw edges give a casual, sporty appearance to the finished garment.

The centered and lapped-seam zippers in this section are hybrid versions of the kind used with regular fabric. Lapped-seam zippers *(overleaf)* are uniquely designed for leather and pseudo suedes—and are the easiest of all zippers to apply, because cumbersome seam allowances are simply cut away.

Buttonholes for the whole leather family must be done by the so-called binding technique, since the usual machine or hand stitching would leave too many close needle holes that cut the leather. Before making buttonholes on any kind of leather, be sure to reinforce the garment with interfacing. Use iron-on interfacing on leather and pseudo suede. For synthetics, glue on the nonwoven interfacing called Pellon.

INSERTING A CENTERED ZIPPER

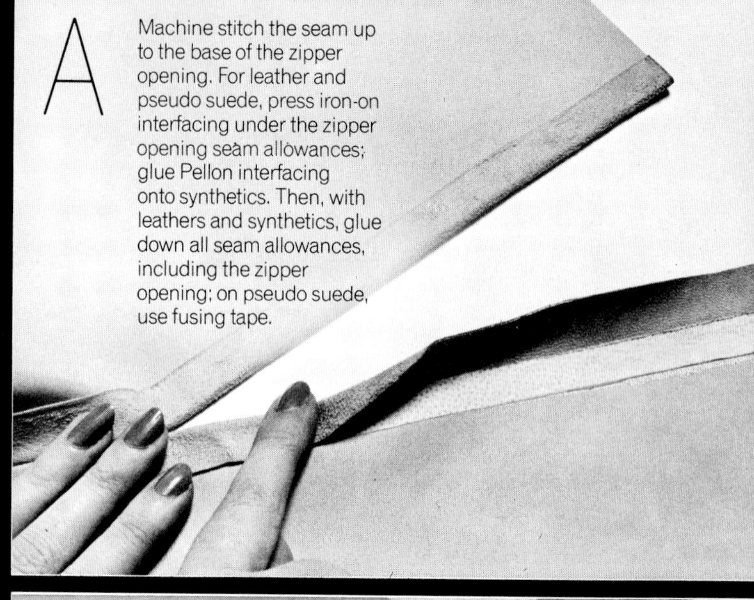

A Machine stitch the seam up to the base of the zipper opening. For leather and pseudo suede, press iron-on interfacing under the zipper opening seam allowances; glue Pellon interfacing onto synthetics. Then, with leathers and synthetics, glue down all seam allowances, including the zipper opening; on pseudo suede, use fusing tape.

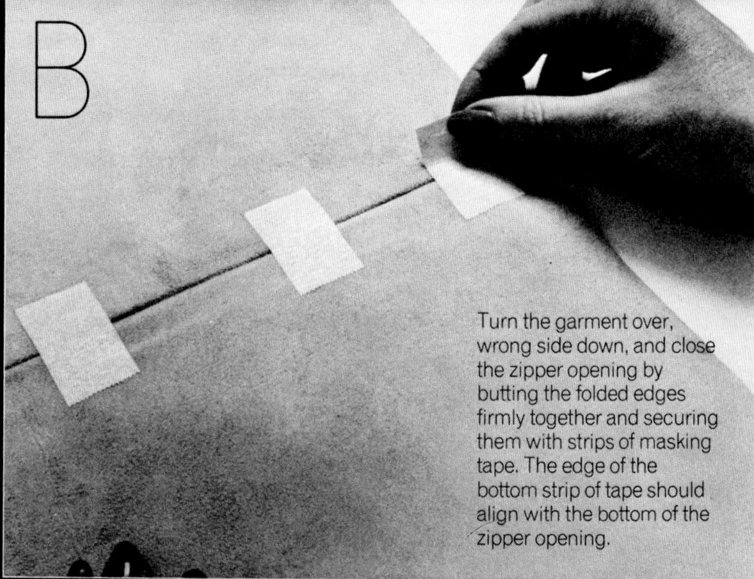

B Turn the garment over, wrong side down, and close the zipper opening by butting the folded edges firmly together and securing them with strips of masking tape. The edge of the bottom strip of tape should align with the bottom of the zipper opening.

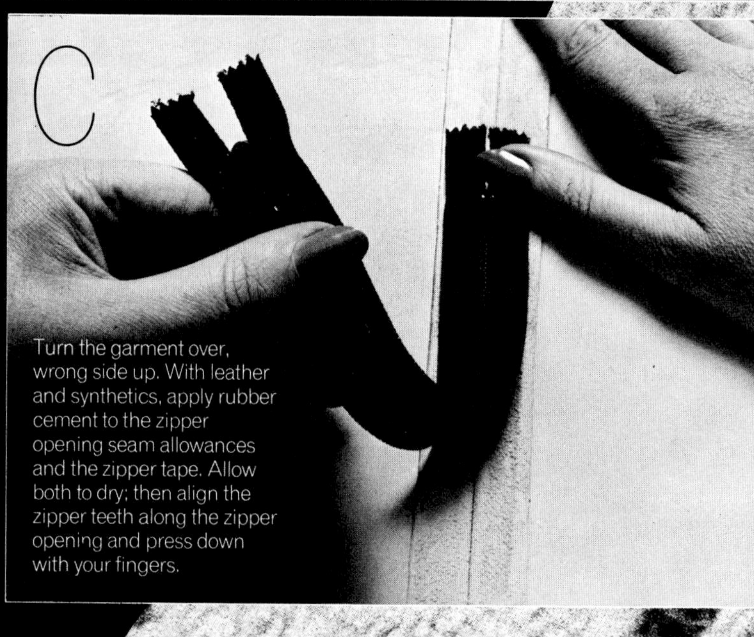

C Turn the garment over, wrong side up. With leather and synthetics, apply rubber cement to the zipper opening seam allowances and the zipper tape. Allow both to dry; then align the zipper teeth along the zipper opening and press down with your fingers.

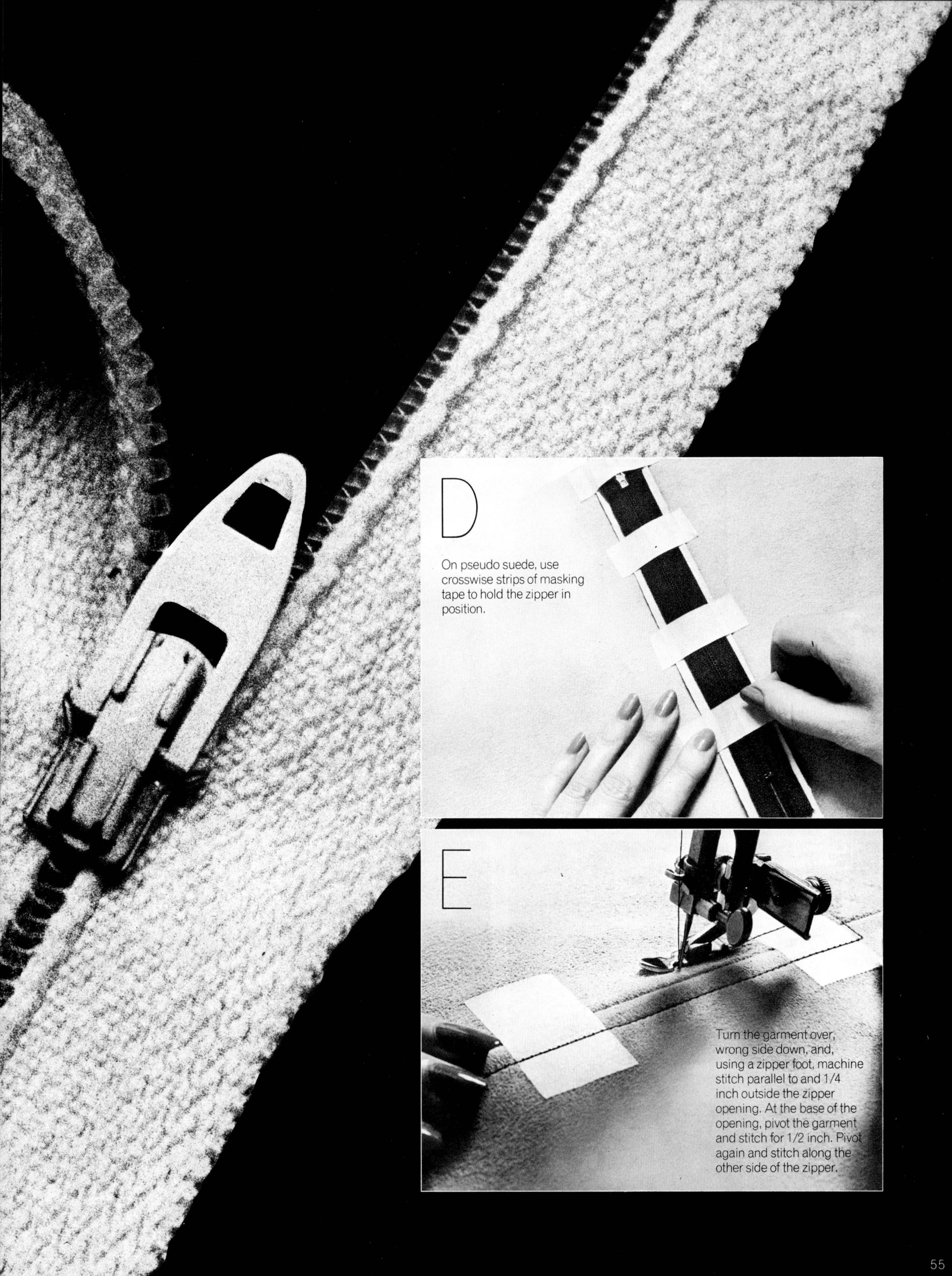

D

On pseudo suede, use crosswise strips of masking tape to hold the zipper in position.

E

Turn the garment over, wrong side down, and, using a zipper foot, machine stitch parallel to and 1/4 inch outside the zipper opening. At the base of the opening, pivot the garment and stitch for 1/2 inch. Pivot again and stitch along the other side of the zipper.

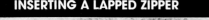

INSERTING A LAPPED ZIPPER

A

Machine stitch the garment seam up to the base of the zipper opening. Make a clip into the left-hand seam allowance 1/8 inch below the base of the zipper opening. Cut to within 1/8 inch of the seam.

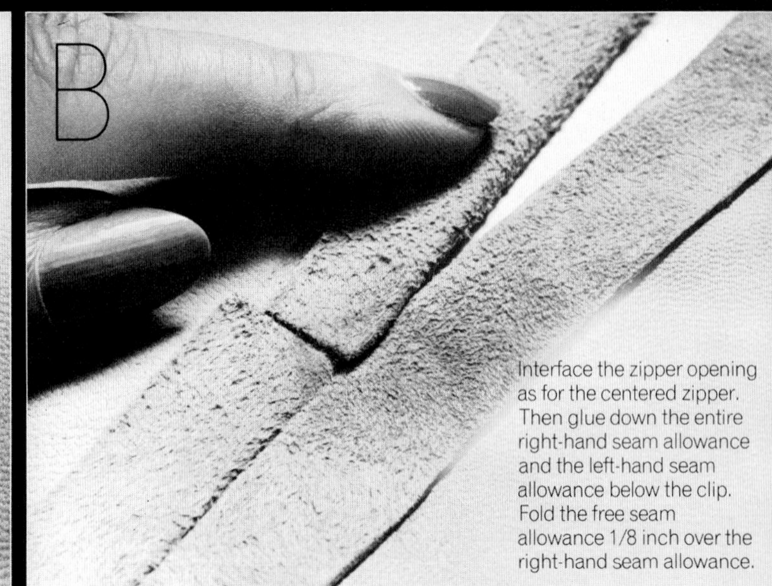

B

Interface the zipper opening as for the centered zipper. Then glue down the entire right-hand seam allowance and the left-hand seam allowance below the clip. Fold the free seam allowance 1/8 inch over the right-hand seam allowance.

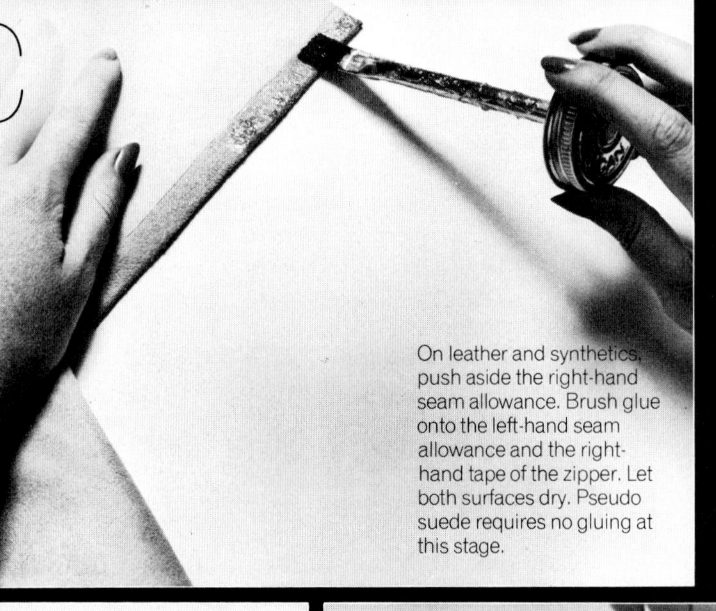

C

On leather and synthetics, push aside the right-hand seam allowance. Brush glue onto the left-hand seam allowance and the right-hand tape of the zipper. Let both surfaces dry. Pseudo suede requires no gluing at this stage.

D

Place the two glued surfaces so that the fold of the left-hand zipper opening is 1/8 inch from the zipper teeth; press down. On pseudo suede, tape the zipper to the seam allowance in the same way with masking tape.

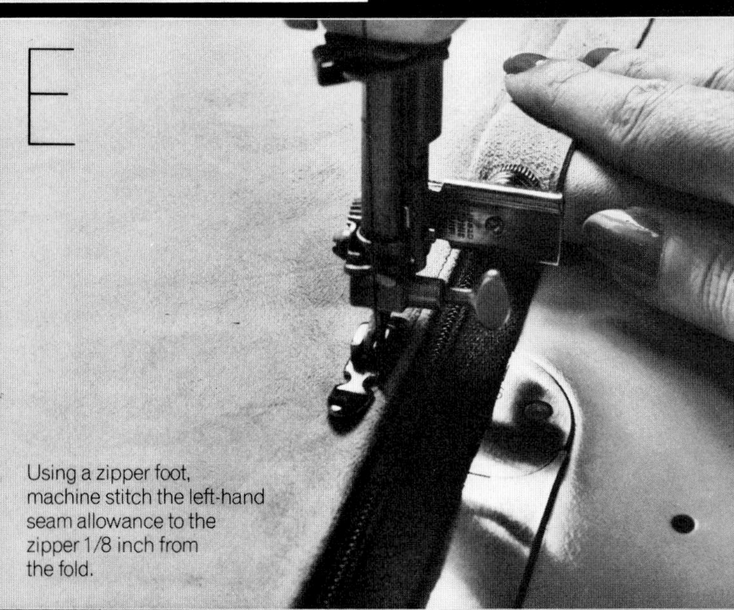

E

Using a zipper foot, machine stitch the left-hand seam allowance to the zipper 1/8 inch from the fold.

F

Close the zipper opening so that the unattached seam allowance extends 1/8 inch over the edge of the attached seam allowance. Secure it with strips of masking tape. Align the bottom strip of tape with the bottom of the zipper opening.

G

Using a zipper foot, topstitch 1/2 inch inside the fold on the overlapped edge. At the base of the zipper, pivot the garment and stitch to the seam.

INSERTING A ZIPPER IN A LEATHER OR PSEUDO-SUEDE LAPPED SEAM

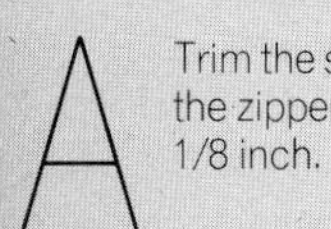

A

Trim the seam allowance on the zipper underlap to 1/8 inch.

B

On leather, glue the right-hand zipper tape to the underside of the indented zipper opening 1/8 inch from the raw edge. On pseudo suede, tape the zipper in position. Stitch as in Box E, opposite.

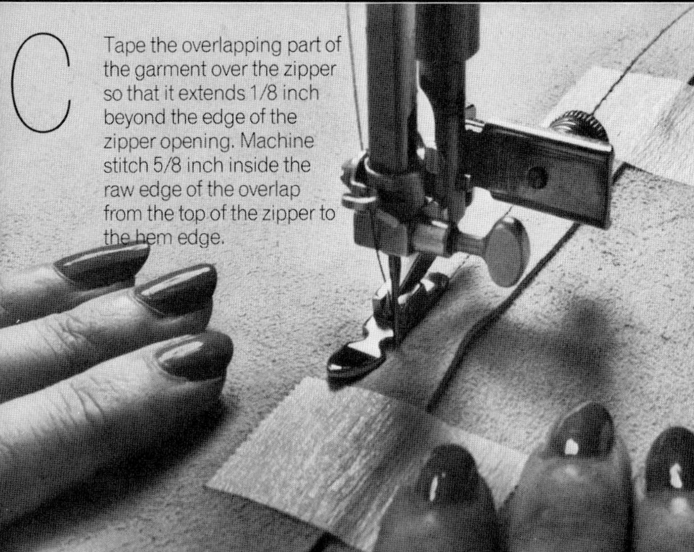

C

Tape the overlapping part of the garment over the zipper so that it extends 1/8 inch beyond the edge of the zipper opening. Machine stitch 5/8 inch inside the raw edge of the overlap from the top of the zipper to the hem edge.

D

Stitch across the bottom of the zipper, starting at the row of stitching made in the preceding step and ending 1/8 inch from the raw edge of the overlap. Pivot the garment and continue to stitch 1/8 inch inside the raw edge of the overlap to the hem edge.

MAKING BUTTONHOLES IN LEATHER

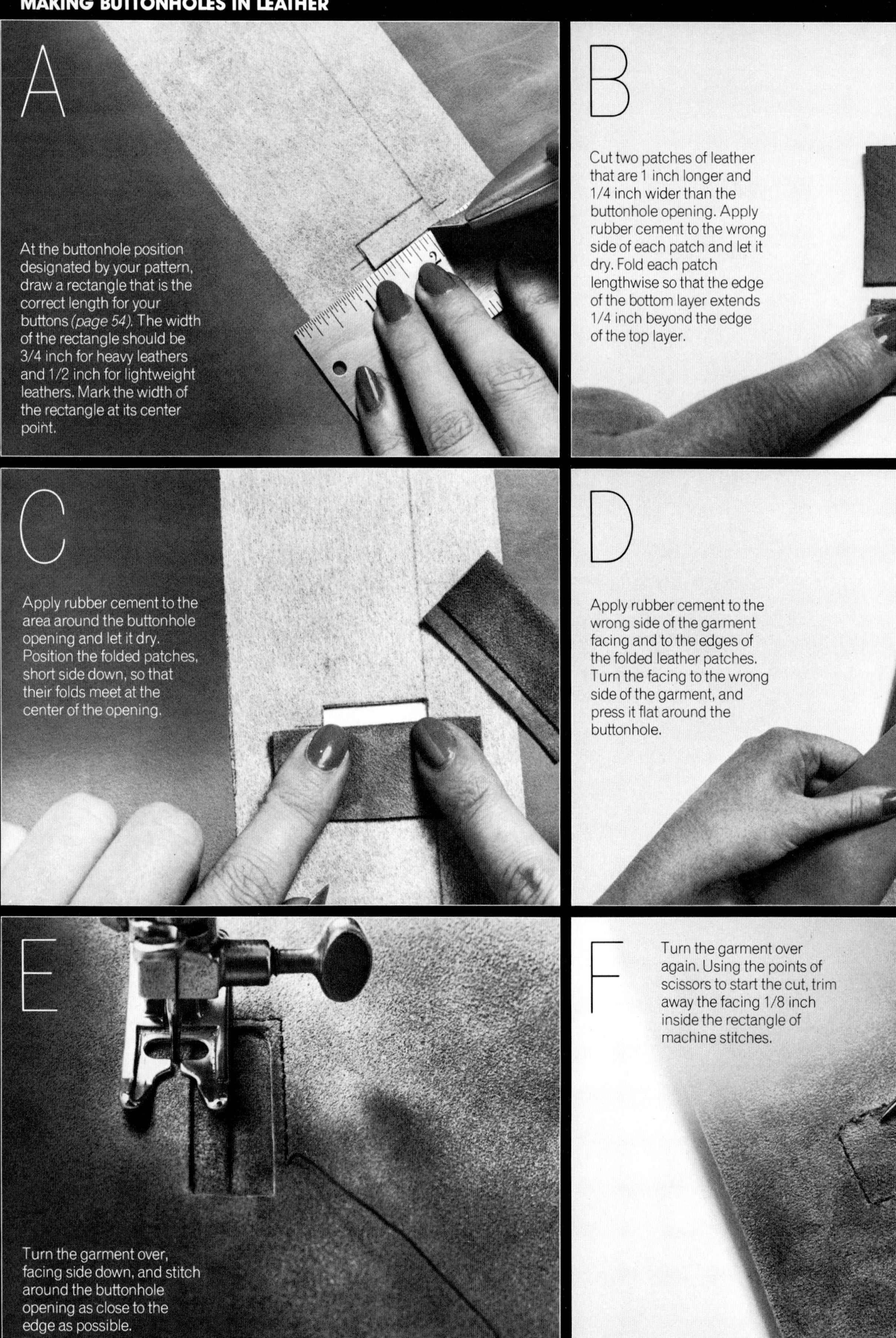

A

At the buttonhole position designated by your pattern, draw a rectangle that is the correct length for your buttons *(page 54)*. The width of the rectangle should be 3/4 inch for heavy leathers and 1/2 inch for lightweight leathers. Mark the width of the rectangle at its center point.

B

Cut two patches of leather that are 1 inch longer and 1/4 inch wider than the buttonhole opening. Apply rubber cement to the wrong side of each patch and let it dry. Fold each patch lengthwise so that the edge of the bottom layer extends 1/4 inch beyond the edge of the top layer.

C

Apply rubber cement to the area around the buttonhole opening and let it dry. Position the folded patches, short side down, so that their folds meet at the center of the opening.

D

Apply rubber cement to the wrong side of the garment facing and to the edges of the folded leather patches. Turn the facing to the wrong side of the garment, and press it flat around the buttonhole.

E

Turn the garment over, facing side down, and stitch around the buttonhole opening as close to the edge as possible.

F

Turn the garment over again. Using the points of scissors to start the cut, trim away the facing 1/8 inch inside the rectangle of machine stitches.

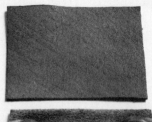

MAKING BUTTONHOLES IN SYNTHETICS AND PSEUDO SUEDE

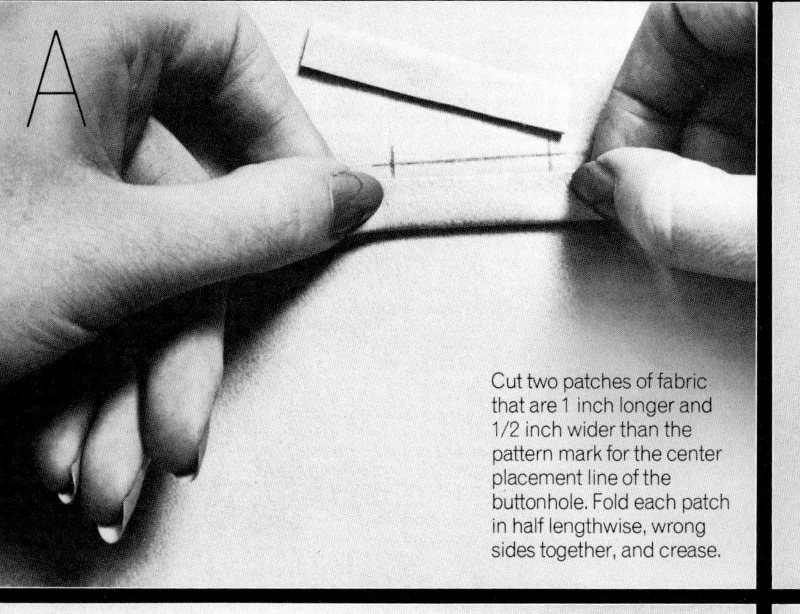

A

Cut two patches of fabric that are 1 inch longer and 1/2 inch wider than the pattern mark for the center placement line of the buttonhole. Fold each patch in half lengthwise, wrong sides together, and crease.

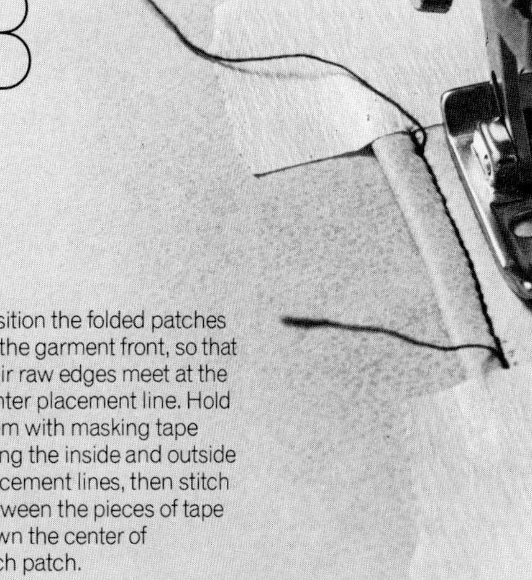

B

Position the folded patches on the garment front, so that their raw edges meet at the center placement line. Hold them with masking tape along the inside and outside placement lines, then stitch between the pieces of tape down the center of each patch.

C

Turn the garment wrong side up. Using the points of scissors, make a 1/4-inch-long cut at the center of the buttonhole parallel to the visible rows of machine stitching. Then make diagonal cuts from the center cut to each of the four corners of the buttonhole.

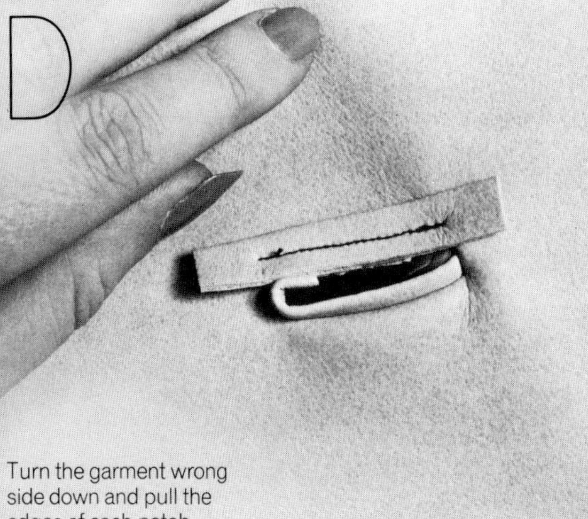

D

Turn the garment wrong side down and pull the edges of each patch through the opening to the wrong side of the garment.

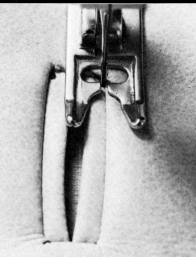

E

Fold the garment along one placement line so that the patch ends extend away from the garment. Machine stitch along the placement line, catching the pointed end of garment fabric and extending 1/8 inch above and below it. Repeat on the other placement line.

F

Turn the facing to the wrong side of the garment and insert paper clips along the outside folded edge, then stitch around the inside edges of the buttonhole to attach the facing. Cut out the facing as shown for leather *(page 58, Box F)*.

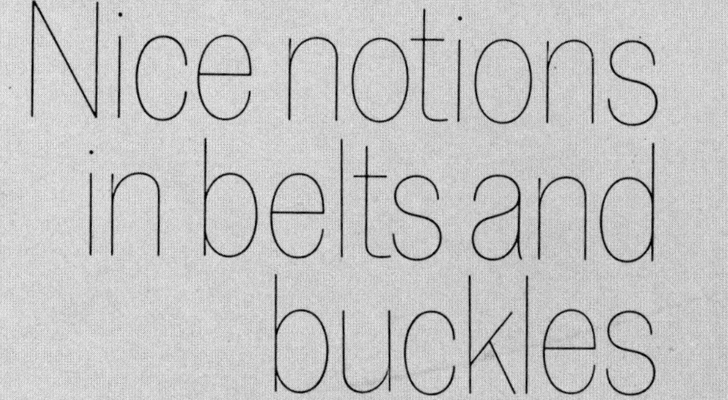

Nice notions in belts and buckles

These three custom belts are, from top to bottom, a sash of pseudo suede with a bone cinch, a classic circlet of brown leather with two gold buckles, and a strip of dyed Madras whip snake backed with kidskin and clasped with a 100-year-old silver buckle. Yet these belts are sisters under the skin. Each was made following the same basic procedure described overleaf: first forming the belt face, then affixing the backing, and finally, attaching the buckle.

Instructions for making the belts

The three belts pictured on the preceding pages are stylish additions to any wardrobe. But they are also excellent examples of the craft of beltmaking, since each is made with a different lining and fastener.

The leather belt is lined with medium-weight cowhide that matches the outside. Its two-tongued buckles fasten through holes made in the leather. The snakeskin belt sports a kidskin lining folded over the top and bottom to frame the outside. The fastener is a two-piece center clasp. Since there is no overlap, the belt must be made precisely to fit your waist. The pseudo-suede belt is lined with rayon. Its buckle holds the fabric in place without a tongue, so that the belt can fit any waist.

To make the belts, you must first familiarize yourself with the basic techniques and equipment used in working with leather. Then, to make the belt holes, you will need a pair of eyelet punching pliers. For interfacing on the leather and snakeskin belts, buy a medium-weight paper such as cover stock (available in art supply stores); for interfacing on the sash belt, use a fusible interfacing.

Once you have mastered the techniques for making these belts, you can change the styling in several ways; experiment with different buckles, change the width, or try a synthetic leather or coated fabric.

A LEATHER BELT WITH TWO BUCKLES

A DETERMINING THE SIZE OF THE BELT

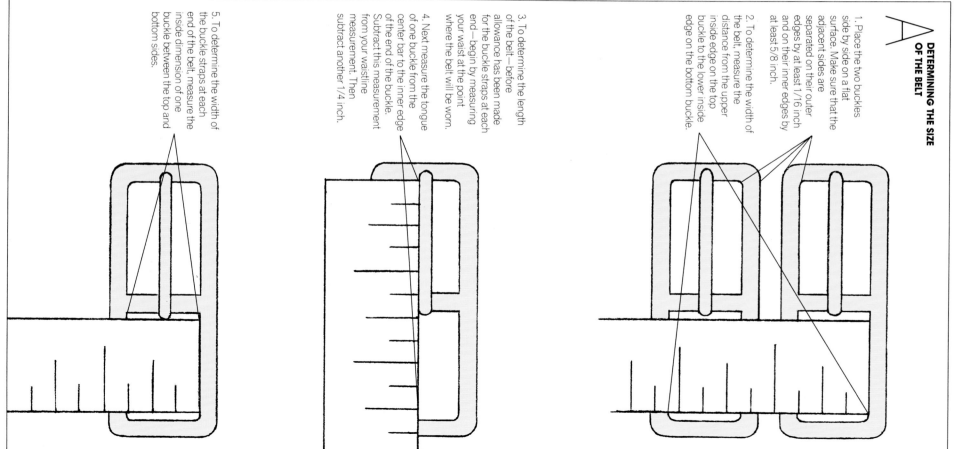

1. Place the two buckles side by side on a flat surface. Make sure that the adjacent sides are separated on their outer edges by at least 1/16 inch and on their inner edges by at least 5/8 inch.

2. To determine the width of the belt, measure the distance from the upper inside edge on the top buckle to the lower inside edge on the bottom buckle.

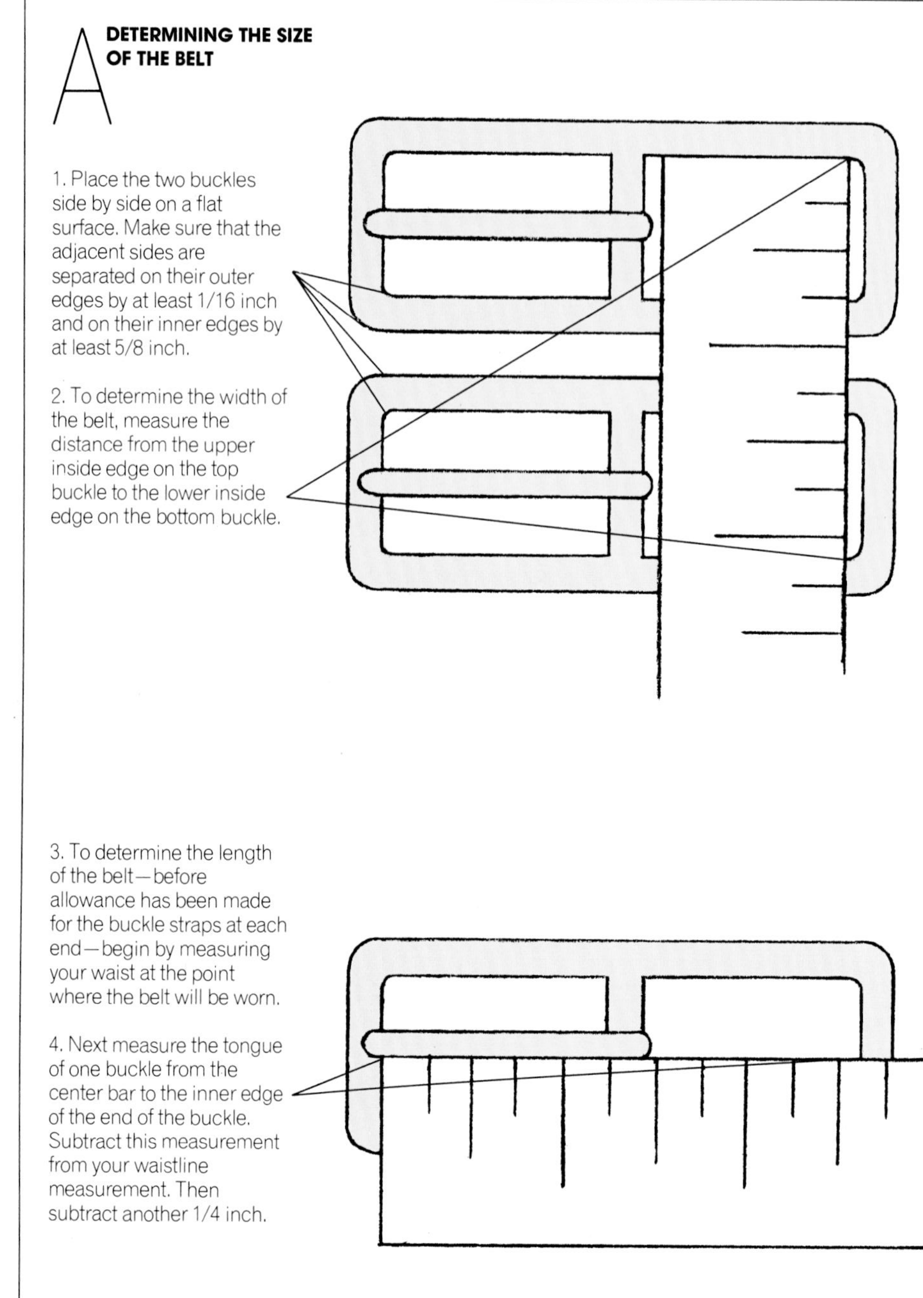

3. To determine the length of the belt—before allowance has been made for the buckle straps at each end—begin by measuring your waist at the point where the belt will be worn.

4. Next measure the tongue of one buckle from the center bar to the inner edge of the end of the buckle. Subtract this measurement from your waistline measurement. Then subtract another 1/4 inch.

5. To determine the width of the buckle straps at each end of the belt, measure the inside dimension of one buckle between the top and bottom sides.

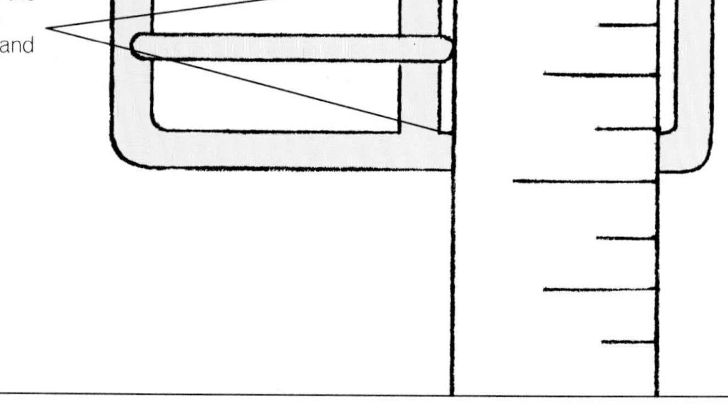

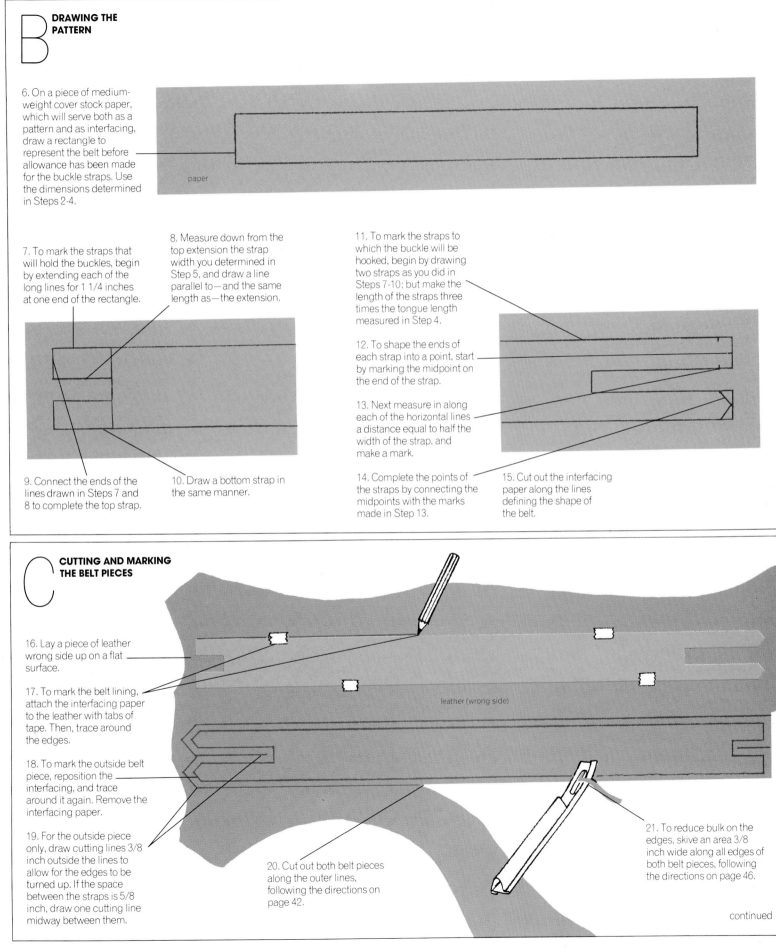

B DRAWING THE PATTERN

6. On a piece of medium-weight cover stock paper, which will serve both as a pattern and as interfacing, draw a rectangle to represent the belt before allowance has been made for the buckle straps. Use the dimensions determined in Steps 2-4.

paper

7. To mark the straps that will hold the buckles, begin by extending each of the long lines for 1 1/4 inches at one end of the rectangle.

8. Measure down from the top extension the strap width you determined in Step 5, and draw a line parallel to—and the same length as—the extension.

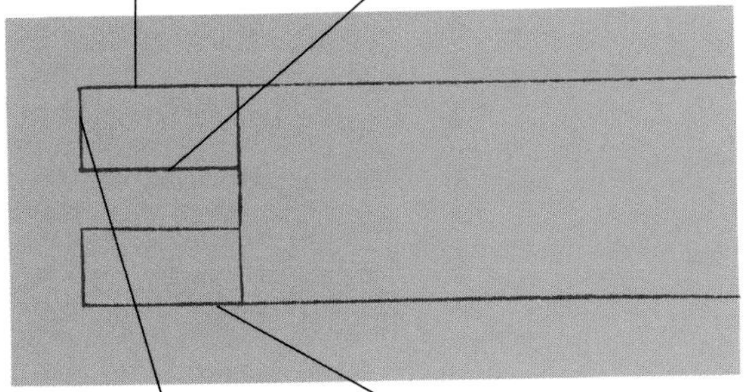

9. Connect the ends of the lines drawn in Steps 7 and 8 to complete the top strap.

10. Draw a bottom strap in the same manner.

11. To mark the straps to which the buckle will be hooked, begin by drawing two straps as you did in Steps 7-10; but make the length of the straps three times the tongue length measured in Step 4.

12. To shape the ends of each strap into a point, start by marking the midpoint on the end of the strap.

13. Next measure in along each of the horizontal lines a distance equal to half the width of the strap, and make a mark.

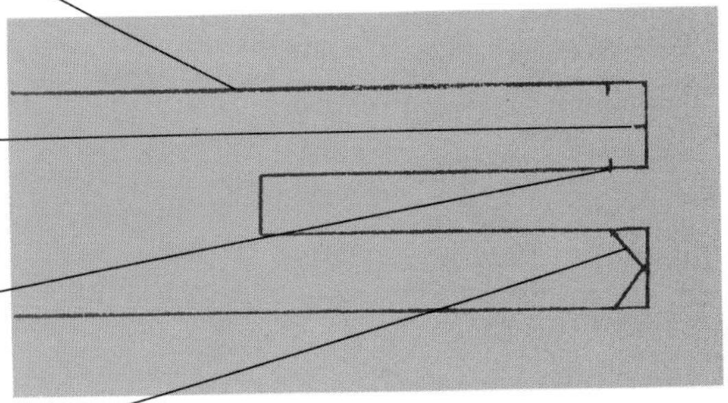

14. Complete the points of the straps by connecting the midpoints with the marks made in Step 13.

15. Cut out the interfacing paper along the lines defining the shape of the belt.

C CUTTING AND MARKING THE BELT PIECES

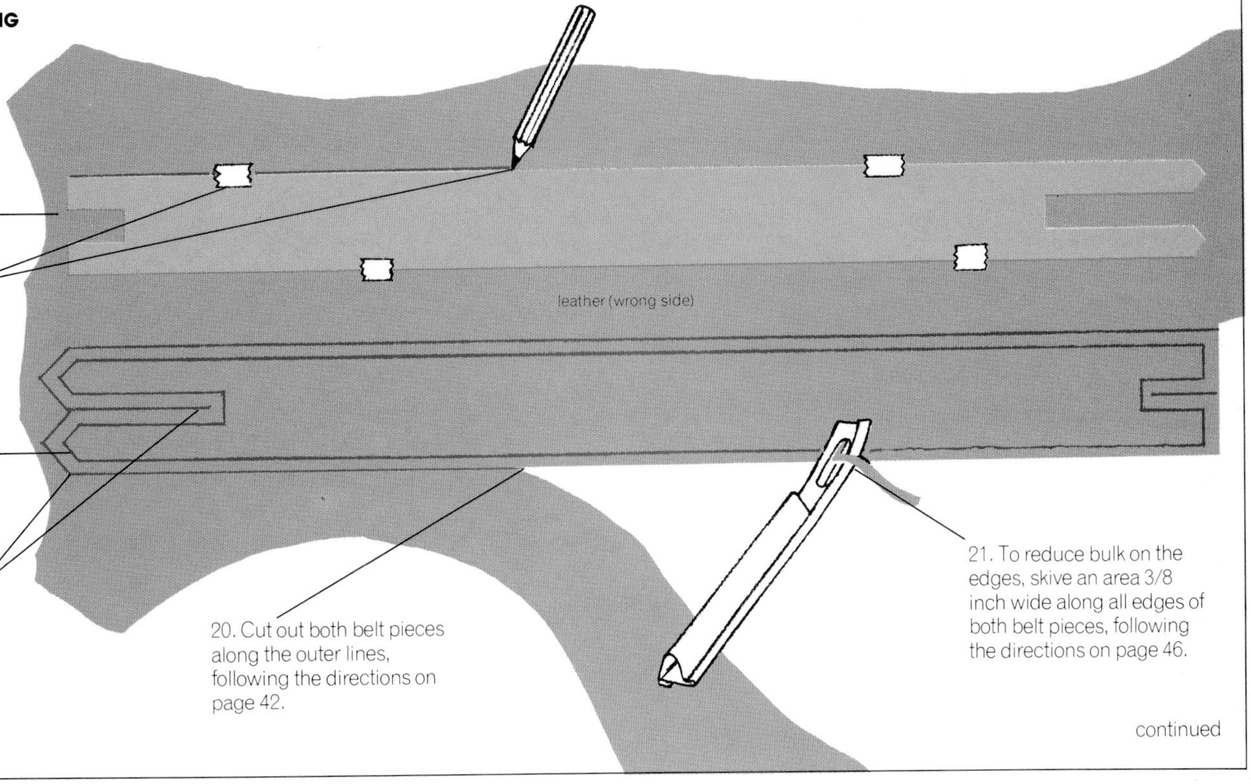

16. Lay a piece of leather wrong side up on a flat surface.

17. To mark the belt lining, attach the interfacing paper to the leather with tabs of tape. Then, trace around the edges.

18. To mark the outside belt piece, reposition the interfacing, and trace around it again. Remove the interfacing paper.

19. For the outside piece only, draw cutting lines 3/8 inch outside the lines to allow for the edges to be turned up. If the space between the straps is 5/8 inch, draw one cutting line midway between them.

leather (wrong side)

20. Cut out both belt pieces along the outer lines, following the directions on page 42.

21. To reduce bulk on the edges, skive an area 3/8 inch wide along all edges of both belt pieces, following the directions on page 46.

continued

D INTERFACING THE BELT

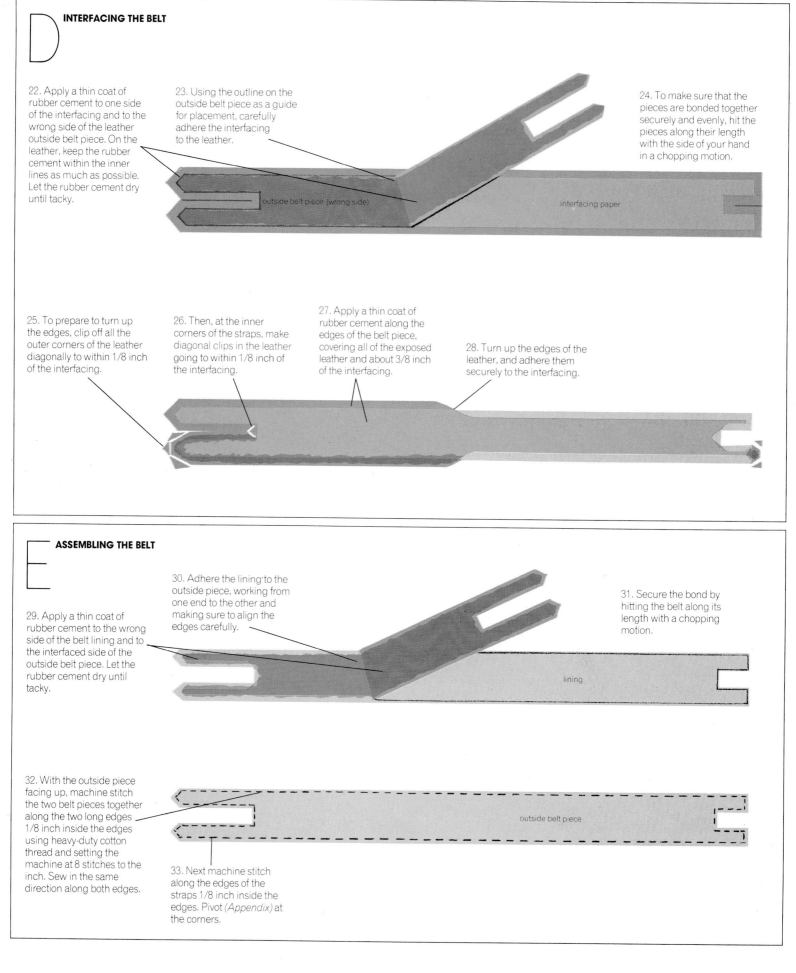

22. Apply a thin coat of rubber cement to one side of the interfacing and to the wrong side of the leather outside belt piece. On the leather, keep the rubber cement within the inner lines as much as possible. Let the rubber cement dry until tacky.

23. Using the outline on the outside belt piece as a guide for placement, carefully adhere the interfacing to the leather.

24. To make sure that the pieces are bonded together securely and evenly, hit the pieces along their length with the side of your hand in a chopping motion.

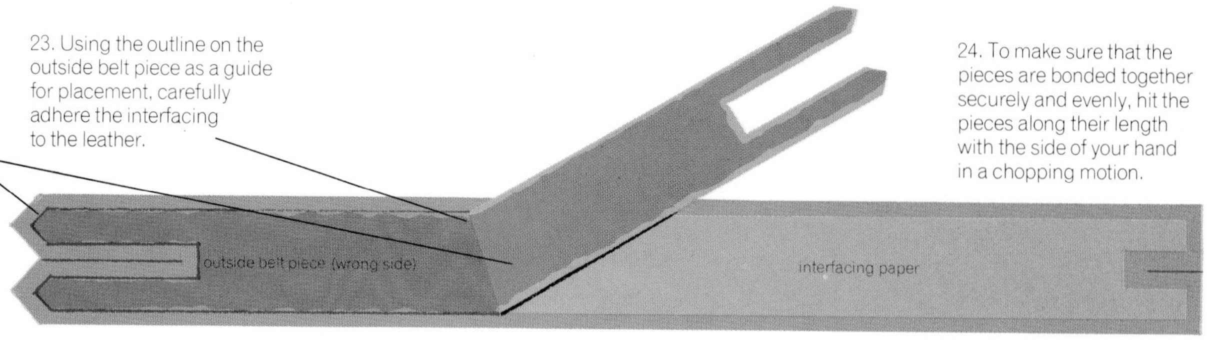

25. To prepare to turn up the edges, clip off all the outer corners of the leather diagonally to within 1/8 inch of the interfacing.

26. Then, at the inner corners of the straps, make diagonal clips in the leather going to within 1/8 inch of the interfacing.

27. Apply a thin coat of rubber cement along the edges of the belt piece, covering all of the exposed leather and about 3/8 inch of the interfacing.

28. Turn up the edges of the leather, and adhere them securely to the interfacing.

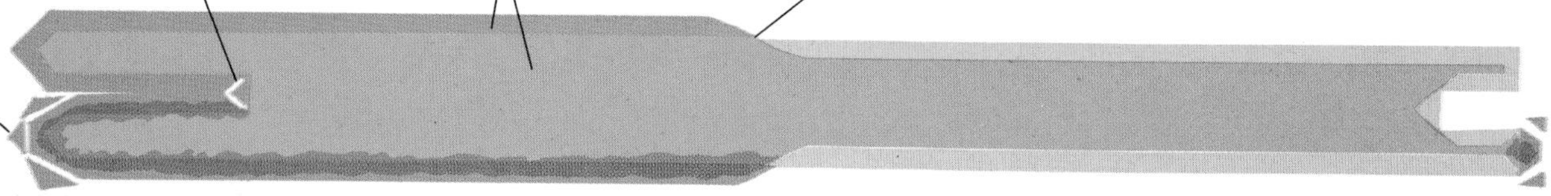

E ASSEMBLING THE BELT

29. Apply a thin coat of rubber cement to the wrong side of the belt lining and to the interfaced side of the outside belt piece. Let the rubber cement dry until tacky.

30. Adhere the lining to the outside piece, working from one end to the other and making sure to align the edges carefully.

31. Secure the bond by hitting the belt along its length with a chopping motion.

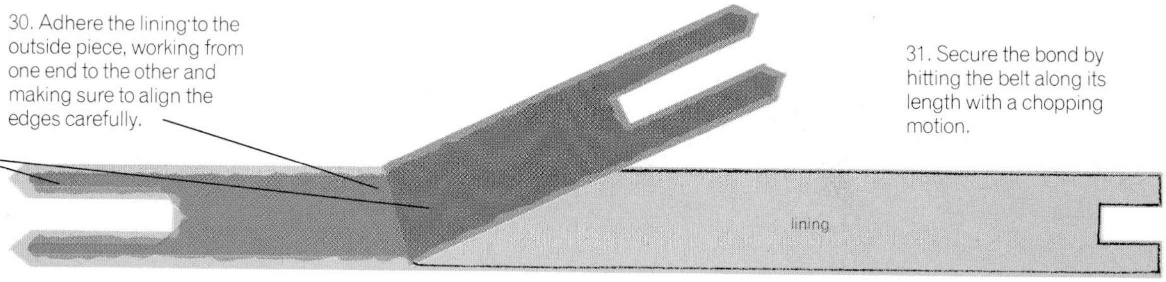

32. With the outside piece facing up, machine stitch the two belt pieces together along the two long edges 1/8 inch inside the edges using heavy-duty cotton thread and setting the machine at 8 stitches to the inch. Sew in the same direction along both edges.

33. Next machine stitch along the edges of the straps 1/8 inch inside the edges. Pivot (*Appendix*) at the corners.

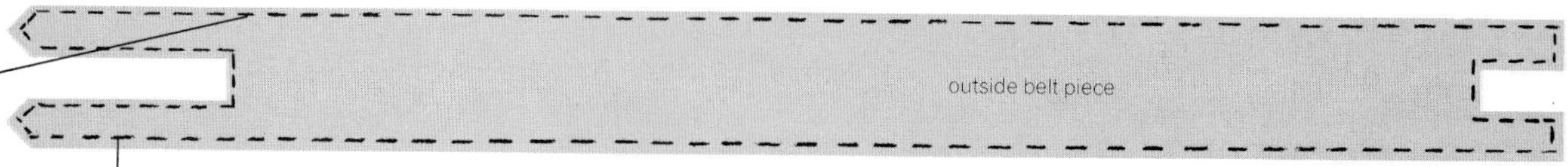

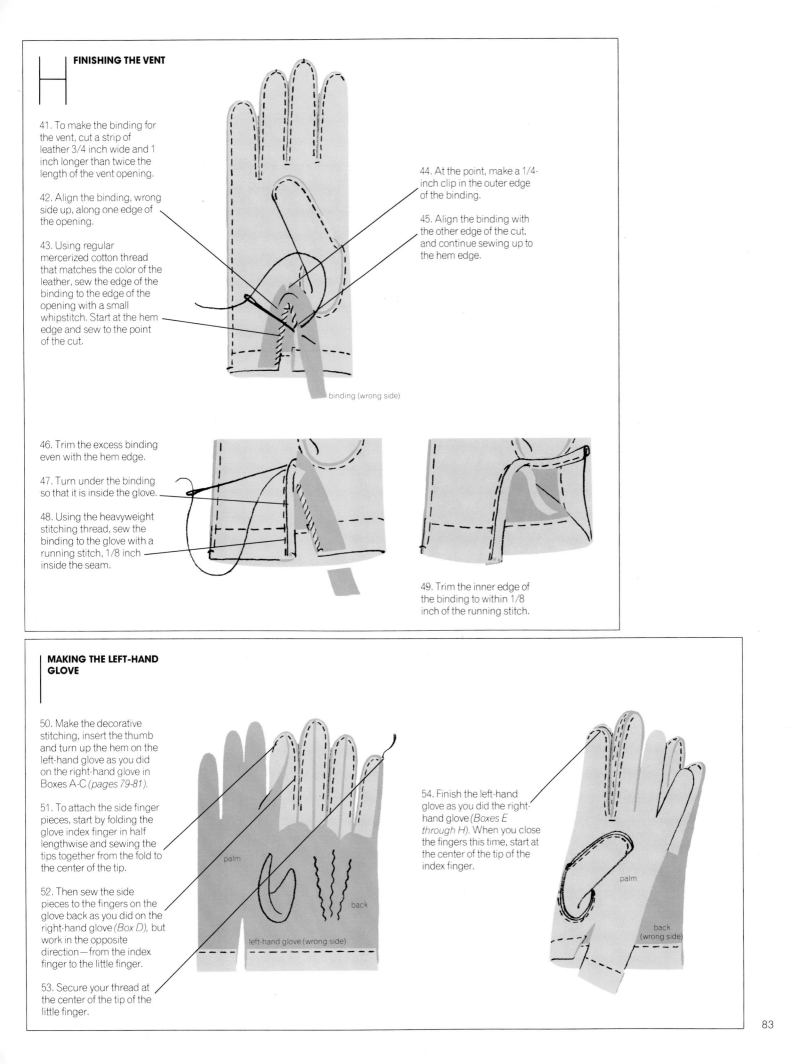

H FINISHING THE VENT

41. To make the binding for the vent, cut a strip of leather 3/4 inch wide and 1 inch longer than twice the length of the vent opening.

42. Align the binding, wrong side up, along one edge of the opening.

43. Using regular mercerized cotton thread that matches the color of the leather, sew the edge of the binding to the edge of the opening with a small whipstitch. Start at the hem edge and sew to the point of the cut.

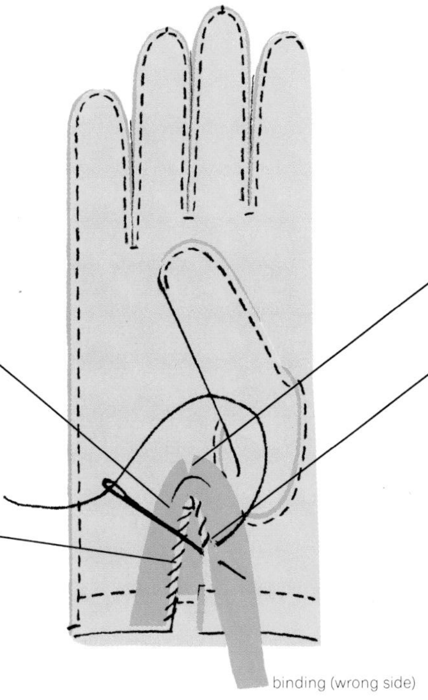

44. At the point, make a 1/4-inch clip in the outer edge of the binding.

45. Align the binding with the other edge of the cut, and continue sewing up to the hem edge.

binding (wrong side)

46. Trim the excess binding even with the hem edge.

47. Turn under the binding so that it is inside the glove.

48. Using the heavyweight stitching thread, sew the binding to the glove with a running stitch, 1/8 inch inside the seam.

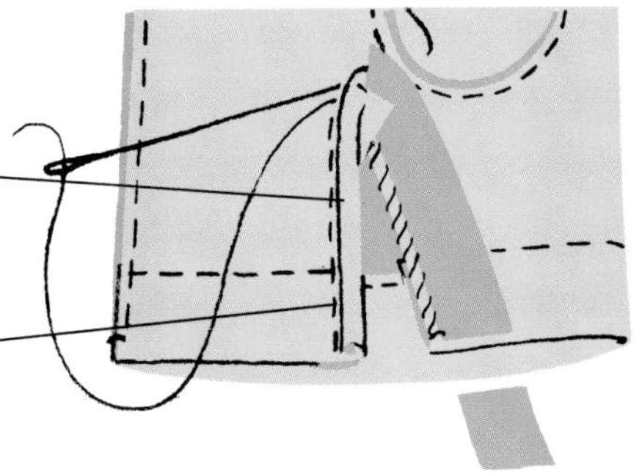

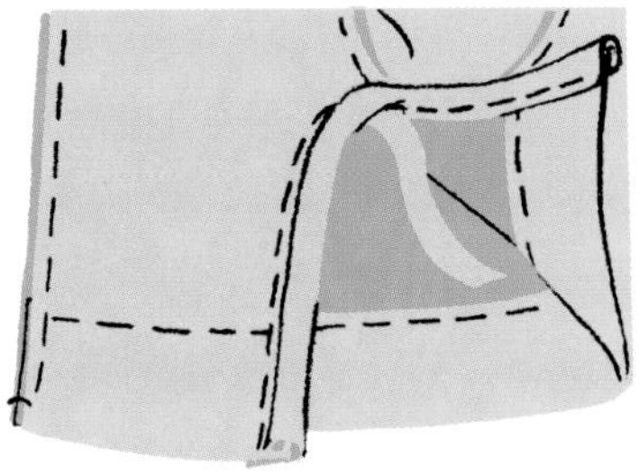

49. Trim the inner edge of the binding to within 1/8 inch of the running stitch.

MAKING THE LEFT-HAND GLOVE

50. Make the decorative stitching, insert the thumb and turn up the hem on the left-hand glove as you did on the right-hand glove in Boxes A-C *(pages 79-81)*.

51. To attach the side finger pieces, start by folding the glove index finger in half lengthwise and sewing the tips together from the fold to the center of the tip.

52. Then sew the side pieces to the fingers on the glove back as you did on the right-hand glove *(Box D)*, but work in the opposite direction—from the index finger to the little finger.

53. Secure your thread at the center of the tip of the little finger.

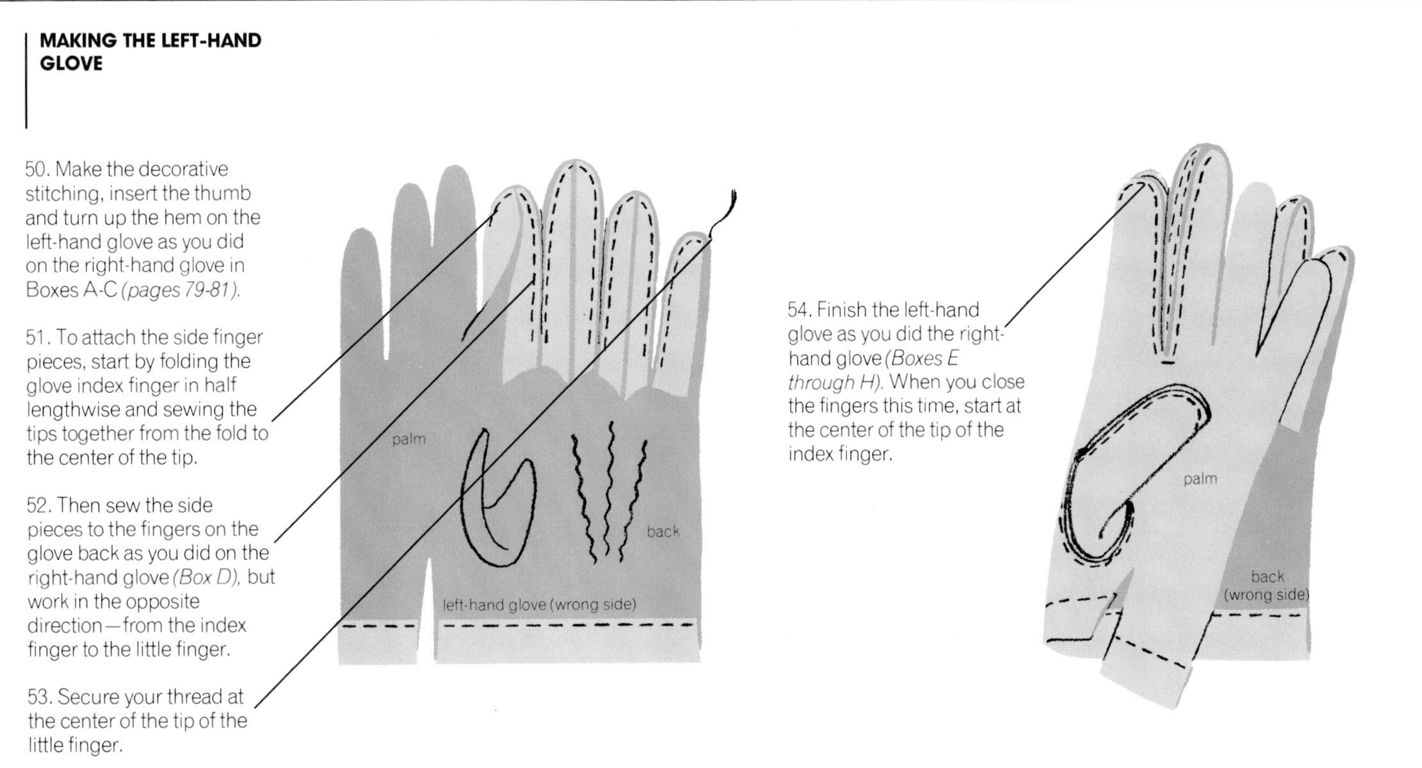

54. Finish the left-hand glove as you did the right-hand glove *(Boxes E through H)*. When you close the fingers this time, start at the center of the tip of the index finger.

A clutch that doubles in brass

Either of these two stylish purses, whose construction is demonstrated overleaf, makes a smashing accessory for dress-up occasions. Both purses are made of lamb suede—although a lambskin or cabretta of similar delicacy can be substituted.

The larger handbag, trimmed in Madras whip snake, is designed to be carried as a clutch; the smaller, also trimmed with whip snake, can serve a dual role and look just as pretty as a shoulder bag. A slender brass chain makes the conversion. It anchors on the underside of the flap fold and can be tucked inside the purse when not in use.

Ways and means of pursemaking

Pattern-making is the most exacting step in producing the trim clutch purse described here and on the following pages. For the smaller purse shown on pages 84 and 85, the grid at right must be drawn precisely in 7/8-inch squares; for the larger purse, the measure is 1 inch. The pattern shapes must be transferred exactly to the grid, as indicated.

Basically, the purse is made in two parts: the outside and the lining. The outer materials are a fine-grained leather such as lamb suede, three matched snakeskins, half a yard of muslin, a sheet of heavyweight cover stock paper (available at art supply stores) and a heavy-duty snap fastener. The lining requires 5/8 yard of upholstery-weight taffeta and another half yard of muslin.

Both the outside and the lining are reinforced with a layer of paper and 3/8 yard of heavyweight Pellon, a nonwoven interfacing. For the shoulder sling version of the bag, two small rings, no larger than 1/2 inch in diameter, and a chain 1 1/4 yards long are needed.

Before following the step-by-step directions given on these pages for assembling the handbag, see the instructions on pages 38-59 for cutting, marking and sewing whatever leather or suede you have chosen.

MAKING THE PATTERN PIECES

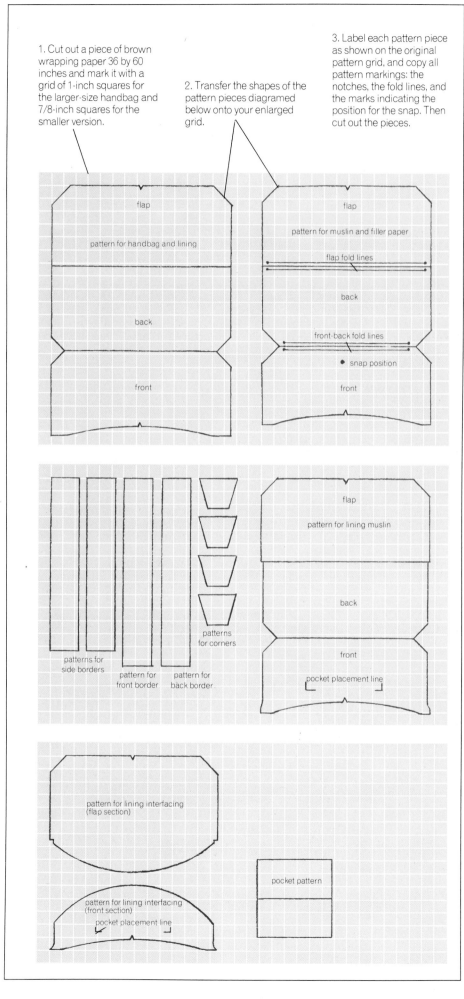

1. Cut out a piece of brown wrapping paper 36 by 60 inches and mark it with a grid of 1-inch squares for the larger-size handbag and 7/8-inch squares for the smaller version.

2. Transfer the shapes of the pattern pieces diagramed below onto your enlarged grid.

3. Label each pattern piece as shown on the original pattern grid, and copy all pattern markings: the notches, the fold lines, and the marks indicating the position for the snap. Then cut out the pieces.

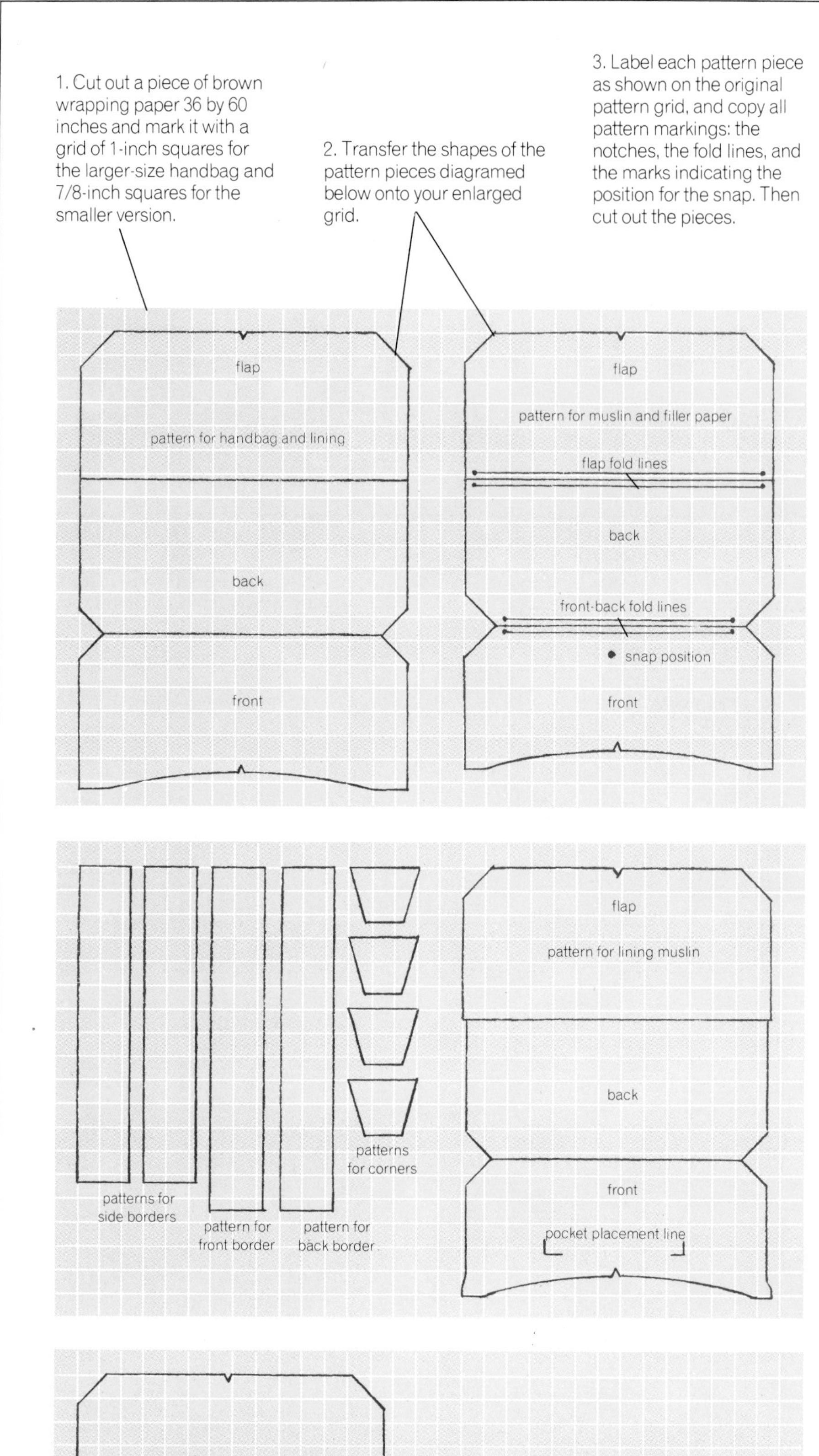

CUTTING OUT THE LEATHER AND THE STIFFENING

A CUTTING OUT THE LEATHER

4. Lay the leather wrong side down on your work board.

5. Place the pattern on top of the leather and cut it out following the directions given on pages 42-44 for the type of leather you are using. Work first on the long edges, then cut the V-shaped wedges and diagonal corners.

6. Cut small notches in the leather to mark the position of the notches on the pattern.

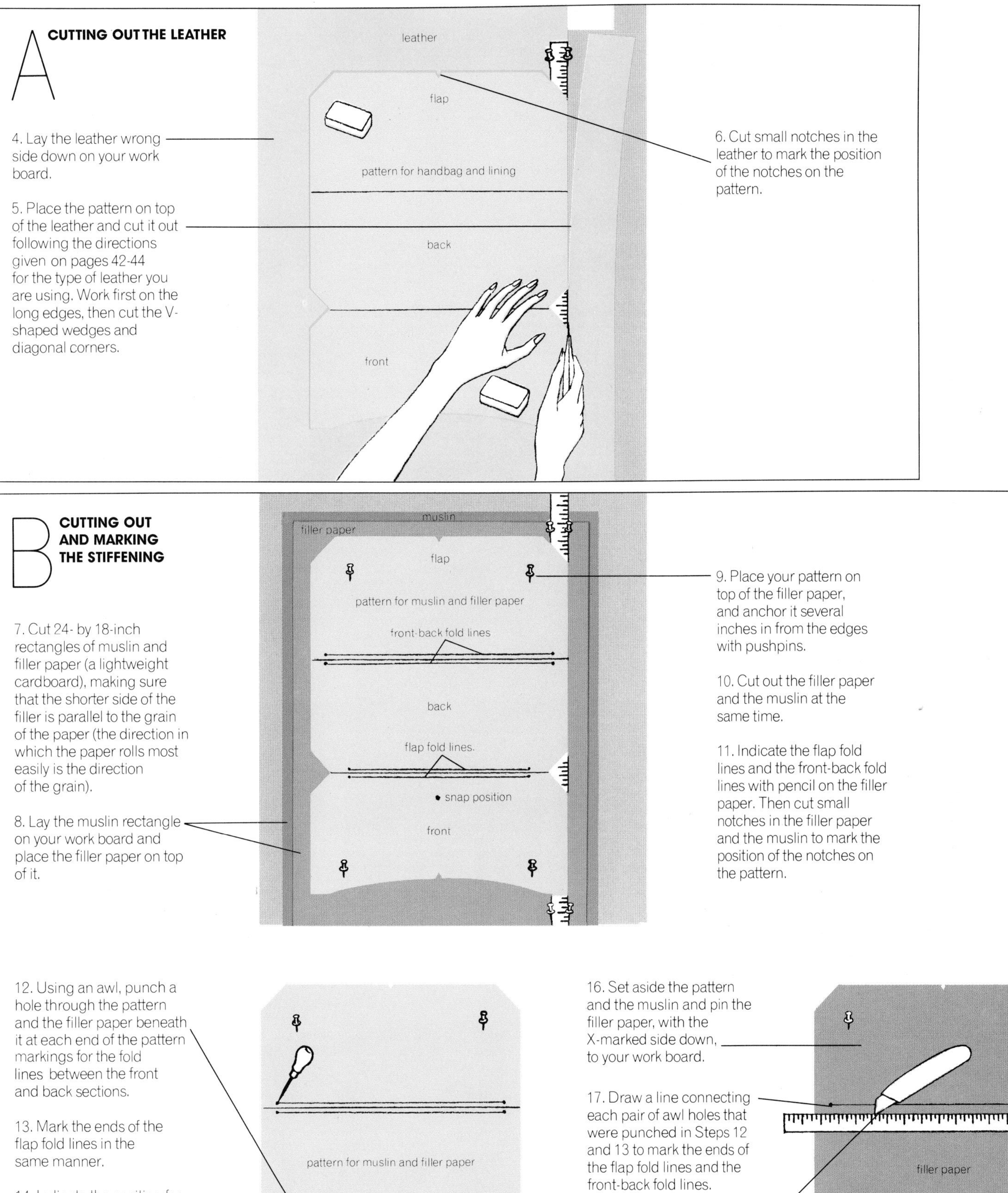

B CUTTING OUT AND MARKING THE STIFFENING

7. Cut 24- by 18-inch rectangles of muslin and filler paper (a lightweight cardboard), making sure that the shorter side of the filler is parallel to the grain of the paper (the direction in which the paper rolls most easily is the direction of the grain).

8. Lay the muslin rectangle on your work board and place the filler paper on top of it.

9. Place your pattern on top of the filler paper, and anchor it several inches in from the edges with pushpins.

10. Cut out the filler paper and the muslin at the same time.

11. Indicate the flap fold lines and the front-back fold lines with pencil on the filler paper. Then cut small notches in the filler paper and the muslin to mark the position of the notches on the pattern.

12. Using an awl, punch a hole through the pattern and the filler paper beneath it at each end of the pattern markings for the fold lines between the front and back sections.

13. Mark the ends of the flap fold lines in the same manner.

14. Indicate the position for the front snap on the filler paper by punching a hole through the pattern marking for the snap.

15. Remove the pushpins and fold back a corner of the pattern and filler paper. Mark the underside of the paper and the upper side of the muslin with an "X."

16. Set aside the pattern and the muslin and pin the filler paper, with the X-marked side down, to your work board.

17. Draw a line connecting each pair of awl holes that were punched in Steps 12 and 13 to mark the ends of the flap fold lines and the front-back fold lines.

18. Using a mat knife and a ruler, slit the filler paper along each of the flap fold and front-back fold lines.

19. Draw an "X" through the hole punched in Step 14 to mark the position of the front snap.

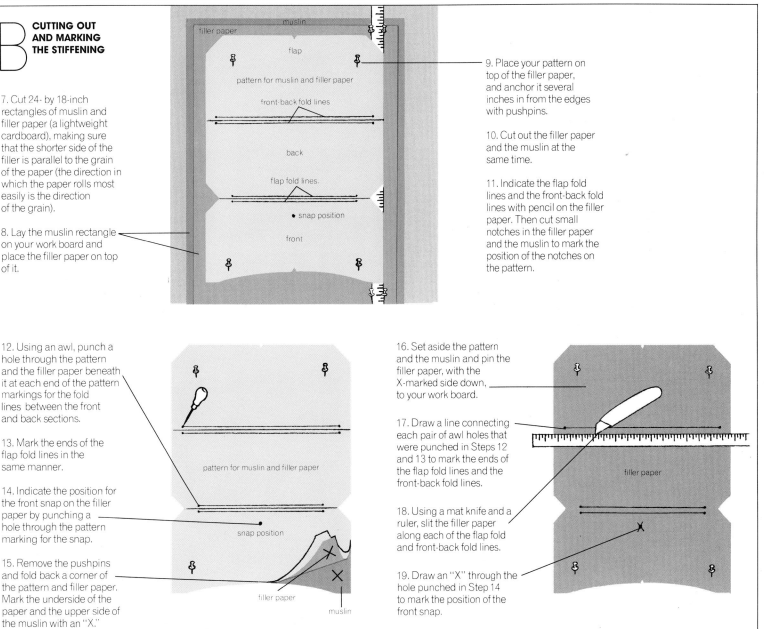

MAKING THE HANDBAG

A ATTACHING THE STIFFENING TO THE LEATHER

1. Place the leather wrong side up on your work board. Then brush a thin coat of rubber cement around all sides of the leather, 1 inch in from the edges. Let it dry.

2. Place the muslin, X-marked side down, on your work board and brush a thin coat of rubber cement around all the edges. Let it dry.

3. Place the glued side of the muslin on top of the leather, centering it so that the notches along the front and flap edges are aligned and the 1/2-inch edge of leather that protrudes is even all around.

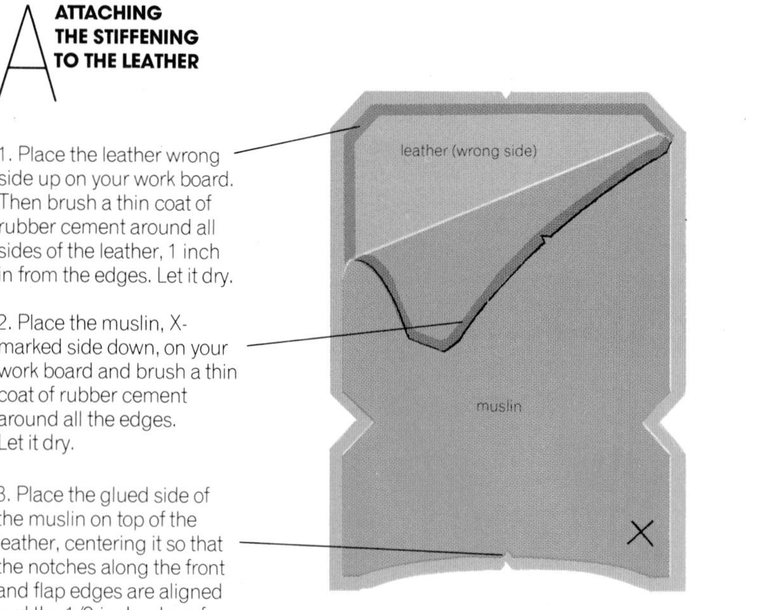

4. Brush a thin coat of rubber cement along all edges of the muslin. Let it dry.

5. Place the filler paper, X-marked side up, on your work board and brush a thin coat of rubber cement along all the edges. Let it dry.

6. Place the glued side of the filler paper on top of the muslin, aligning all the edges.

7. To remove a narrow strip of the stiff filler paper along the flap fold line and the front-back fold line, take a mat knife and make a cut at both ends of the horizontal fold-line cuts made in Step 18, page 87. Be careful not to cut into the muslin and leather beneath the filler paper. Set aside the cut-out strips.

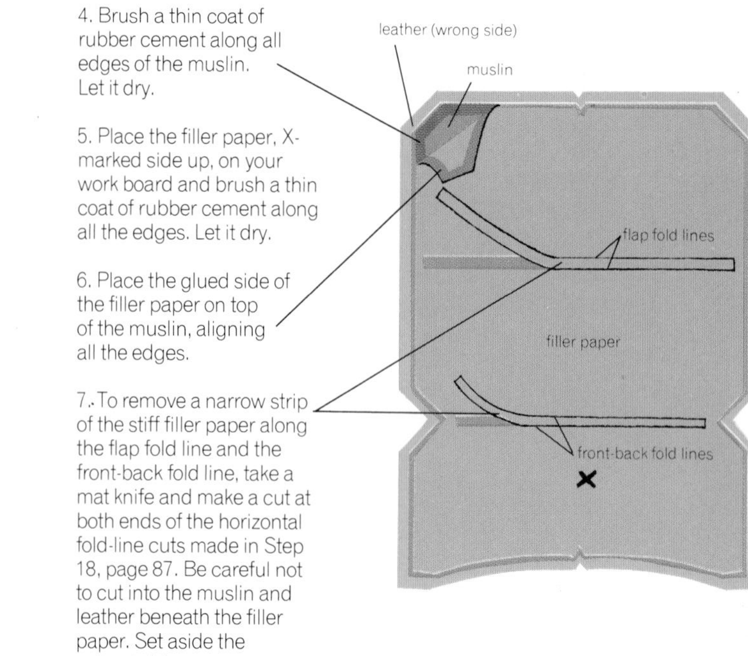

8. Apply a thin coat of rubber cement along the edges of the filler paper and the protruding 1/2 inch of leather, brushing outward toward the edge of the leather as you work.

9. After the rubber cement is dry, clip the protruding leather edge at each V-shaped wedge, cutting to within 1/8 inch of the point.

10. Trim the front corners diagonally 1/8 inch away from the paper. Then clip at 1/2-inch intervals around the curved front edge, cutting to within 1/8 inch of the paper.

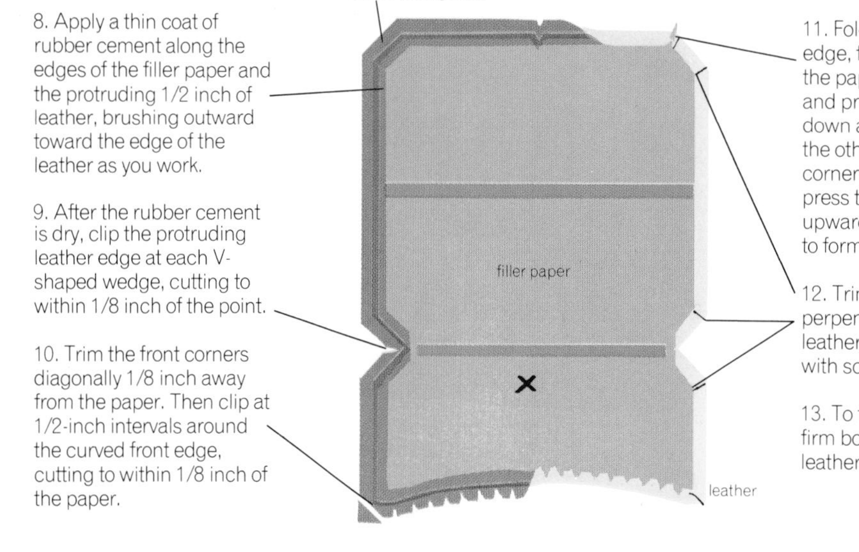

11. Fold over the leather edge, feeling for the edge of the paper with one hand, and pressing the leather down against the paper with the other. Work toward the corners, and at each corner, press the excess leather upward perpendicularly to form a point.

12. Trim off the perpendicular points of leather at the corners with scissors.

13. To flatten and ensure a firm bond, hammer the leather down with a mallet.

B PREPARING THE SNAKESKIN BORDER

14. Cut out the snakeskin and the interfacing, using the original border pattern pieces. Then trim away 1/2 inch along all sides of the interfacing for the wedge-shaped corners and along the long edges only of the interfacing strips.

15. Lay the snakeskin wrong side up. Brush rubber cement down the center of each strip and in the center of the wedges. Repeat on the interfacing.

16. Place the interfacing, glued sides down, on top of the matching snakeskin strips, centering them between the long edges and aligning the short ends. Center the wedge-shaped interfacing pieces on the matching snakeskin sections; trim the snakeskin diagonally at the corners, cutting 1/8 inch from the interfacing.

17. Brush a light coat of rubber cement onto the protruding edges of the snakeskin and along all edges of interfacing. Let it dry.

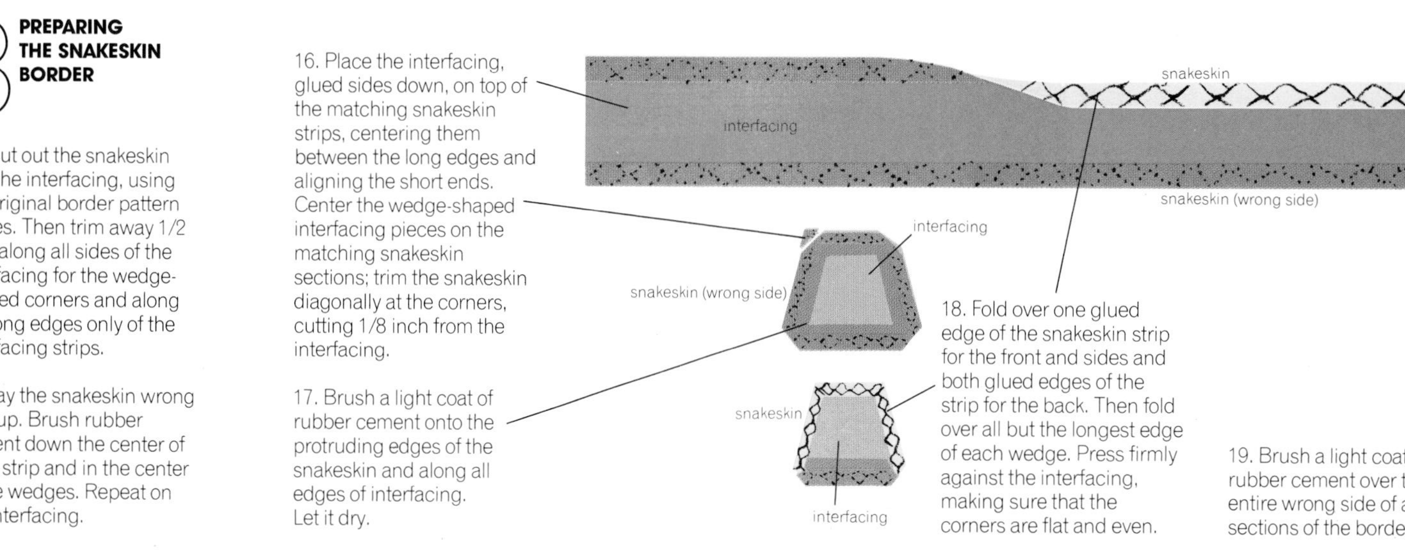

18. Fold over one glued edge of the snakeskin strip for the front and sides and both glued edges of the strip for the back. Then fold over all but the longest edge of each wedge. Press firmly against the interfacing, making sure that the corners are flat and even.

19. Brush a light coat of rubber cement over the entire wrong side of all sections of the border.

FLATTENING EDGES OF REAL AND FAKE FUR

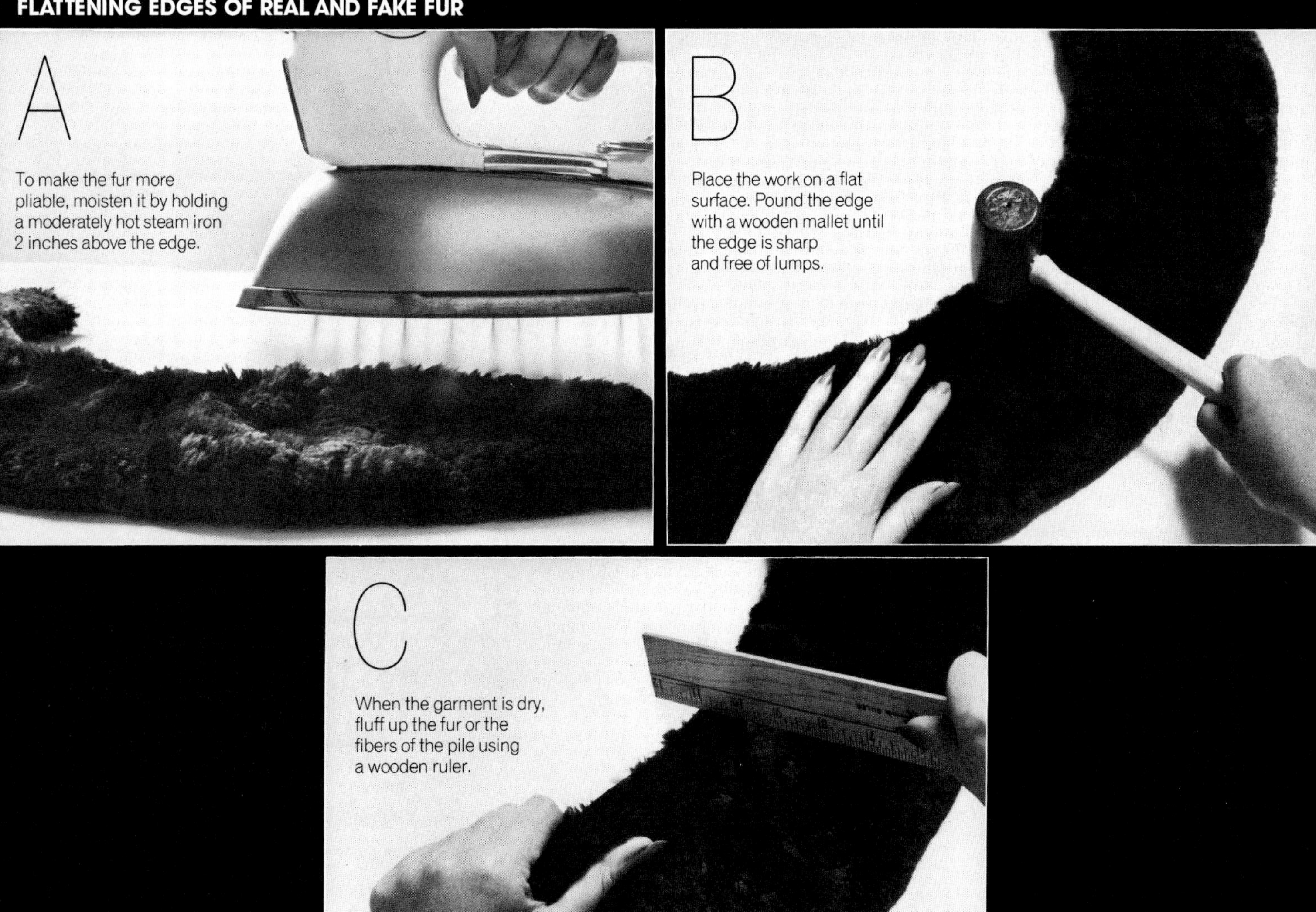

A

To make the fur more pliable, moisten it by holding a moderately hot steam iron 2 inches above the edge.

B

Place the work on a flat surface. Pound the edge with a wooden mallet until the edge is sharp and free of lumps.

C

When the garment is dry, fluff up the fur or the fibers of the pile using a wooden ruler.

Reviving tired old fur

When an old fur is brought out of retirement to be restyled into a chic hat or collar, the fur should be thoroughly inspected for moth holes or worn areas. Test it for moth infestation by beating with a yardstick or the wooden handle of a mallet and, if necessary, repair it, as shown overleaf. If the fur is in good condition, it needs only to be freshened with a soft brush lightly dampened and then groomed with a wire brush to fluff it up. But if the fur shows evidence of moths—whitish dust from crumbled moth eggs or larvae—it should be cleaned by a professional furrier. Never send a fur to a dry cleaner and never attempt to do the job yourself with cleaning fluid.

Transplanted patches from waste pieces of the fur can be used to cover worn spots or holes. The patches should be cut in zigzag lines in order to achieve inconspicuous seams.

TESTING THE SKIN OF REAL FUR

A To test the skin to see if it is still in good condition, first wet a rag with water and rub it on the skin to moisten it.

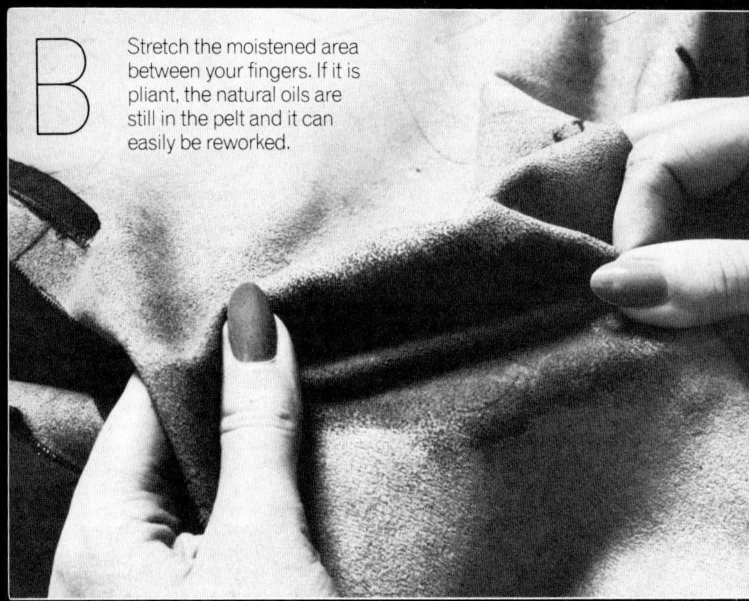

B Stretch the moistened area between your fingers. If it is pliant, the natural oils are still in the pelt and it can easily be reworked.

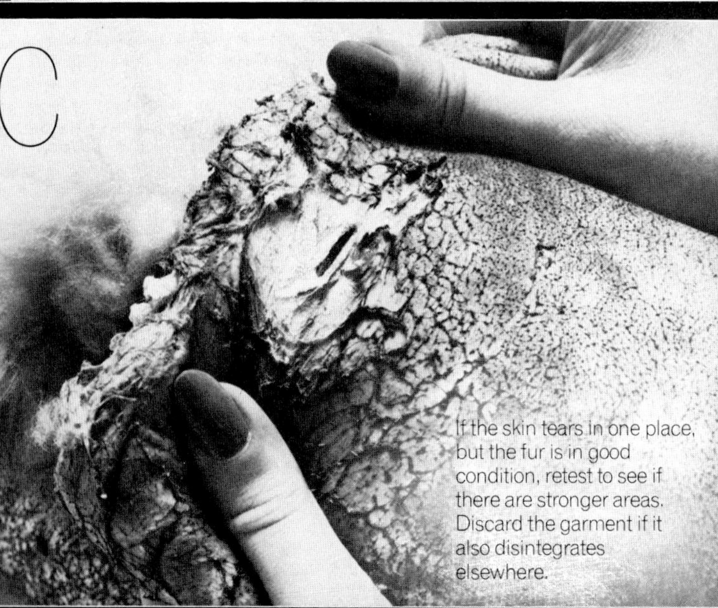

C If the skin tears in one place, but the fur is in good condition, retest to see if there are stronger areas. Discard the garment if it also disintegrates elsewhere.

EXAMINING THE FUR ITSELF

A Beat the fur vigorously with a wooden handle or a yardstick. If evidence of moths appears, have the garment cleaned by a professional furrier.

B If cleaning is not necessary, eliminate mustiness or dust by sponging the fur with a soft brush dipped in plain water.

C Hang the fur up to dry. Then smooth out the hair using a wire grooming brush designed for pets. Brush first against the nap, then in the direction in which the hair lies.

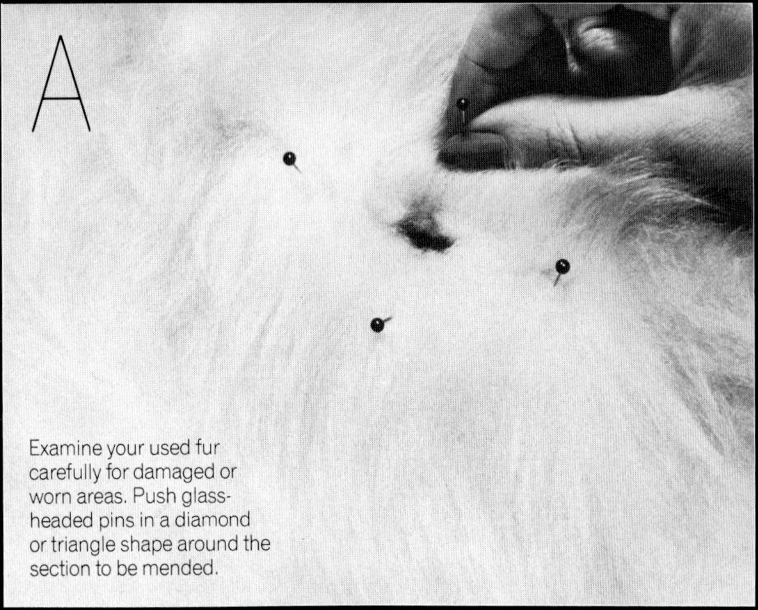

A

Examine your used fur carefully for damaged or worn areas. Push glass-headed pins in a diamond or triangle shape around the section to be mended.

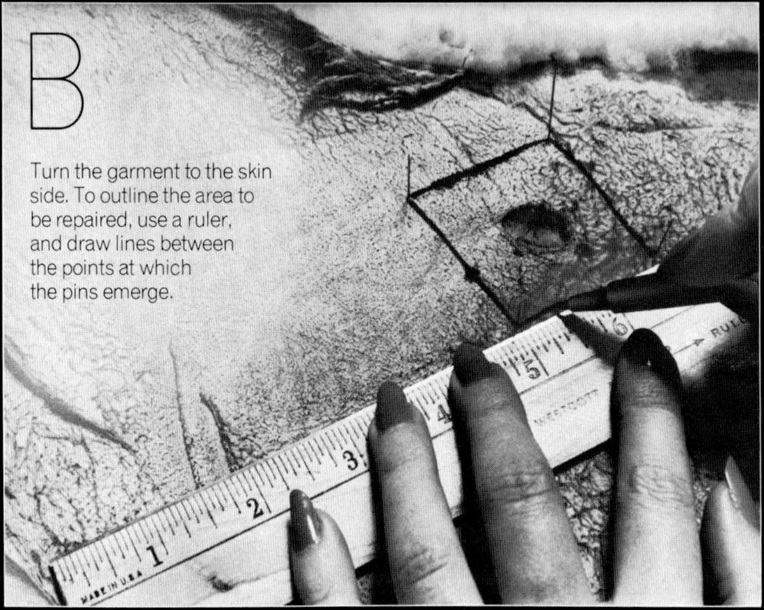

B

Turn the garment to the skin side. To outline the area to be repaired, use a ruler, and draw lines between the points at which the pins emerge.

C

Remove the pins. Cut along the marked outline, using a sharp, single-edged razor blade. Lift out the patch, separating the hairs gently.

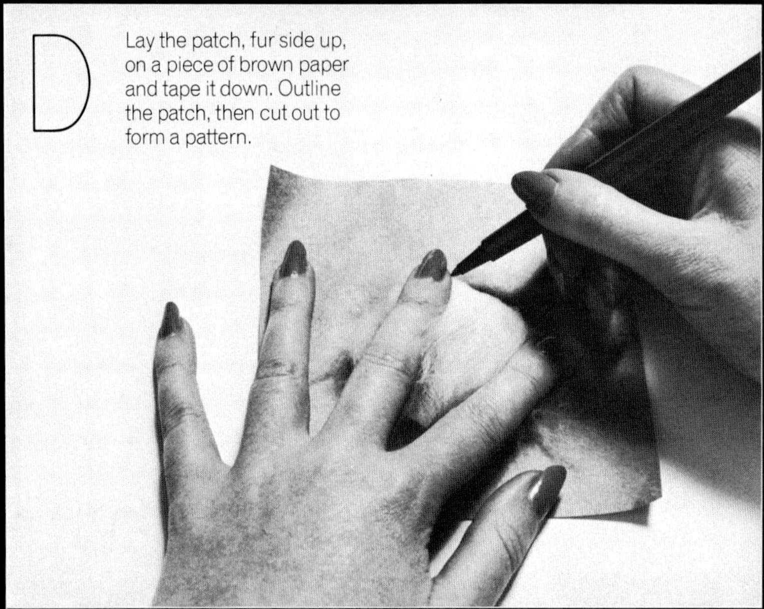

D

Lay the patch, fur side up, on a piece of brown paper and tape it down. Outline the patch, then cut out to form a pattern.

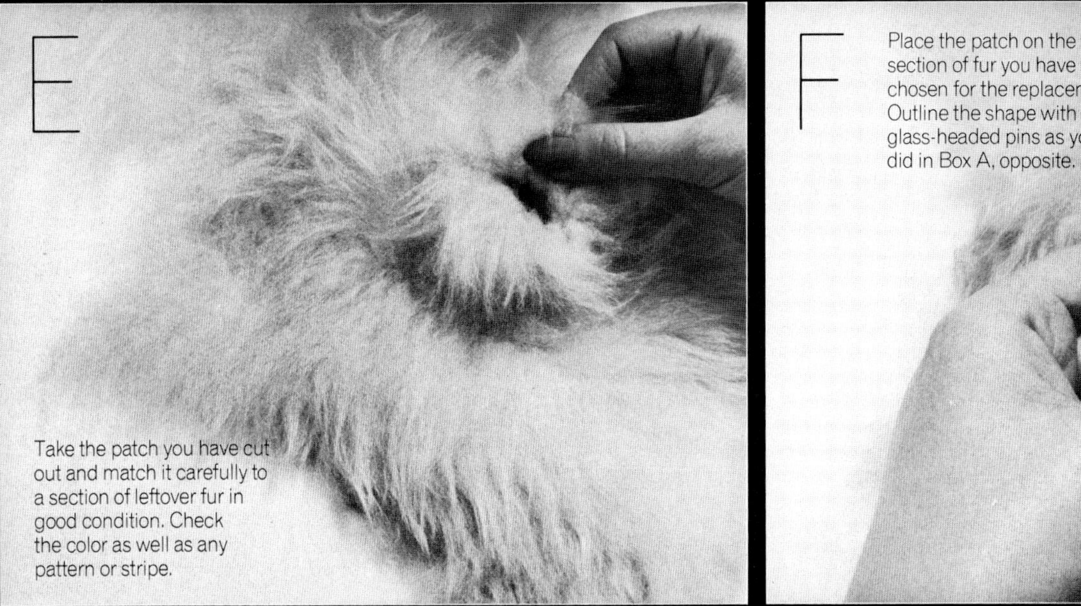

E

Take the patch you have cut out and match it carefully to a section of leftover fur in good condition. Check the color as well as any pattern or stripe.

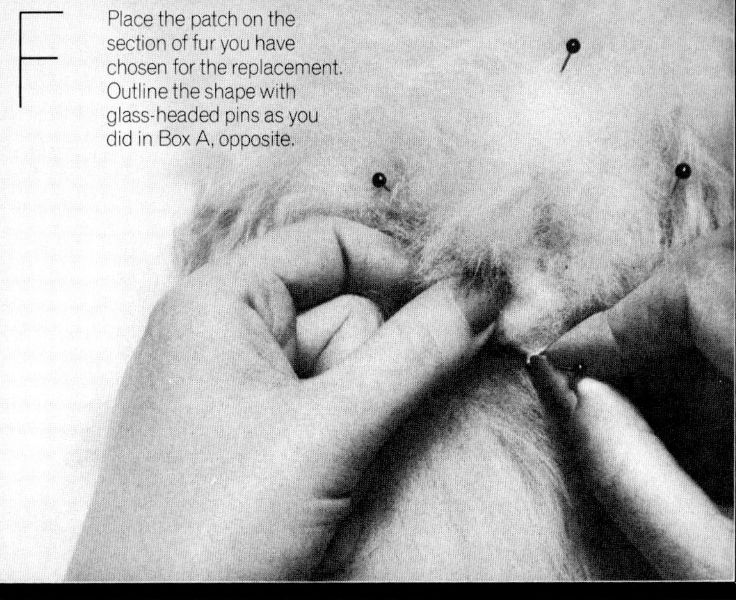

F

Place the patch on the section of fur you have chosen for the replacement. Outline the shape with glass-headed pins as you did in Box A, opposite.

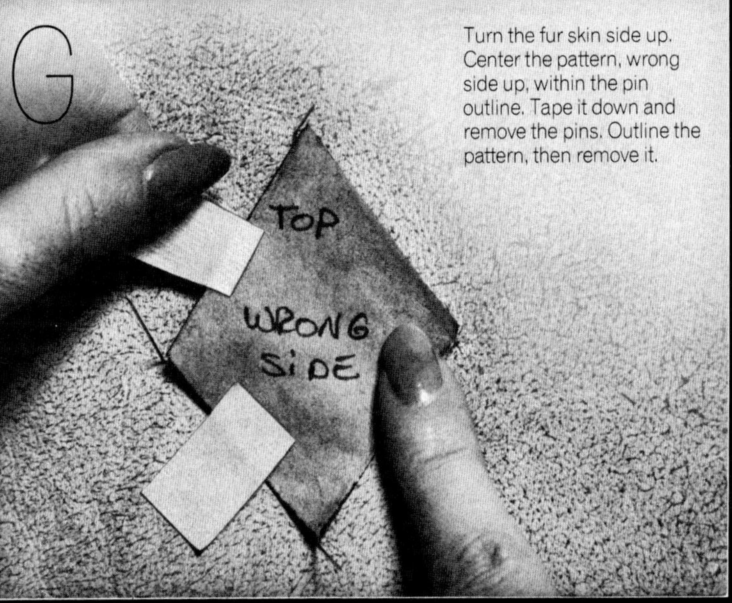

G

Turn the fur skin side up. Center the pattern, wrong side up, within the pin outline. Tape it down and remove the pins. Outline the pattern, then remove it.

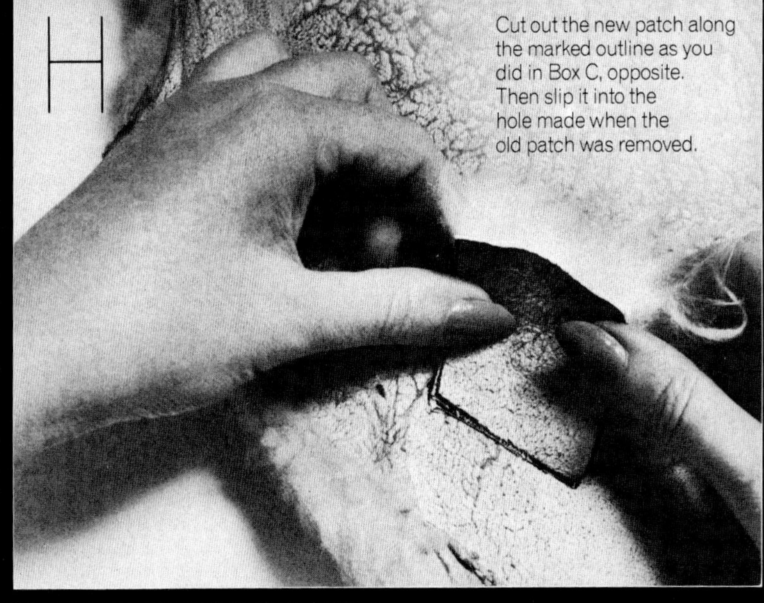

H

Cut out the new patch along the marked outline as you did in Box C, opposite. Then slip it into the hole made when the old patch was removed.

I

Tape the new patch down along three sides. Sew the edges together and flatten them as shown in Boxes B-E, pages 112-113.

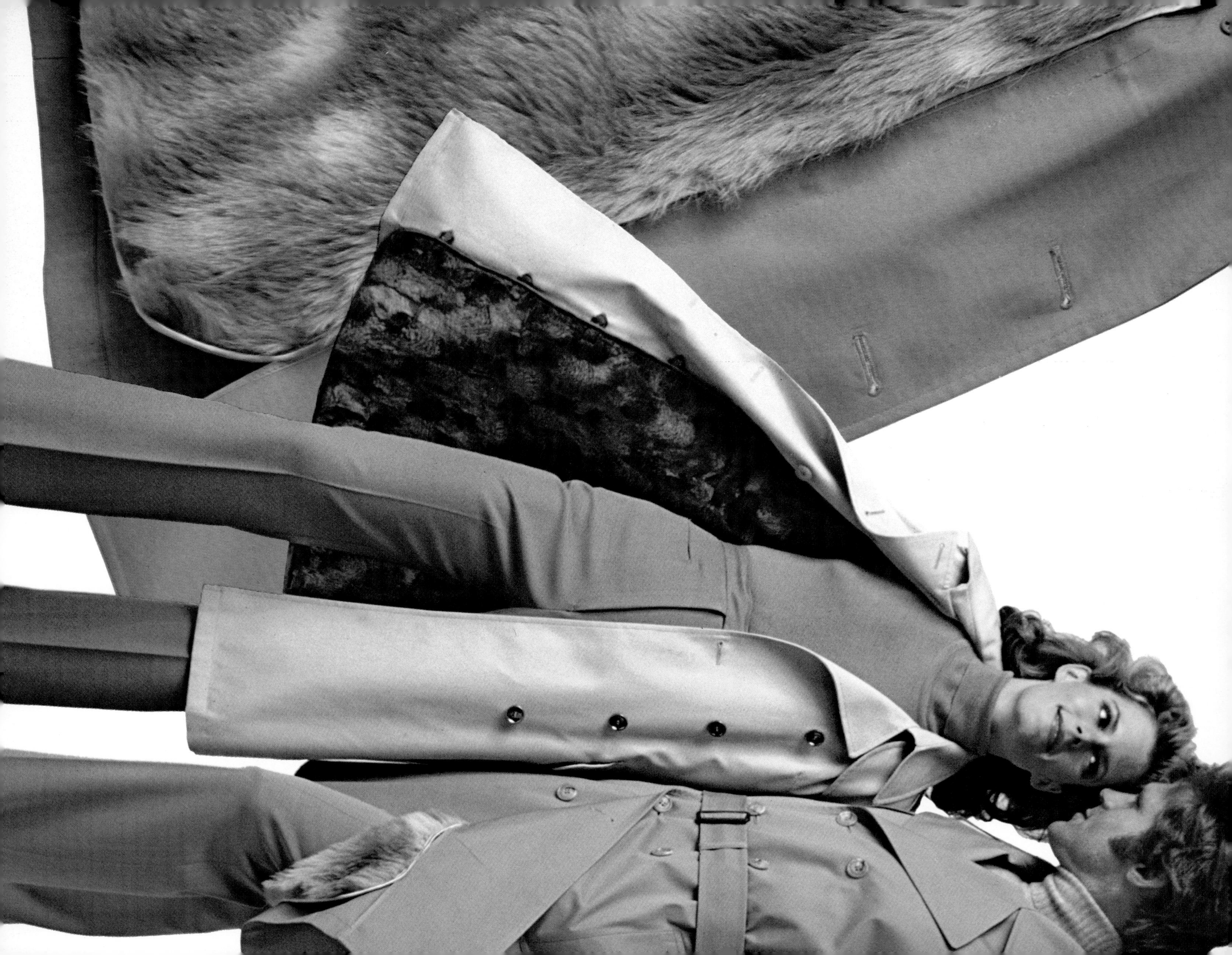

Frauds for an inside job

Normally a trench coat functions as little more than weatherproofing. But, fancied up with a detachable fur lining, the coat takes on an understated elegance. Most real furs are too extravagant for such undercover work, but the same sense of luxury can be achieved with fake fur. Shown here and demonstrated overleaf are a fake broadtail used to custom-line an off-the-rack woman's manteau, and a fake stone marten to upgrade a man's ready-made coat.

Lining a coat with bogus fur

Detachable fur coat linings, like the ones shown on the preceding pages, are better made of fake furs than of real pelts. Real fur is expensive; and besides, finding enough sizable segments of old fur to piece together may be difficult.

In selecting a new coat to be lined, remember that fake furs vary in bulkiness; for example, if you plan to use a thick-piled fake, buy a coat that is one size too large.

Your choice of linings is, of course, more limited with an old coat. If the coat has a fitted waist, the pile should not exceed 1/4 inch. With straight or flared coats, make a pinning test to determine how thick the lining can be: pin the coat in on both sides, 1 1/2 inches from the seams. Now try on the coat; if it is comfortable when buttoned, your pile lining can be as thick as 3/4 inch. If the pinned coat pulls, use 1/4-inch pile.

Trace the pattern, as shown on the following pages. The pieces will fit side by side on a standard roll of fake fur. To determine how many yards of fabric you need, add 2 inches to the pattern length; the extra inches will allow margin for error. You will also need 5/8-inch buttons or grip fasteners to hold the lining in place at 3- to 5-inch intervals.

Cut, sew and mark your lining according to the instructions given for particular fake fur on pages 102-103.

MAKING THE PATTERN FOR A COAT WITH SET-IN SLEEVES

A TRACING THE OUTLINE OF THE COAT

1. Lay the coat for which you are making a lining on a flat surface so that one front section is facing up. Lay a large sheet of firm tissue paper over the front. Tape together several sheets of paper, if necessary.

2. Pin the paper in place.

3. Using a dull pencil with a soft lead, mark the outline of the coat front on the paper with a series of dashes. Trace along the front and hem edges, and the neck, shoulder, arm and side seams. Make sure to mark at closer intervals along curved seams.

4. Unpin the paper, and place it on a flat surface.

5. Connect the marks to complete the outline of the front. Use a ruler for straight lines; draw curves freehand.

6. Make an outline of half of the coat back by repeating Steps 1-5. But this time align one long edge of the tissue paper with the center-back seam or the center-back fold of the folded coat.

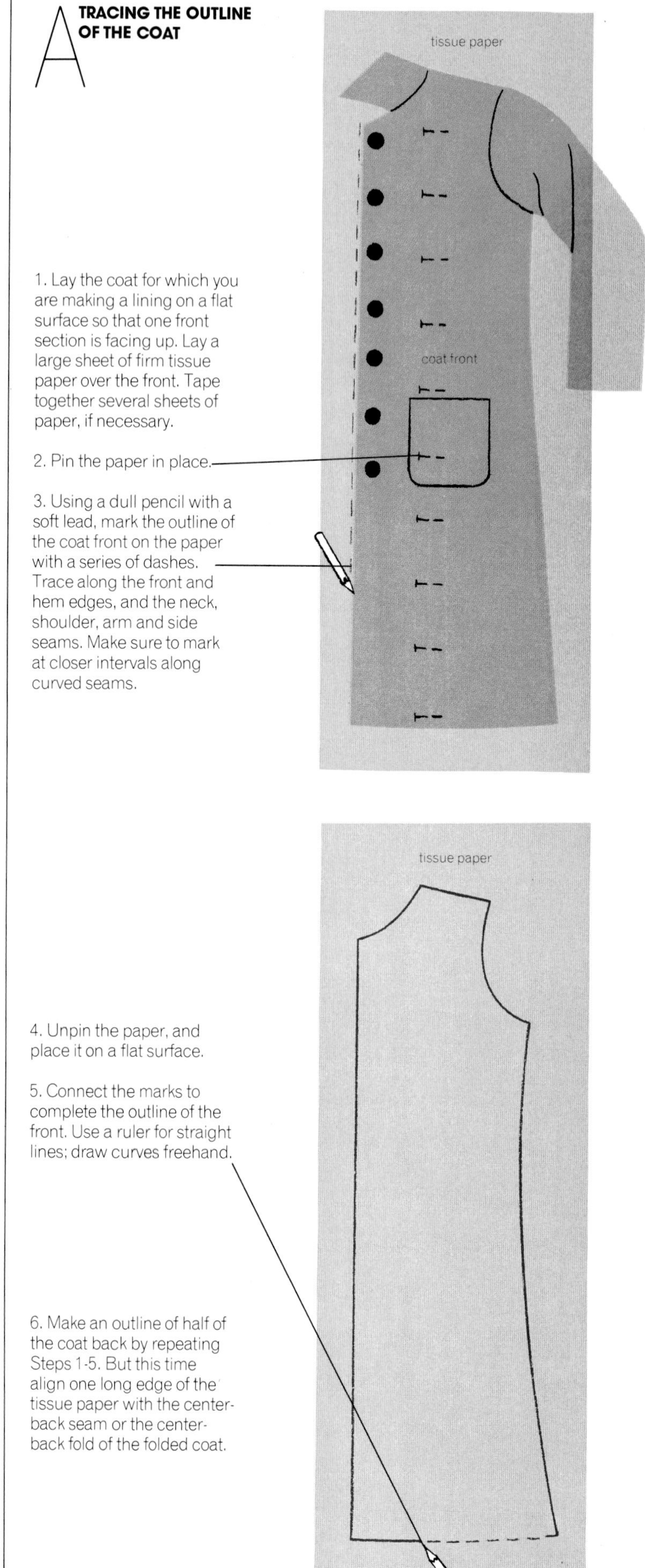

B MAKING THE FRONT PATTERN

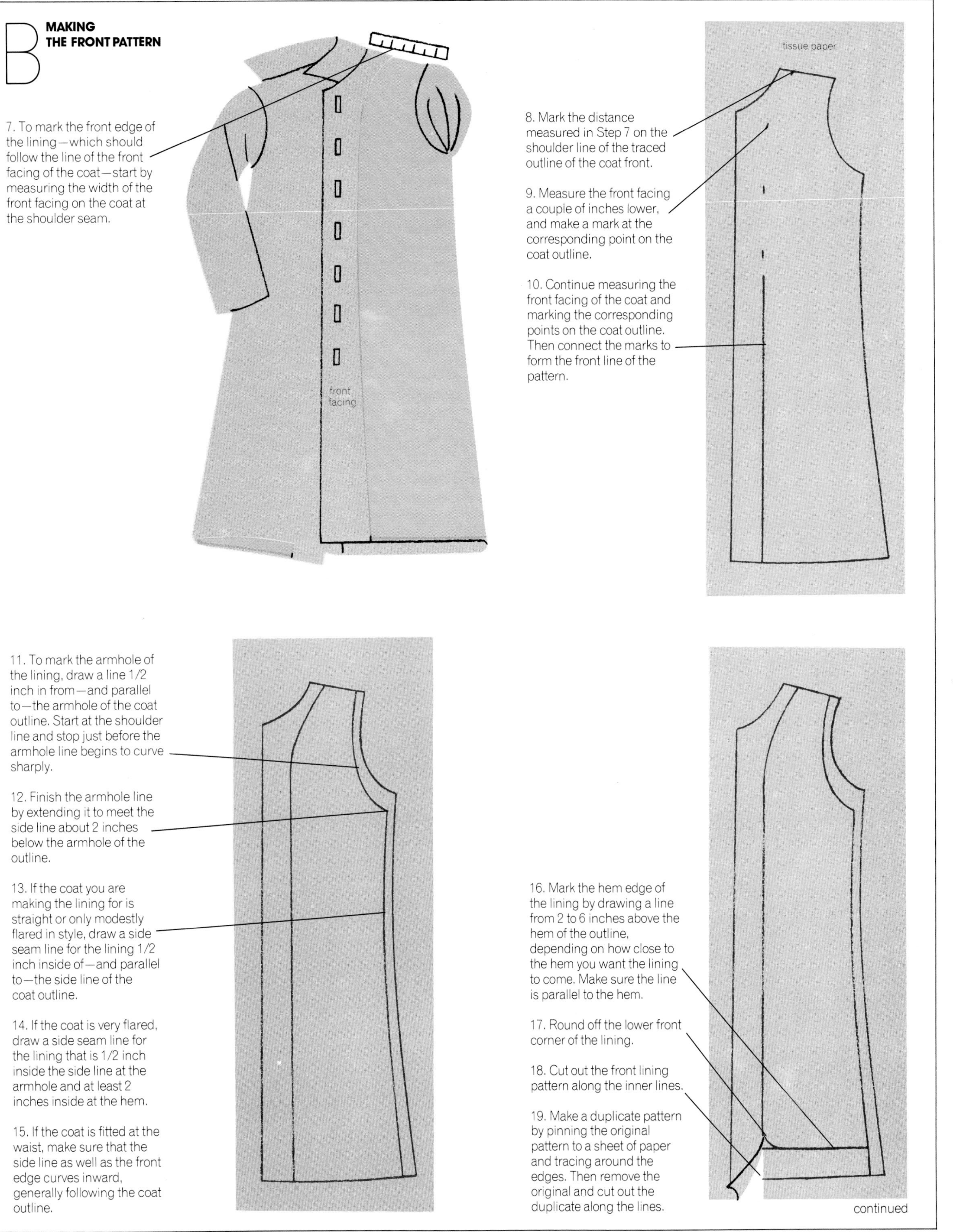

7. To mark the front edge of the lining—which should follow the line of the front facing of the coat—start by measuring the width of the front facing on the coat at the shoulder seam.

8. Mark the distance measured in Step 7 on the shoulder line of the traced outline of the coat front.

9. Measure the front facing a couple of inches lower, and make a mark at the corresponding point on the coat outline.

10. Continue measuring the front facing of the coat and marking the corresponding points on the coat outline. Then connect the marks to form the front line of the pattern.

11. To mark the armhole of the lining, draw a line 1/2 inch in from—and parallel to—the armhole of the coat outline. Start at the shoulder line and stop just before the armhole line begins to curve sharply.

12. Finish the armhole line by extending it to meet the side line about 2 inches below the armhole of the outline.

13. If the coat you are making the lining for is straight or only modestly flared in style, draw a side seam line for the lining 1/2 inch inside of—and parallel to—the side line of the coat outline.

14. If the coat is very flared, draw a side seam line for the lining that is 1/2 inch inside the side line at the armhole and at least 2 inches inside at the hem.

15. If the coat is fitted at the waist, make sure that the side line as well as the front edge curves inward, generally following the coat outline.

16. Mark the hem edge of the lining by drawing a line from 2 to 6 inches above the hem of the outline, depending on how close to the hem you want the lining to come. Make sure the line is parallel to the hem.

17. Round off the lower front corner of the lining.

18. Cut out the front lining pattern along the inner lines.

19. Make a duplicate pattern by pinning the original pattern to a sheet of paper and tracing around the edges. Then remove the original and cut out the duplicate along the lines.

continued

A TRACING THE OUTLINE OF THE COAT

1. Try on the coat for which you are making a lining, and insert a pin at the end of one shoulder.

2. Lay the coat on a flat surface with the pin-marked front section facing up. Lay a large sheet of firm tissue paper over the front. Tape together several sheets of paper if necessary.

3. Pin the paper in place.

4. Using a dull pencil with a soft lead, mark the outline of the coat front on the paper with a series of dashes. Trace along the front and hem edges and the neck and side seams. Mark the top shoulder seam between the neck seam and the pin.

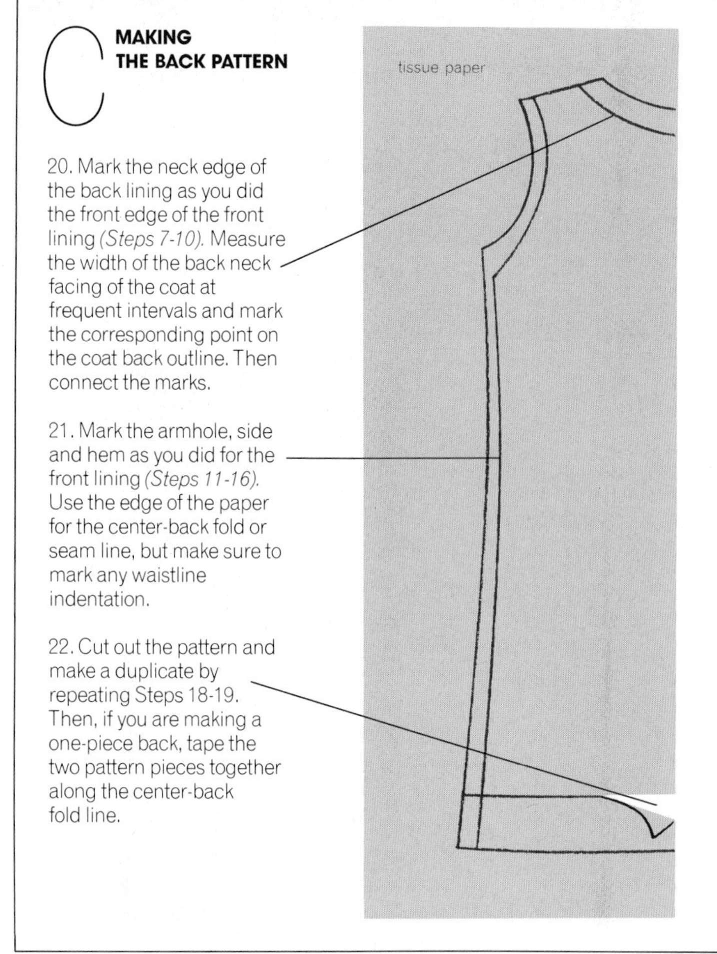

5. Unpin the paper, and place it on a flat surface.

6. Connect the pencil marks to complete the outline of the front. Use a ruler for straight lines; draw curves freehand. To complete the armhole, draw a straight line from the outer end of the shoulder line to the top of the side line.

7. Make the outline of half the coat back by repeating Steps 2-6. But this time align one long edge of the paper with the center-back seam or the center-back fold of the folded coat.

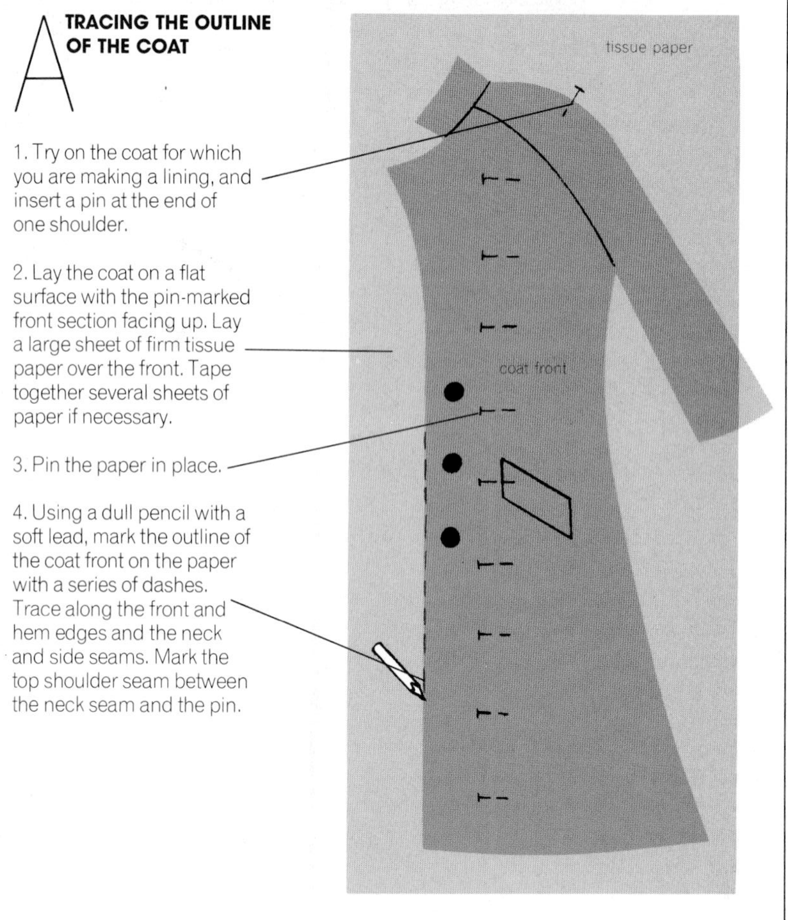

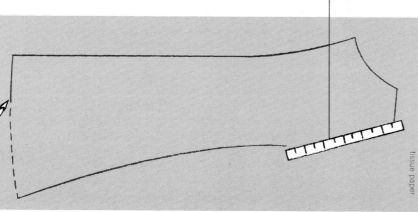

C MAKING THE BACK PATTERN

20. Mark the neck edge of the back lining as you did the front edge of the front lining *(Steps 7-10).* Measure the width of the back neck facing of the coat at frequent intervals and mark the corresponding point on the coat back outline. Then connect the marks.

21. Mark the armhole, side and hem as you did for the front lining *(Steps 11-16).* Use the edge of the paper for the center-back fold or seam line, but make sure to mark any waistline indentation.

22. Cut out the pattern and make a duplicate by repeating Steps 18-19. Then, if you are making a one-piece back, tape the two pattern pieces together along the center-back fold line.

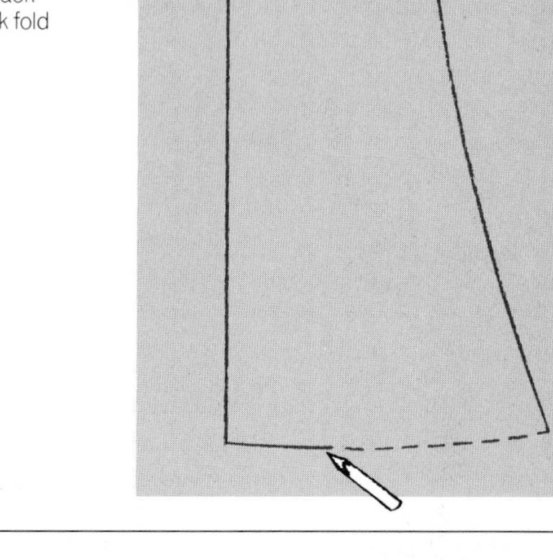

B MAKING THE PATTERN PIECES

8. To mark the front edge of the lining, follow the instructions for making a pattern for a coat with set-in sleeves *(page 127, Steps 7-10).*

9. To mark the armhole of the lining, start by measuring in 2 inches from the midpoint of the straight line connecting the shoulder and side lines. Make a mark.

10. Next measure down 2 inches from the lower end of the straight line along the side line and make a mark.

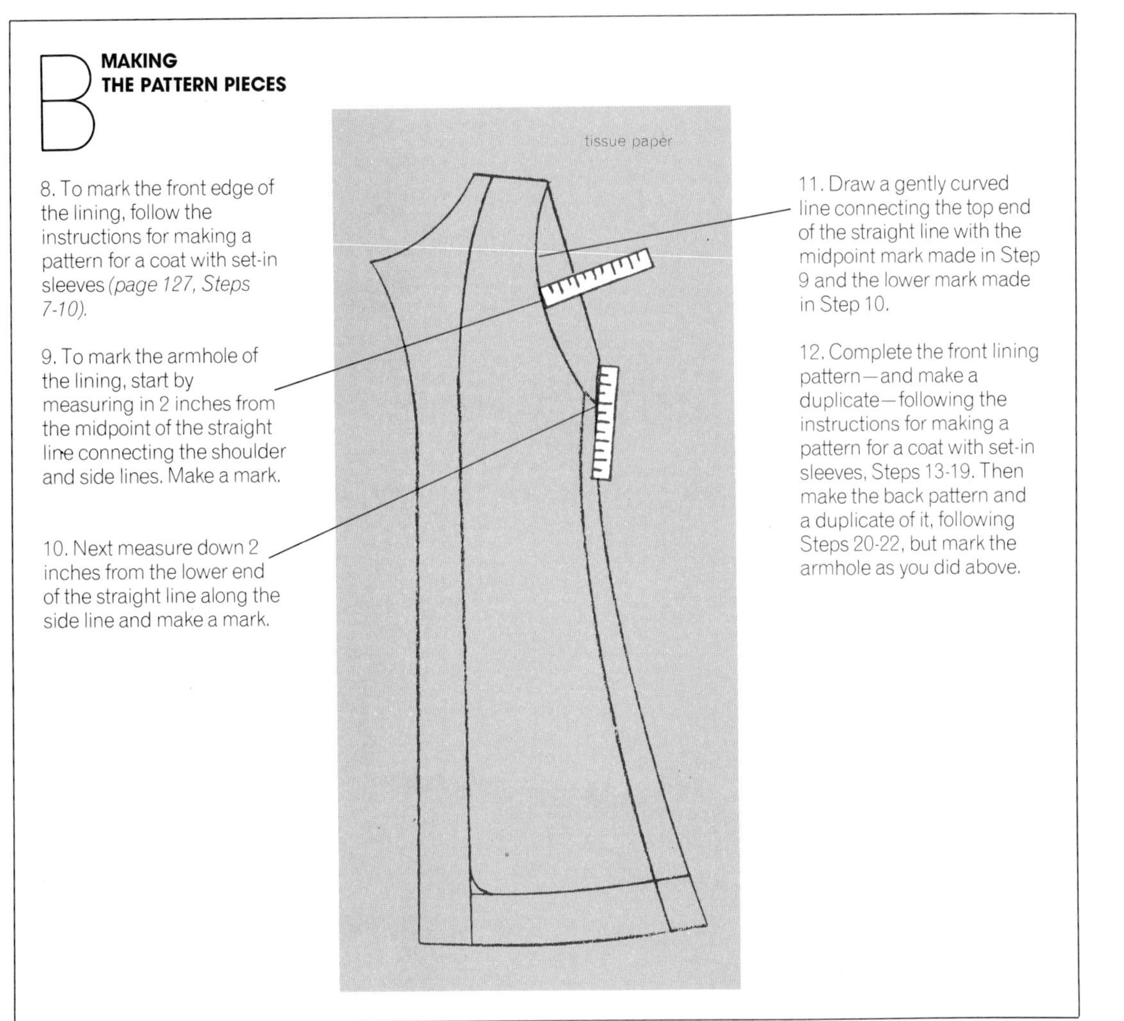

11. Draw a gently curved line connecting the top end of the straight line with the midpoint mark made in Step 9 and the lower mark made in Step 10.

12. Complete the front lining pattern—and make a duplicate—following the instructions for making a pattern for a coat with set-in sleeves, Steps 13-19. Then make the back pattern and a duplicate of it, following Steps 20-22, but mark the armhole as you did above.

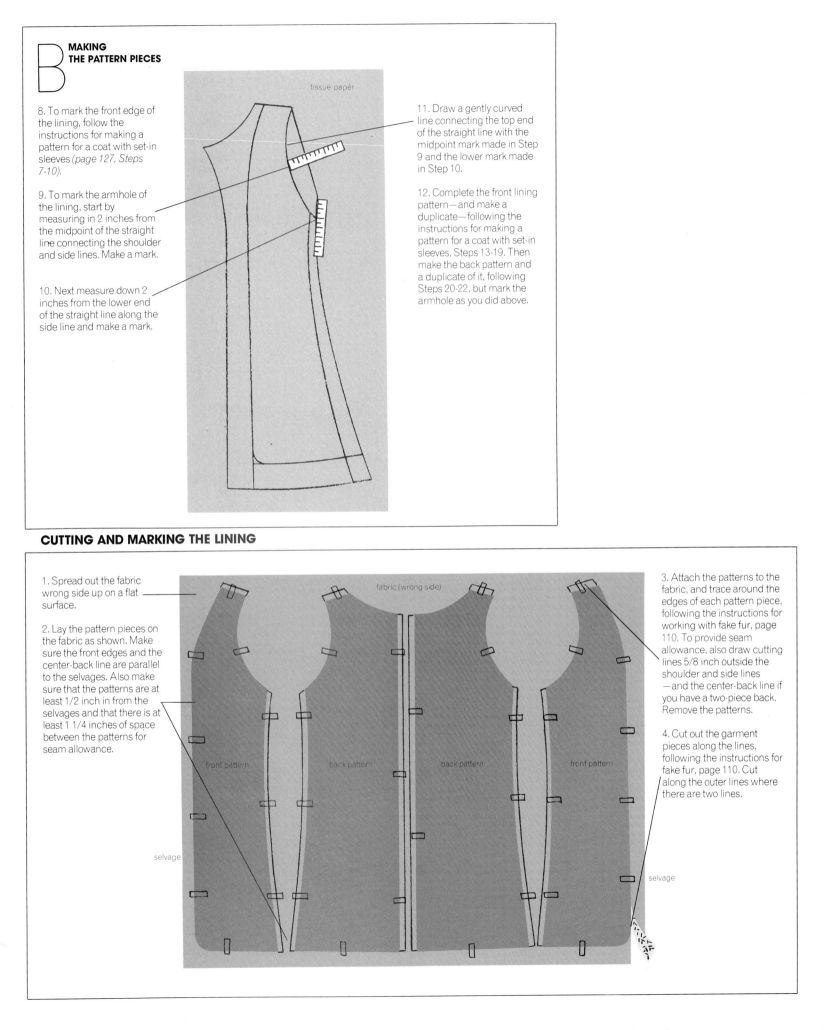

CUTTING AND MARKING THE LINING

1. Spread out the fabric wrong side up on a flat surface.

2. Lay the pattern pieces on the fabric as shown. Make sure the front edges and the center-back line are parallel to the selvages. Also make sure that the patterns are at least 1/2 inch in from the selvages and that there is at least 1 1/4 inches of space between the patterns for seam allowance.

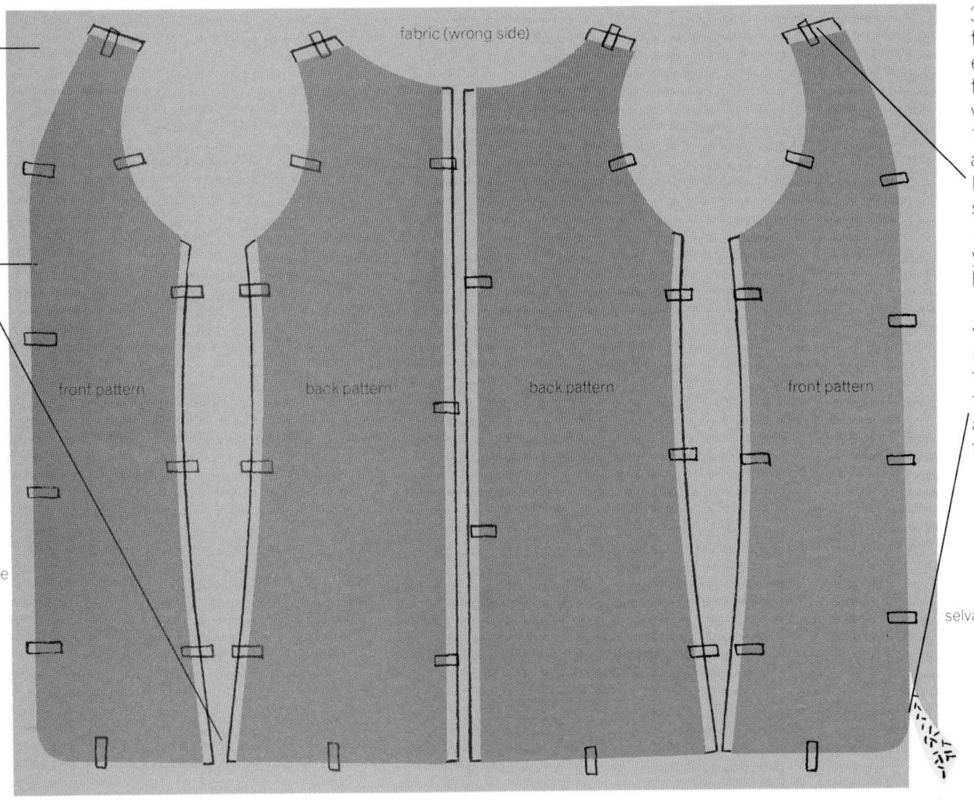

fabric (wrong side) — front pattern — back pattern — back pattern — front pattern — selvage — selvage

3. Attach the patterns to the fabric, and trace around the edges of each pattern piece, following the instructions for working with fake fur, page 110. To provide seam allowance, also draw cutting lines 5/8 inch outside the shoulder and side lines —and the center-back line if you have a two-piece back. Remove the patterns.

4. Cut out the garment pieces along the lines, following the instructions for fake fur, page 110. Cut along the outer lines where there are two lines.

CONSTRUCTING THE LINING

A ASSEMBLING THE LINING PIECES

1. If your lining has two back pieces, close the center-back seam, following the instructions for sewing fake fur, pages 114-115.

2. Attach the fronts to the back by closing the shoulder and side seams.

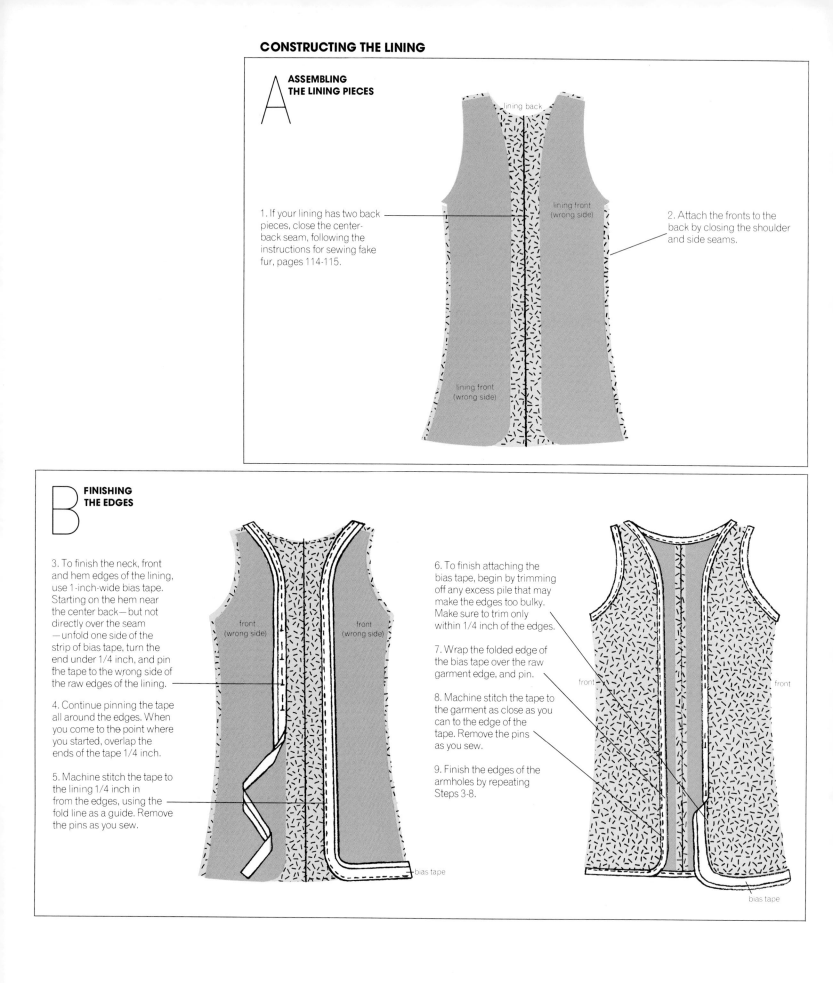

B FINISHING THE EDGES

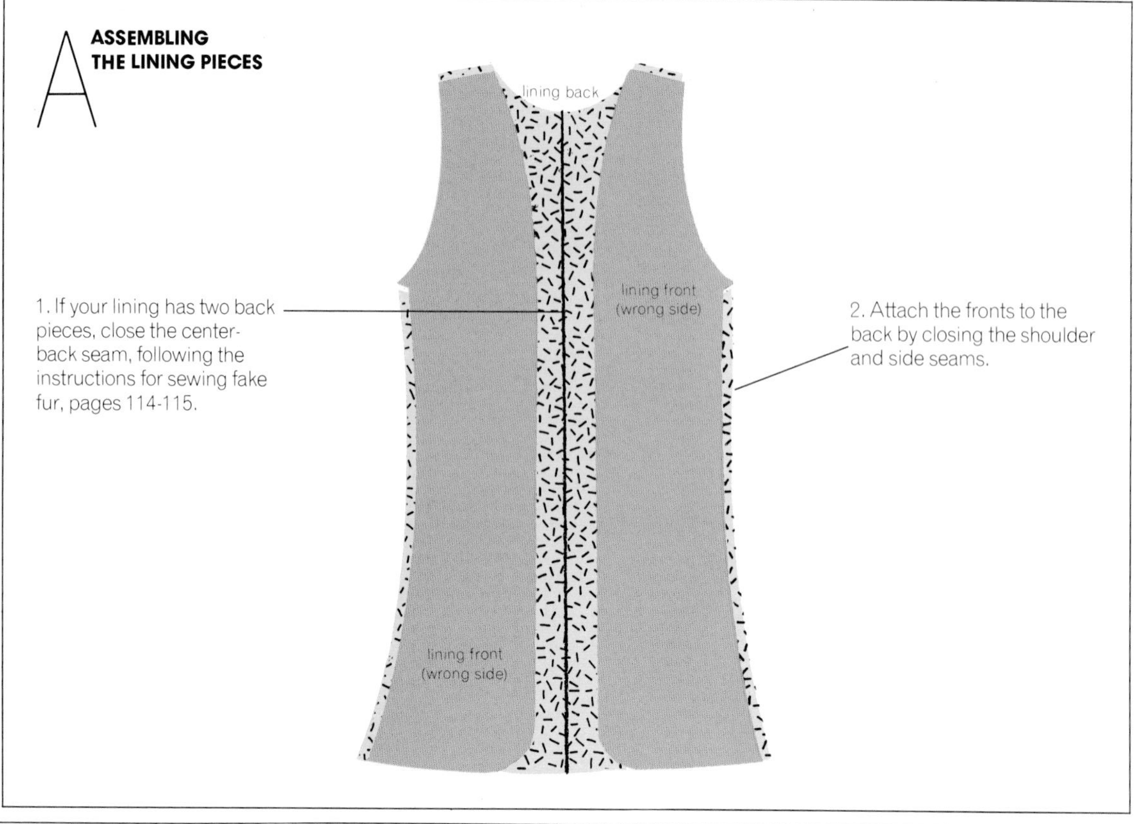

3. To finish the neck, front and hem edges of the lining, use 1-inch-wide bias tape. Starting on the hem near the center back—but not directly over the seam—unfold one side of the strip of bias tape, turn the end under 1/4 inch, and pin the tape to the wrong side of the raw edges of the lining.

4. Continue pinning the tape all around the edges. When you come to the point where you started, overlap the ends of the tape 1/4 inch.

5. Machine stitch the tape to the lining 1/4 inch in from the edges, using the fold line as a guide. Remove the pins as you sew.

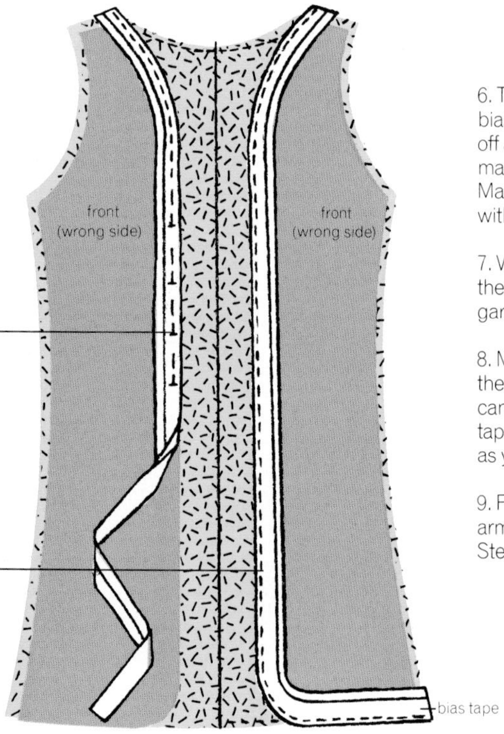

6. To finish attaching the bias tape, begin by trimming off any excess pile that may make the edges too bulky. Make sure to trim only within 1/4 inch of the edges.

7. Wrap the folded edge of the bias tape over the raw garment edge, and pin.

8. Machine stitch the tape to the garment as close as you can to the edge of the tape. Remove the pins as you sew.

9. Finish the edges of the armholes by repeating Steps 3-8.

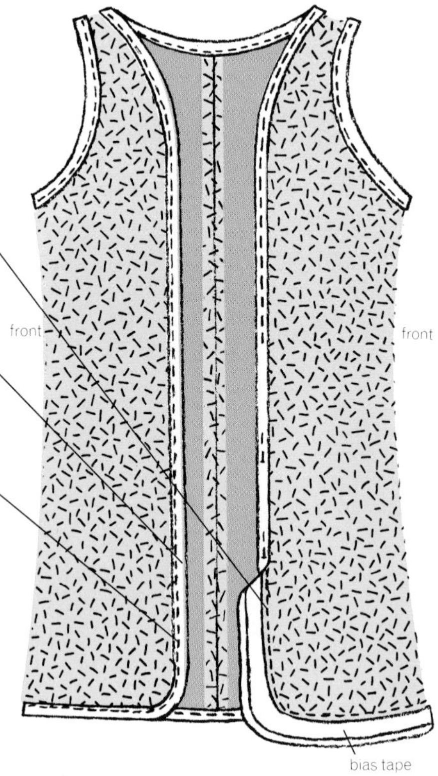

ATTACHING THE LINING WITH BUTTON LOOPS

A MAKING THE BUTTON LOOPS

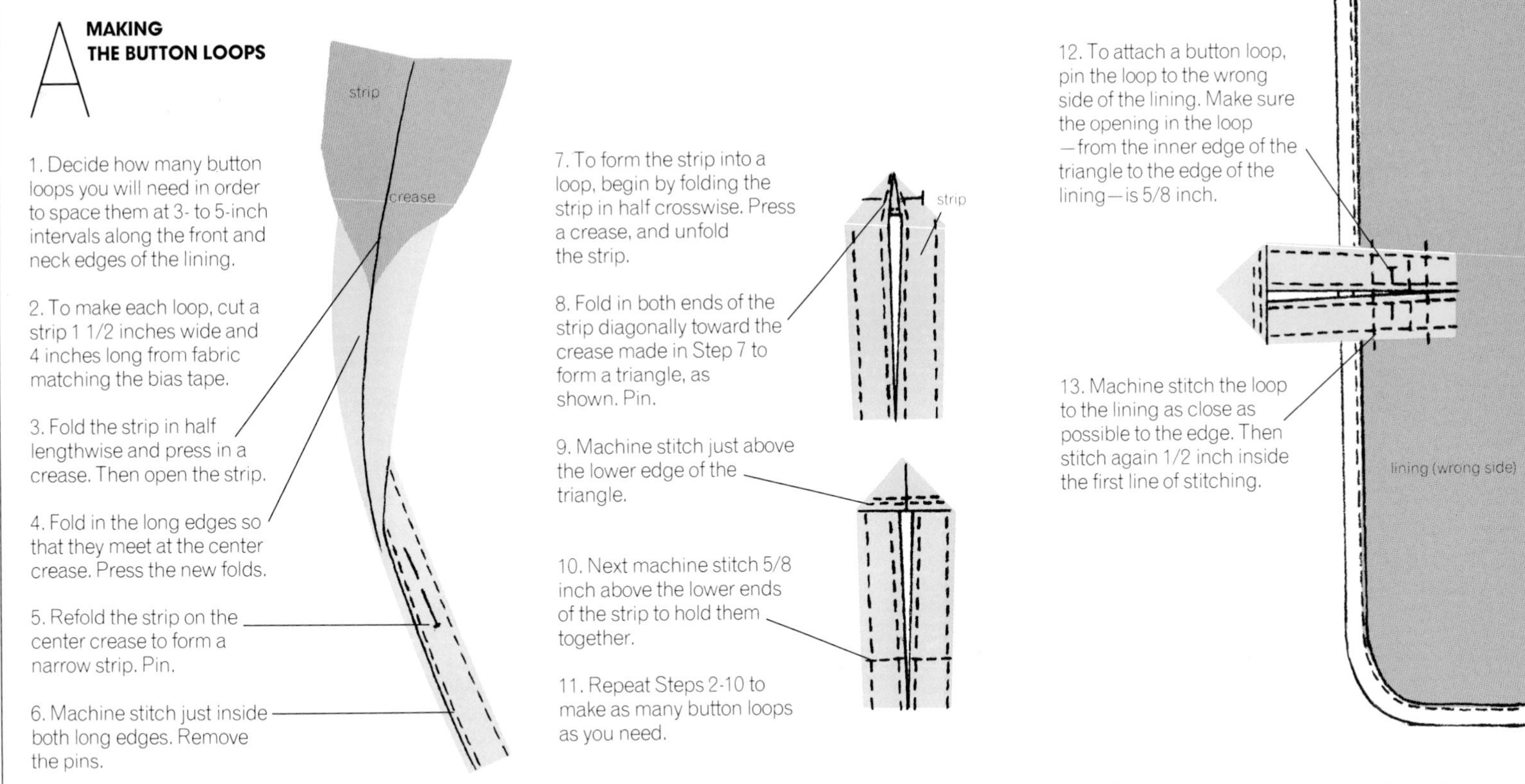

1. Decide how many button loops you will need in order to space them at 3- to 5-inch intervals along the front and neck edges of the lining.

2. To make each loop, cut a strip 1 1/2 inches wide and 4 inches long from fabric matching the bias tape.

3. Fold the strip in half lengthwise and press in a crease. Then open the strip.

4. Fold in the long edges so that they meet at the center crease. Press the new folds.

5. Refold the strip on the center crease to form a narrow strip. Pin.

6. Machine stitch just inside both long edges. Remove the pins.

7. To form the strip into a loop, begin by folding the strip in half crosswise. Press a crease, and unfold the strip.

8. Fold in both ends of the strip diagonally toward the crease made in Step 7 to form a triangle, as shown. Pin.

9. Machine stitch just above the lower edge of the triangle.

10. Next machine stitch 5/8 inch above the lower ends of the strip to hold them together.

11. Repeat Steps 2-10 to make as many button loops as you need.

12. To attach a button loop, pin the loop to the wrong side of the lining. Make sure the opening in the loop —from the inner edge of the triangle to the edge of the lining—is 5/8 inch.

13. Machine stitch the loop to the lining as close as possible to the edge. Then stitch again 1/2 inch inside the first line of stitching.

B ATTACHING THE BUTTONS

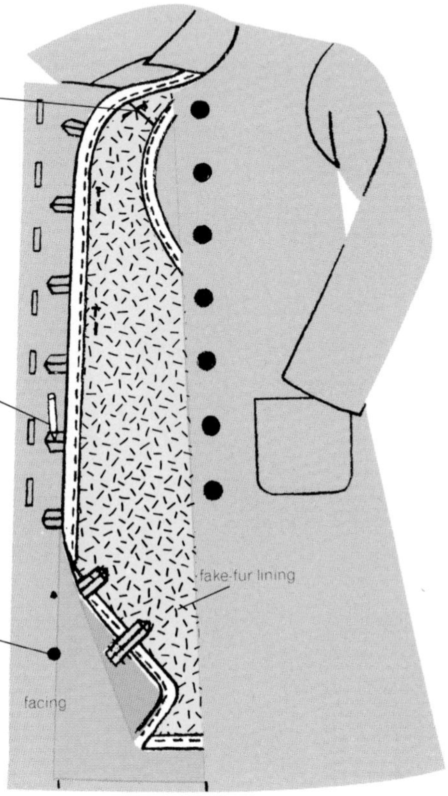

14. Slip the lining into the coat so that its wrong side is against the coat. Align the neck and front edges of the lining with the edges of the facings in the coat, making sure to match the shoulder seams. Pin the lining in place.

15. Mark the position of the buttons on the coat facings by making a chalk mark through the opening in each loop at the outer triangular end of the loop.

16. Remove the lining from the coat.

17. Hand sew a button with a 1/2-inch diameter to the facing at each of the marks, making sure to center the button over the mark. Be careful to catch only the facing in your stitches so that they will not show on the outside of the coat.

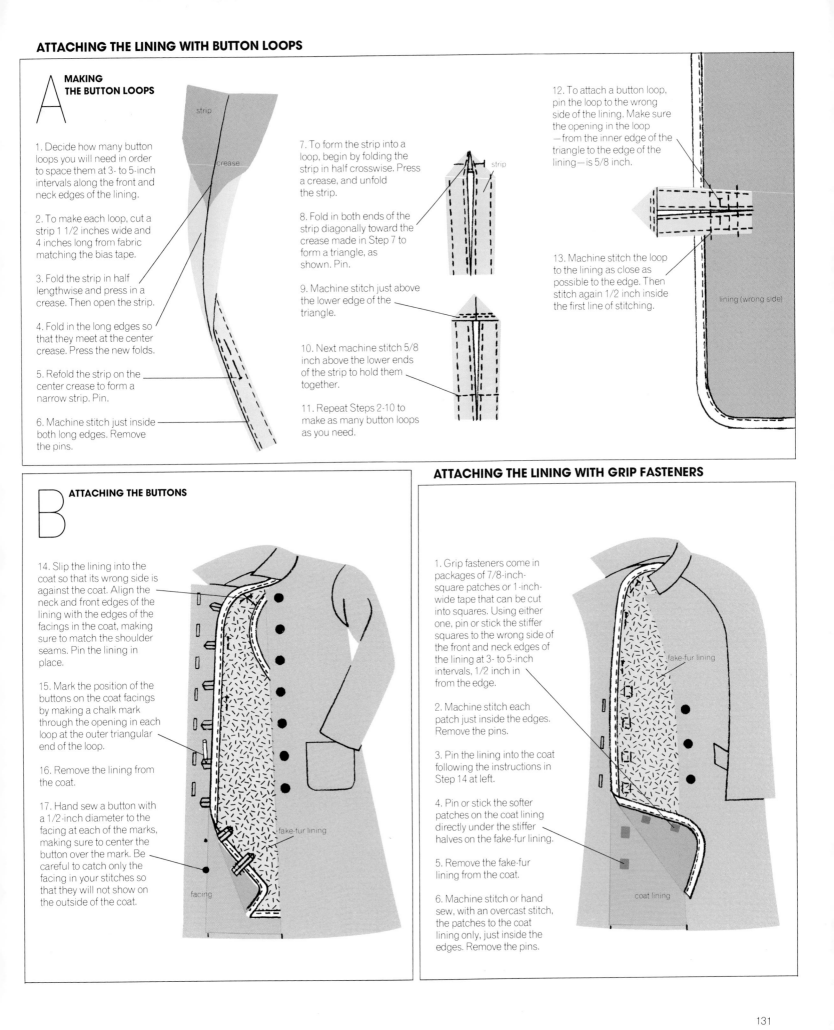

fake-fur lining

facing

ATTACHING THE LINING WITH GRIP FASTENERS

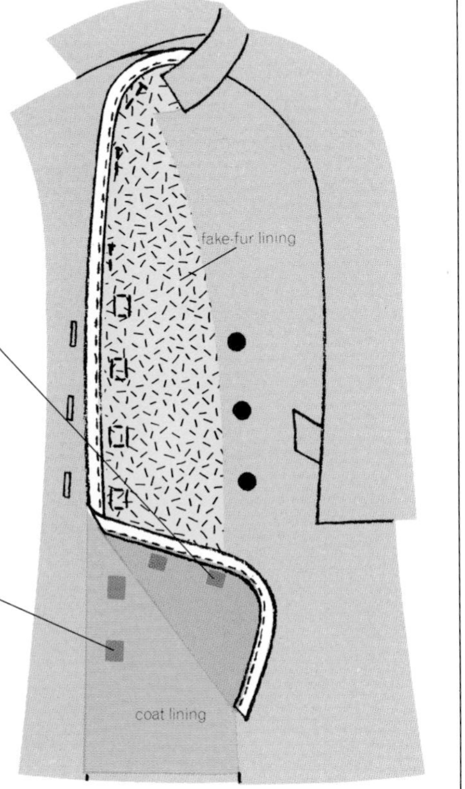

1. Grip fasteners come in packages of 7/8-inch-square patches or 1-inch-wide tape that can be cut into squares. Using either one, pin or stick the stiffer squares to the wrong side of the front and neck edges of the lining at 3- to 5-inch intervals, 1/2 inch in from the edge.

2. Machine stitch each patch just inside the edges. Remove the pins.

3. Pin the lining into the coat following the instructions in Step 14 at left.

4. Pin or stick the softer patches on the coat lining directly under the stiffer halves on the fake-fur lining.

5. Remove the fake-fur lining from the coat.

6. Machine stitch or hand sew, with an overcast stitch, the patches to the coat lining only, just inside the edges. Remove the pins.

fake-fur lining

coat lining

Topped off for winter

Fur, be it natural or fake, is unsurpassed as winter trim. Two ways to top off with fur are shown here—and detailed overleaf. The short-haired hat with matching collar and cuffs *(right)* has been recut from an old squirrel stole. The popover hat at far right is made of fake long-haired brown and white stone marten. The same brown trims the cardigan.

Making the hats, collars and cuffs

The instructions given here are for making the fur hats and accessories on the previous pages. The cloche and Peter Pan collar are most suited to a short-haired fur; the large beret and shawl collar look best in a longer pile fur. As shown, the cloche is made of well-preserved old fur and the beret fur is fake.

Before constructing these garments, check the techniques on pages 106-123 for cutting, marking and stitching fur. Take care how you position the nap. In the cloche the nap runs upward to the crown; in the beret it runs downward. On all cuffs the nap goes around the wrist.

For the cloche and collar you will need a prepared skin, a yard of rayon taffeta, a Size 5 glover's needle, and heavy-duty mercerized cotton thread the color of the fur. The hat requires 1/4 yard of matching felt and 1 1/2 yards of 3/4-inch-wide grosgrain ribbon for the hatband. For the collar and cuffs purchase 1/2 yard of interfacing and a package of 1/2-inch-wide twill or seam tape.

The beret and collar require: two colors of long-pile fake—1/4 yard of each color for the beret and 3/4 yard more of the darker color for collar and cuffs; a yard of rayon taffeta; and polyester thread. Finally, buy 3/4 yard of elastic, 3/4 inch wide, for the hat and seam or twill tape, 1/2 inch wide, for the collar and cuffs.

THE REAL FUR HAT

A MAKING THE PATTERN

1. Cut out a piece of brown wrapping paper 14 inches wide and 26 inches long. Mark it with a grid of 1-inch squares.

2. Transfer the shapes of the pattern pieces diagramed below onto your enlarged grid.

3. To determine your correct head size, measure the circumference of your head with a tape measure. Add 3/4 inch to this measurement for a comfortable fit. Then enlarge or reduce the pattern, which is for an average size 22, accordingly.

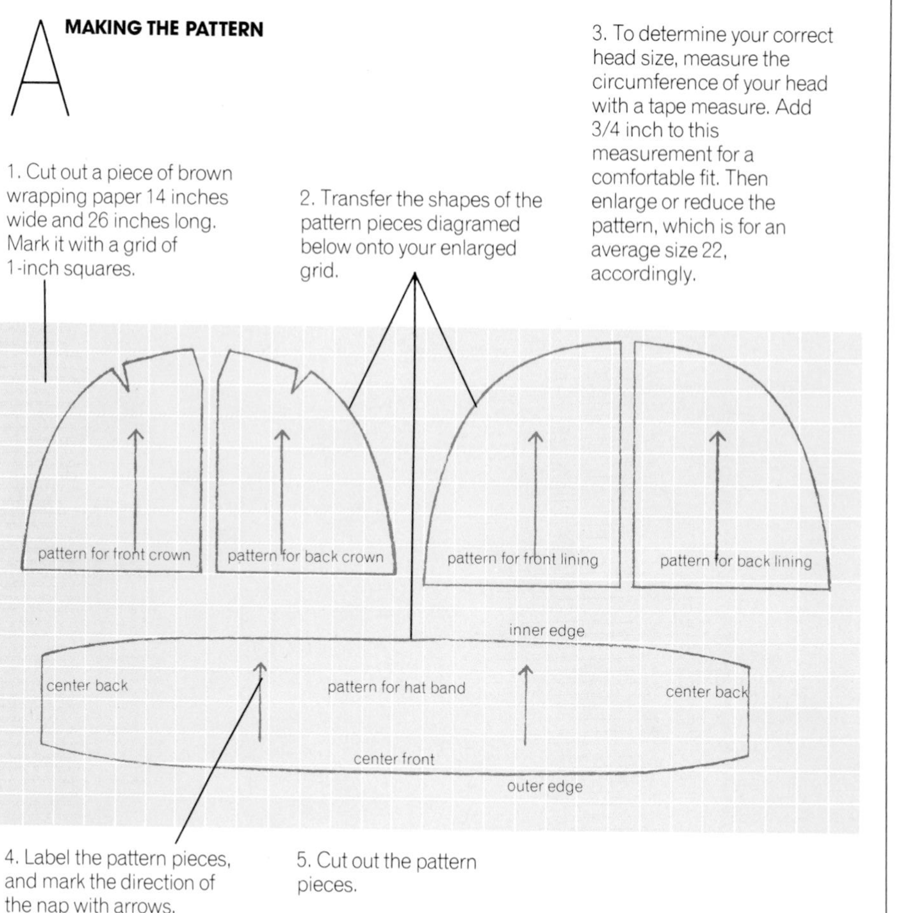

4. Label the pattern pieces, and mark the direction of the nap with arrows.

5. Cut out the pattern pieces.

B MARKING AND CUTTING OUT THE FUR

6. Determine and mark the direction of the nap on your fur *(page 106)*.

7. Rotate the fur so that the arrows are pointing up.

8. Position the band and crown pattern pieces on the fur as shown, making sure to match the direction of the arrows. Tape them in place, and outline them *(page 108)*.

9. Reposition the crown pattern pieces as indicated by the dash lines, and outline them.

10. Set aside the pattern pieces, and transfer the labels to the skin. Cut out the pieces along the marked outlines *(page 109)*.

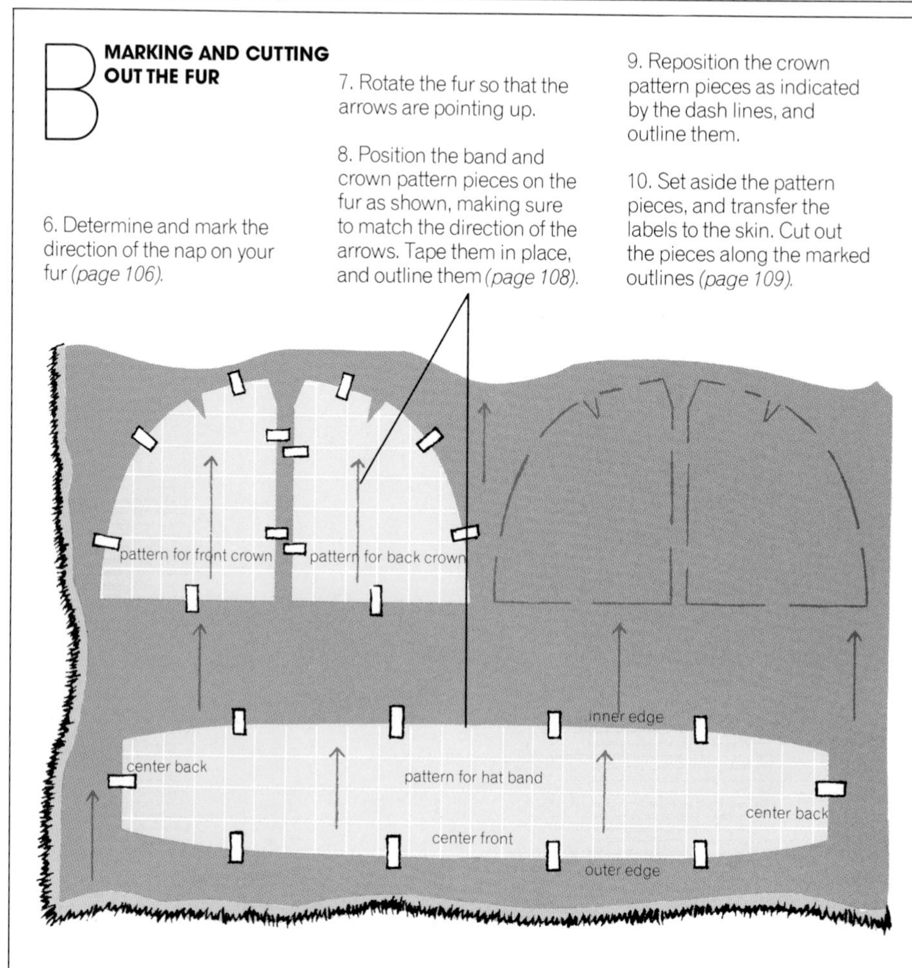

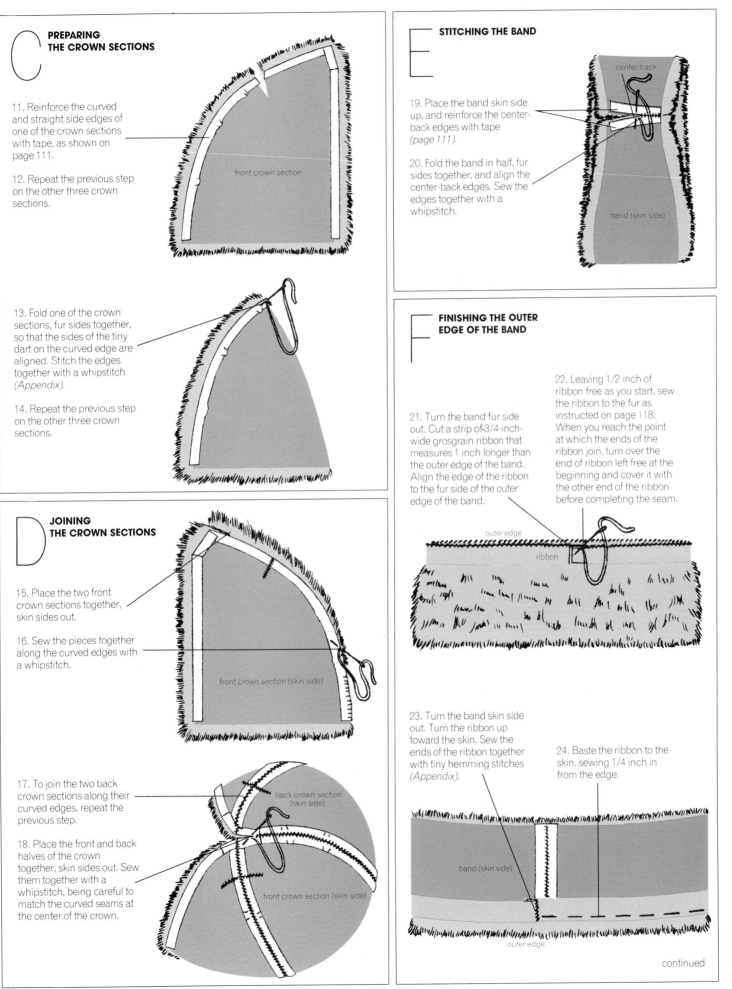

C PREPARING THE CROWN SECTIONS

11. Reinforce the curved and straight side edges of one of the crown sections with tape, as shown on page 111.

12. Repeat the previous step on the other three crown sections.

13. Fold one of the crown sections, fur sides together, so that the sides of the tiny dart on the curved edge are aligned. Stitch the edges together with a whipstitch *(Appendix).*

14. Repeat the previous step on the other three crown sections.

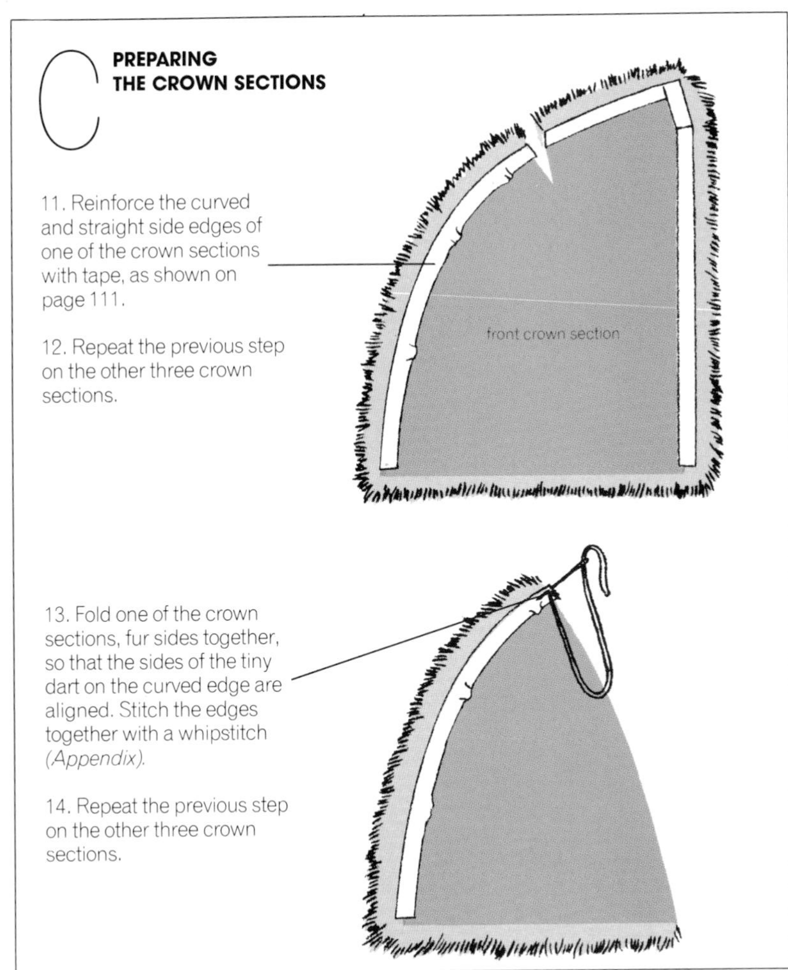

D JOINING THE CROWN SECTIONS

15. Place the two front crown sections together, skin sides out.

16. Sew the pieces together along the curved edges with a whipstitch.

17. To join the two back crown sections along their curved edges, repeat the previous step.

18. Place the front and back halves of the crown together, skin sides out. Sew them together with a whipstitch, being careful to match the curved seams at the center of the crown.

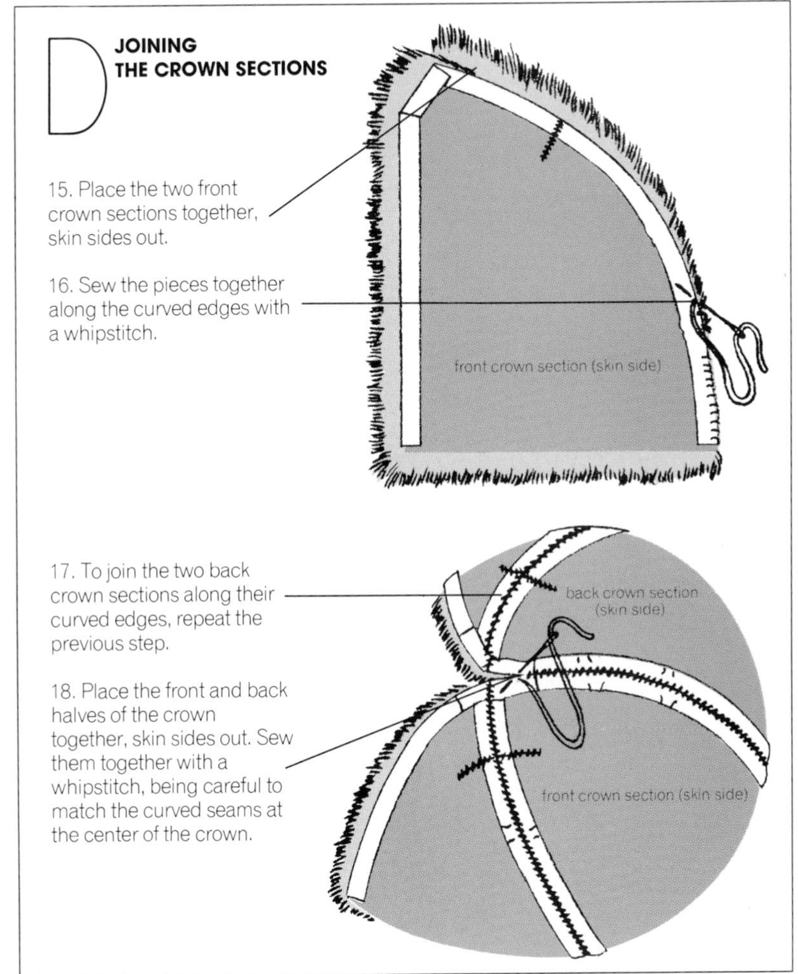

E STITCHING THE BAND

19. Place the band skin side up, and reinforce the center-back edges with tape *(page 111).*

20. Fold the band in half, fur sides together, and align the center-back edges. Sew the edges together with a whipstitch.

center back

band (skin side)

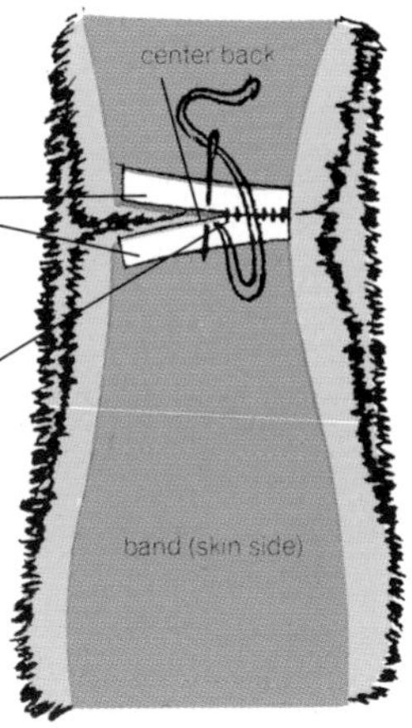

F FINISHING THE OUTER EDGE OF THE BAND

21. Turn the band fur side out. Cut a strip of 3/4-inch-wide grosgrain ribbon that measures 1 inch longer than the outer edge of the band. Align the edge of the ribbon to the fur side of the outer edge of the band.

22. Leaving 1/2 inch of ribbon free as you start, sew the ribbon to the fur as instructed on page 118. When you reach the point at which the ends of the ribbon join, turn over the end of ribbon left free at the beginning and cover it with the other end of the ribbon before completing the seam.

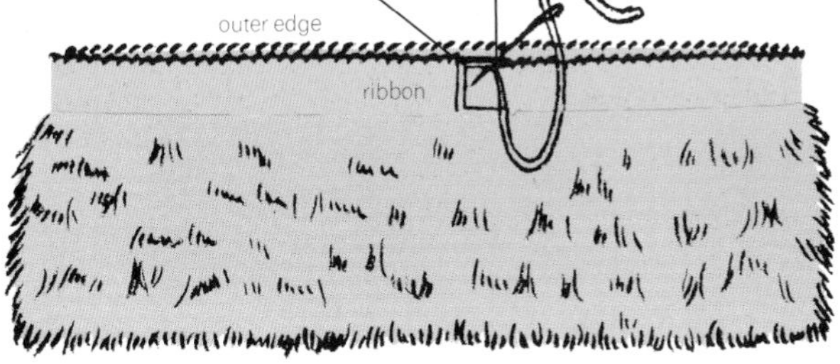

outer edge

ribbon

23. Turn the band skin side out. Turn the ribbon up toward the skin. Sew the ends of the ribbon together with tiny hemming stitches *(Appendix).*

24. Baste the ribbon to the skin, sewing 1/4 inch in from the edge.

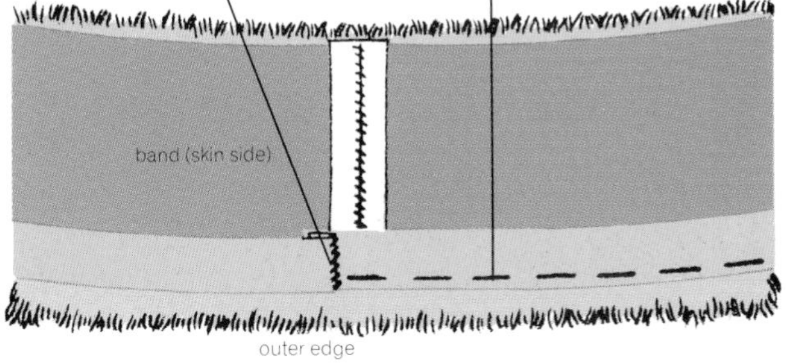

band (skin side)

outer edge

continued

G MAKING THE LINING OF THE BAND

25. Using the original pattern piece for the band, cut out a piece of felt in a color that blends in with the color of your fur. Add 1/4 inch at each center-back edge and 3/4 inch along the inner and outer edges for seam allowance.

26. Fold the felt in half and machine stitch the center-back edges together, sewing 1/4 inch in from the edge. Press open the seam.

27. Turn the felt so that the seam faces toward the inside. Slip it over the band, placing the outer edges and the wrong sides together and aligning the center-back seams.

28. Turn under the outer edge of the felt 3/4 inch, using the free edge of the ribbon as a guide. Match the folded edge of the felt with the seam joining the ribbon to the band and pin them together.

29. Attach the felt to the ribbon, using a slip stitch *(Appendix)*. Remove the pins as you sew.

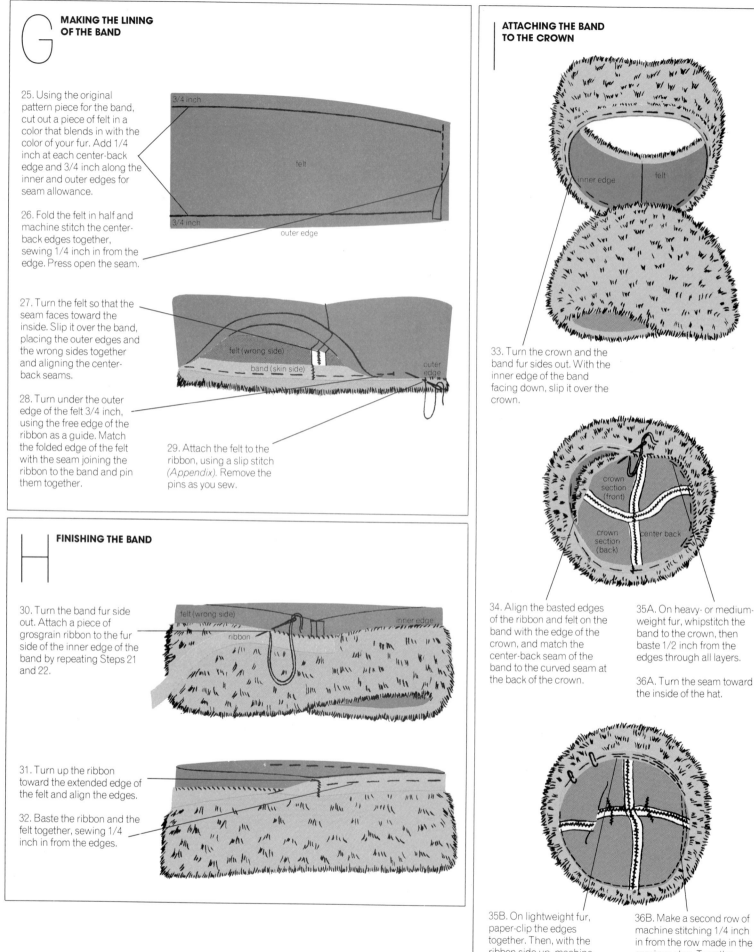

H FINISHING THE BAND

30. Turn the band fur side out. Attach a piece of grosgrain ribbon to the fur side of the inner edge of the band by repeating Steps 21 and 22.

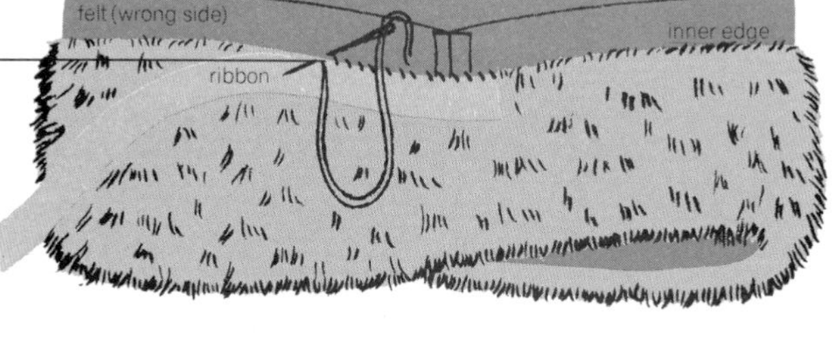

31. Turn up the ribbon toward the extended edge of the felt and align the edges.

32. Baste the ribbon and the felt together, sewing 1/4 inch in from the edges.

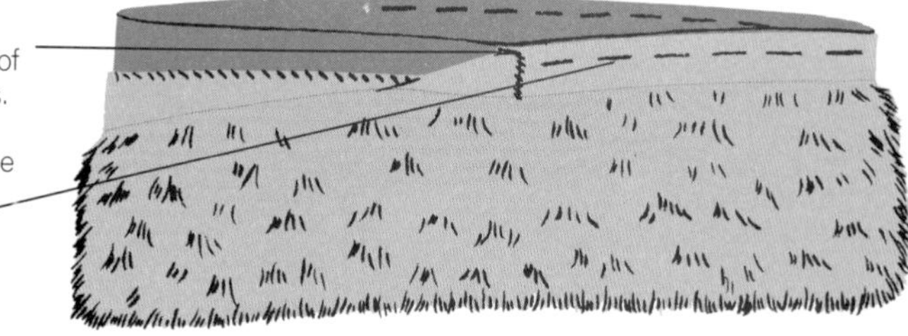

ATTACHING THE BAND TO THE CROWN

33. Turn the crown and the band fur sides out. With the inner edge of the band facing down, slip it over the crown.

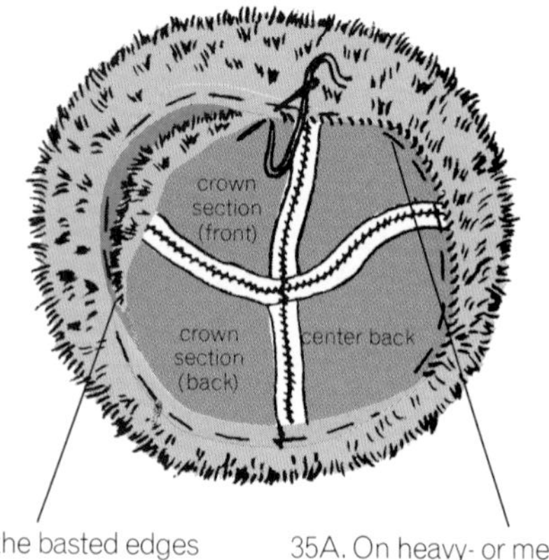

34. Align the basted edges of the ribbon and felt on the band with the edge of the crown, and match the center-back seam of the band to the curved seam at the back of the crown.

35A. On heavy- or medium-weight fur, whipstitch the band to the crown, then baste 1/2 inch from the edges through all layers.

36A. Turn the seam toward the inside of the hat.

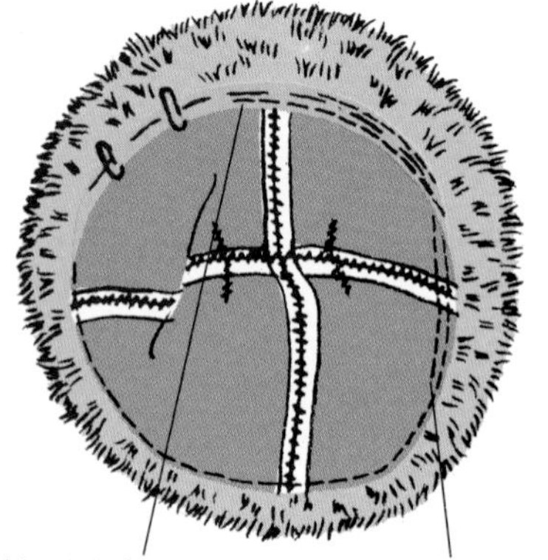

35B. On lightweight fur, paper-clip the edges together. Then, with the ribbon side up, machine stitch 1/8 inch in from the edge through all layers.

36B. Make a second row of machine stitching 1/4 inch in from the row made in the previous step. Turn the seam toward the crown.

J MAKING THE LINING OF THE CROWN

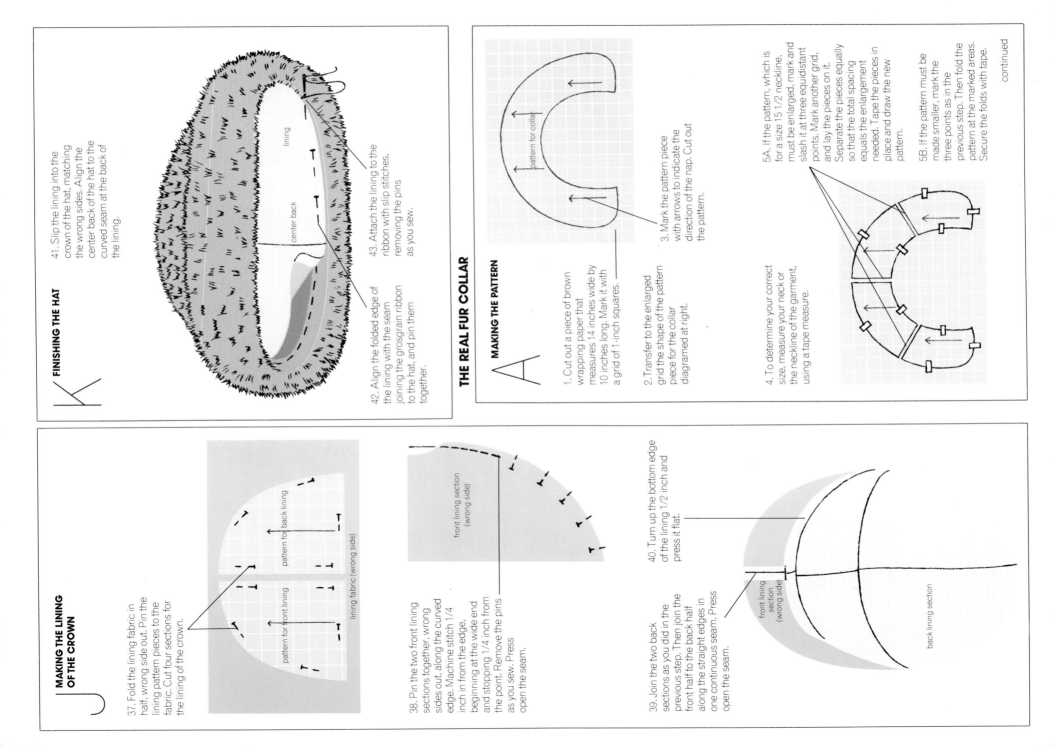

37. Fold the lining fabric in half, wrong side out. Pin the lining pattern pieces to the fabric. Cut four sections for the lining of the crown.

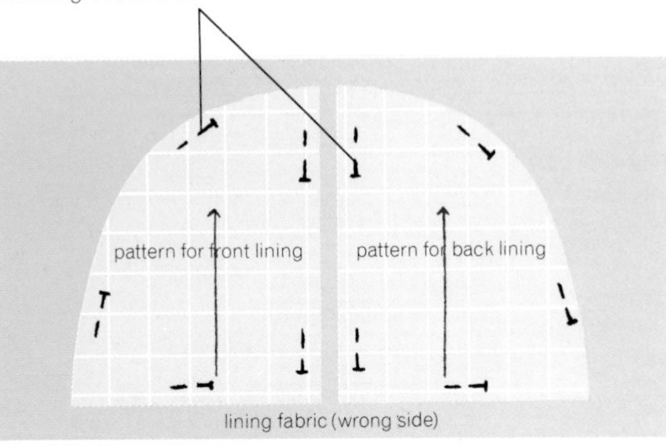

38. Pin the two front lining sections together, wrong sides out, along the curved edge. Machine stitch 1/4 inch in from the edge, beginning at the wide end and stopping 1/4 inch from the point. Remove the pins as you sew. Press open the seam.

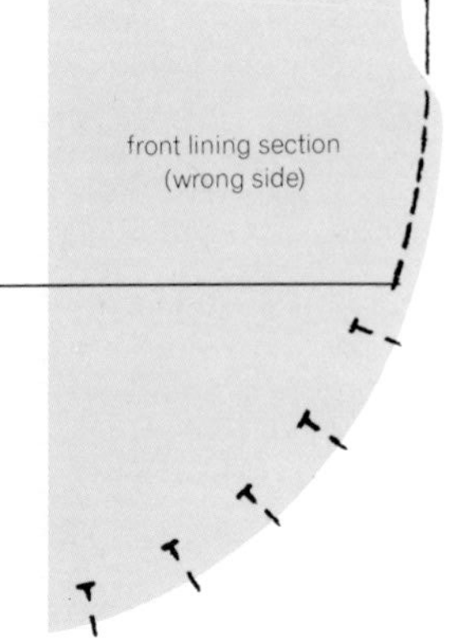

39. Join the two back sections as you did in the previous step. Then join the front half to the back half along the straight edges in one continuous seam. Press open the seam.

40. Turn up the bottom edge of the lining 1/2 inch and press it flat.

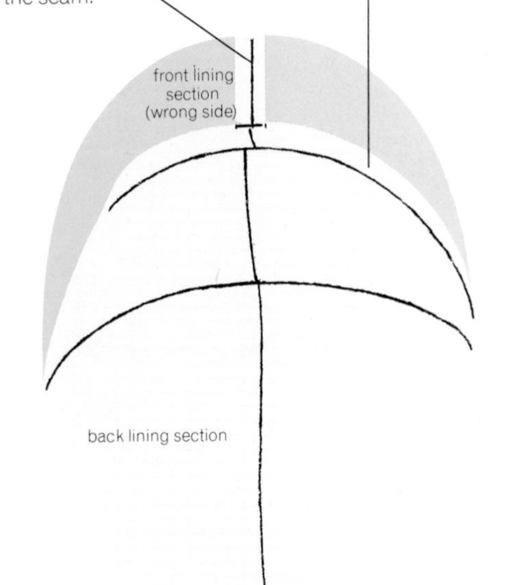

K FINISHING THE HAT

41. Slip the lining into the crown of the hat, matching the wrong sides. Align the center back of the hat to the curved seam at the back of the lining.

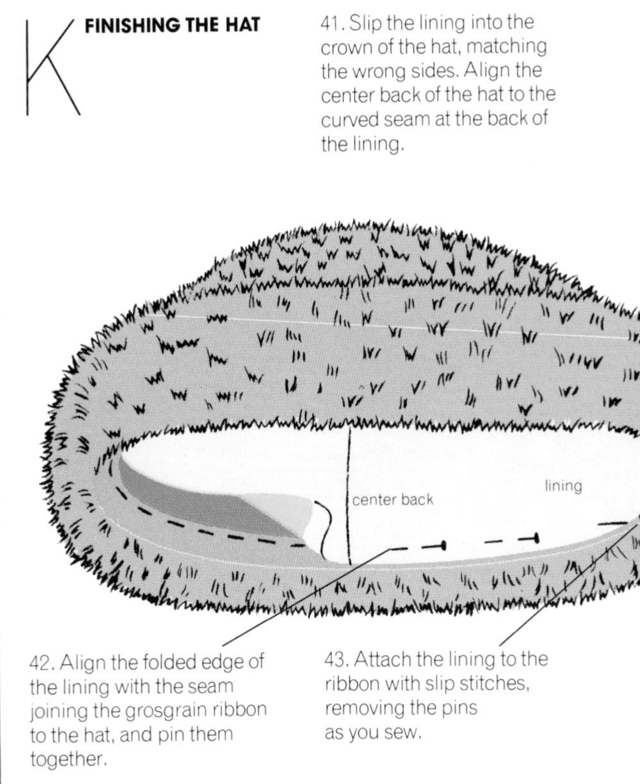

42. Align the folded edge of the lining with the seam joining the grosgrain ribbon to the hat, and pin them together.

43. Attach the lining to the ribbon with slip stitches, removing the pins as you sew.

THE REAL FUR COLLAR

A MAKING THE PATTERN

1. Cut out a piece of brown wrapping paper that measures 14 inches wide by 10 inches long. Mark it with a grid of 1-inch squares.

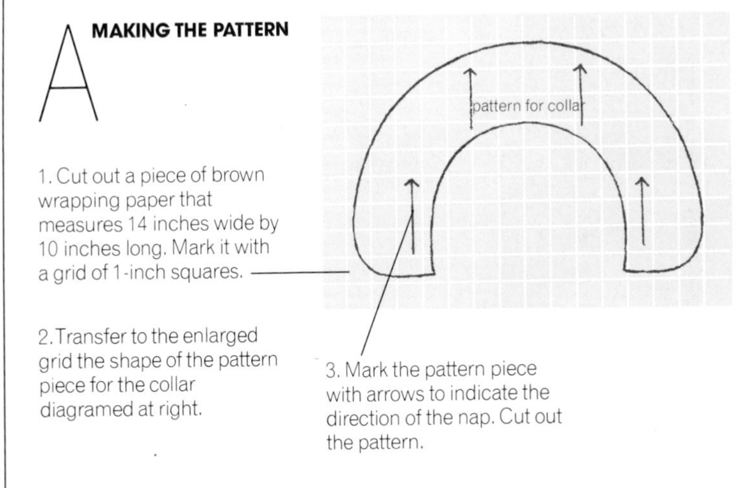

2. Transfer to the enlarged grid the shape of the pattern piece for the collar diagramed at right.

3. Mark the pattern piece with arrows to indicate the direction of the nap. Cut out the pattern.

4. To determine your correct size, measure your neck or the neckline of the garment, using a tape measure.

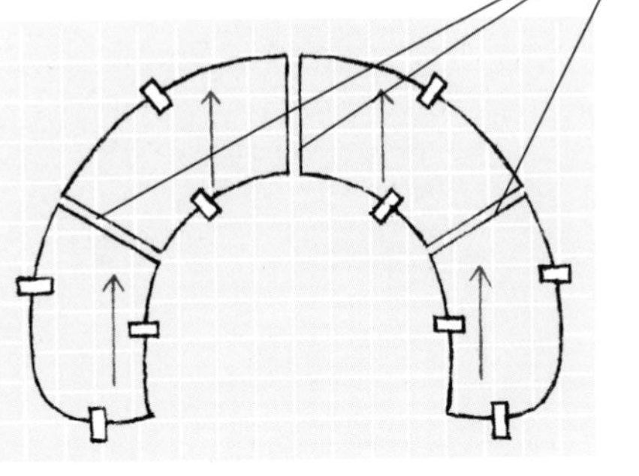

5A. If the pattern, which is for a size 15 1/2 neckline, must be enlarged, mark and slash it at three equidistant points. Mark another grid, and lay the pieces on it. Separate the pieces equally so that the total spacing equals the enlargement needed. Tape the pieces in place and draw the new pattern.

5B. If the pattern must be made smaller, mark the three points as in the previous step. Then fold the pattern at the marked areas. Secure the folds with tape.

continued

B MARKING THE FUR

6. Determine the direction of the nap on your fur and mark with arrows *(page 106)*.

7. Rotate the fur so that the arrows are pointing up.

8. Tape the pattern on the fur, as shown, making sure to match the direction of the arrows. Outline the pattern, then cut out the collar as shown on pages 108-109.

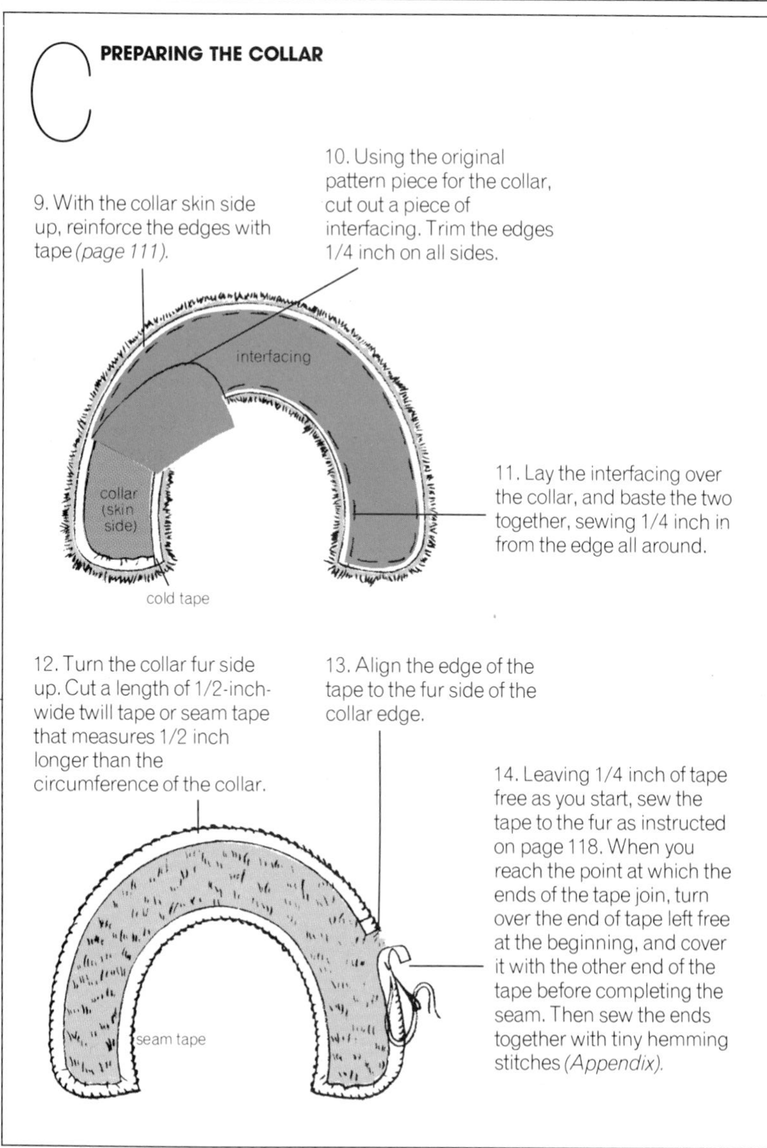

C PREPARING THE COLLAR

9. With the collar skin side up, reinforce the edges with tape *(page 111)*.

10. Using the original pattern piece for the collar, cut out a piece of interfacing. Trim the edges 1/4 inch on all sides.

11. Lay the interfacing over the collar, and baste the two together, sewing 1/4 inch in from the edge all around.

12. Turn the collar fur side up. Cut a length of 1/2-inch-wide twill tape or seam tape that measures 1/2 inch longer than the circumference of the collar.

13. Align the edge of the tape to the fur side of the collar edge.

14. Leaving 1/4 inch of tape free as you start, sew the tape to the fur as instructed on page 118. When you reach the point at which the ends of the tape join, turn over the end of tape left free at the beginning, and cover it with the other end of the tape before completing the seam. Then sew the ends together with tiny hemming stitches *(Appendix)*.

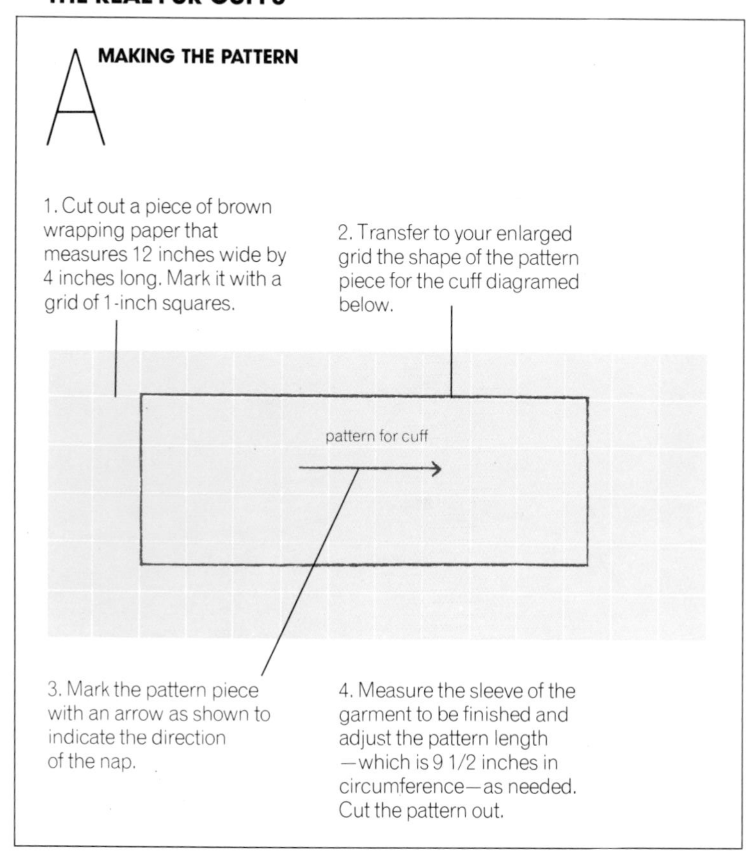

D MAKING THE LINING

15. Pin the original pattern piece for the collar to a single thickness of lining fabric. Add 1/2 inch around the edge, and mark the new outline. Cut out the lining.

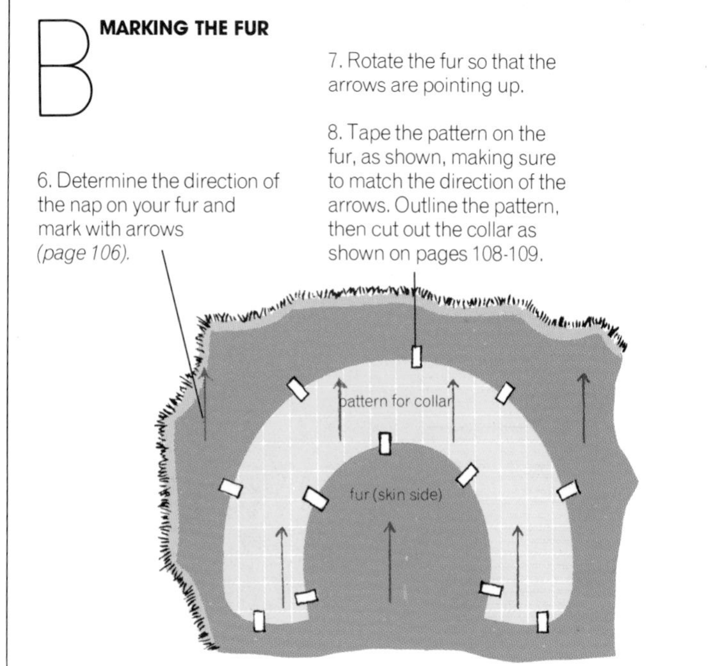

E FINISHING THE COLLAR

16. Turn under the edges of the lining 1/2 inch, and press.

17. Turn the tape attached in Steps 13-14 toward the skin side. Baste the tape to the skin.

18. With the wrong sides together, lay the lining over the collar. Pin the lining and the collar together along the edges.

19. Attach the lining to the collar along the edges with a slip stitch *(Appendix)*, removing the pins as you sew.

20. Place the collar, fur side out, around the neckline of the garment to be finished, and slip stitch them together.

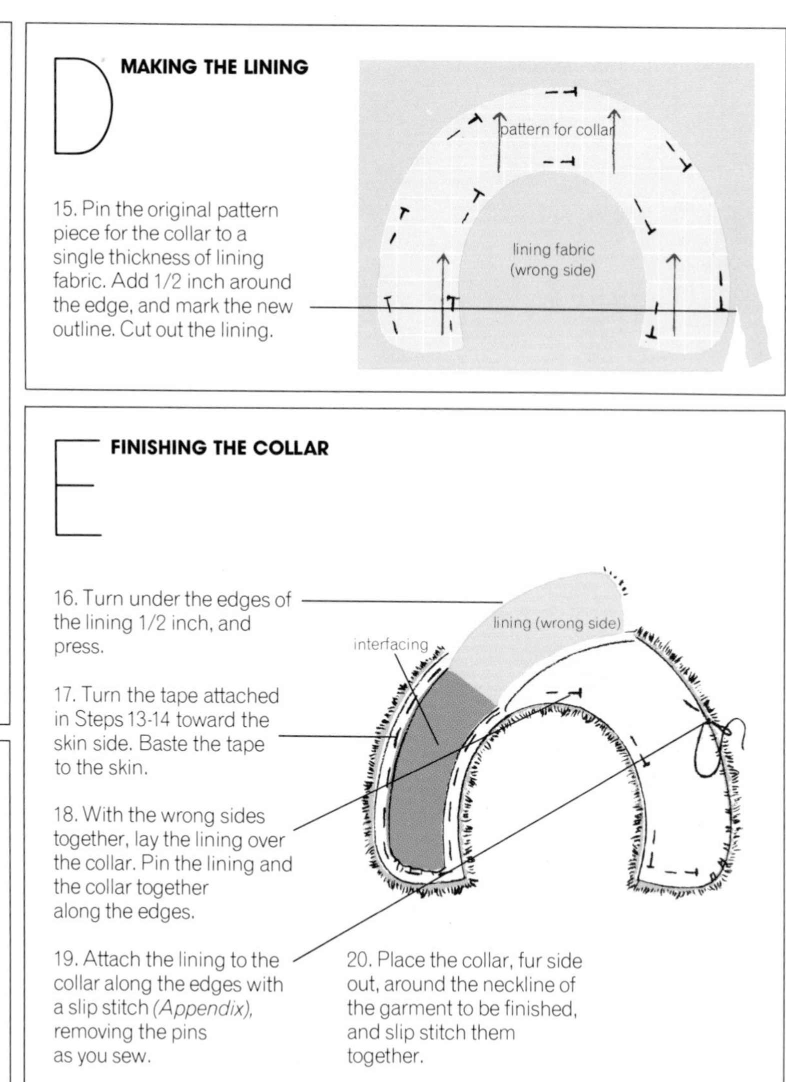

THE REAL FUR CUFFS

A MAKING THE PATTERN

1. Cut out a piece of brown wrapping paper that measures 12 inches wide by 4 inches long. Mark it with a grid of 1-inch squares.

2. Transfer to your enlarged grid the shape of the pattern piece for the cuff diagramed below.

pattern for cuff

3. Mark the pattern piece with an arrow as shown to indicate the direction of the nap.

4. Measure the sleeve of the garment to be finished and adjust the pattern length —which is 9 1/2 inches in circumference—as needed. Cut the pattern out.

B MARKING THE FUR

5. Determine the direction of the nap on your fur and mark with arrows *(page 106).*

6. Rotate the fur so that the arrows are pointing to the right.

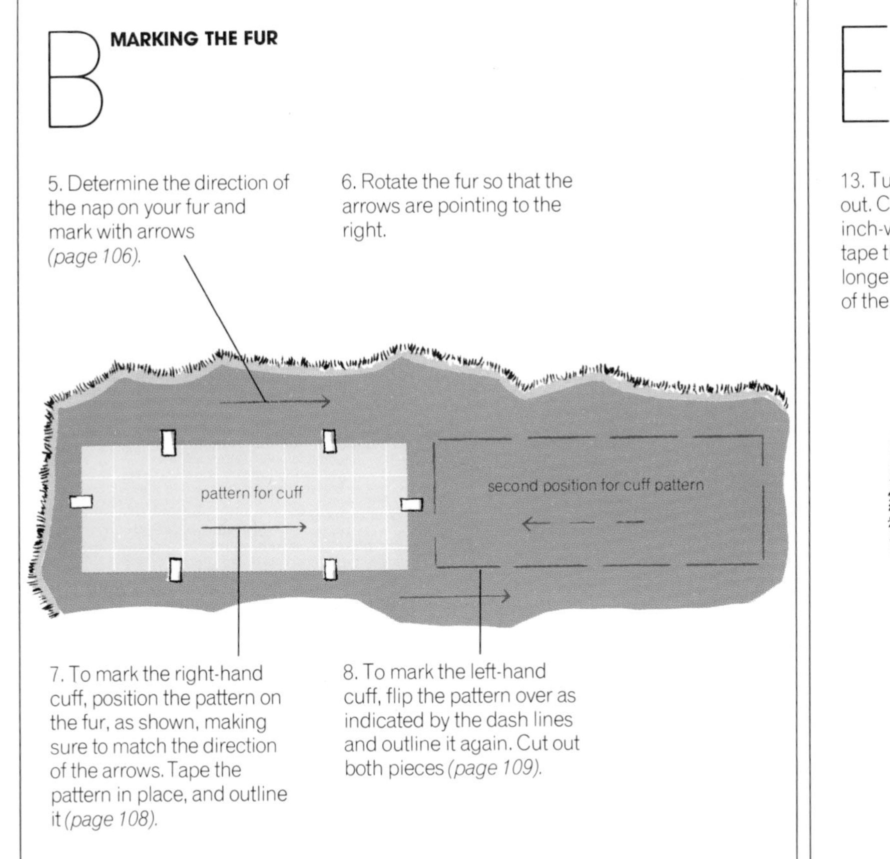

7. To mark the right-hand cuff, position the pattern on the fur, as shown, making sure to match the direction of the arrows. Tape the pattern in place, and outline it *(page 108).*

8. To mark the left-hand cuff, flip the pattern over as indicated by the dash lines and outline it again. Cut out both pieces *(page 109).*

C PREPARING THE CUFF

9. Lay one of the cuffs skin side up, and reinforce the edges with tape *(page 111).*

10. Using the original pattern for the cuff, cut out two pieces of interfacing and trim the edges 1/4 inch on all sides.

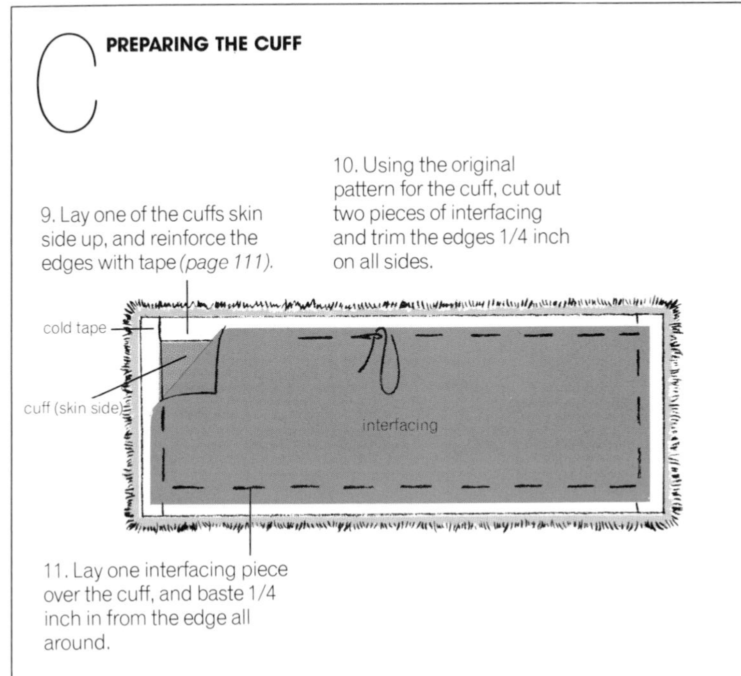

11. Lay one interfacing piece over the cuff, and baste 1/4 inch in from the edge all around.

D STITCHING THE ENDS OF THE CUFF

12. Fold the cuff in half, fur sides together. Stitch the ends together with a whipstitch as shown on pages 112-113.

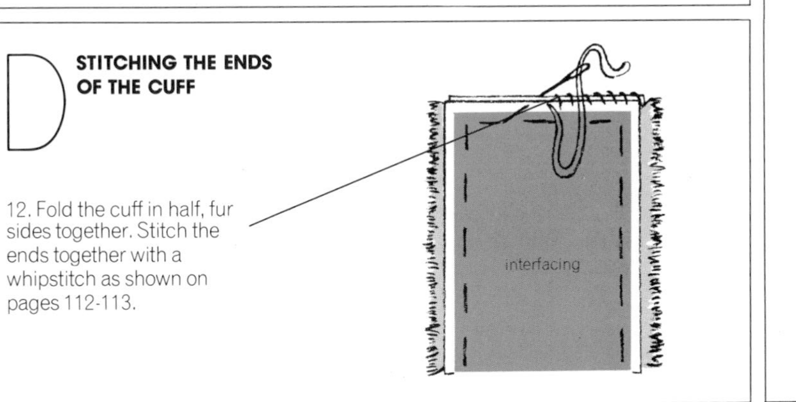

E FINISHING THE EDGES OF THE CUFF

13. Turn the cuff fur side out. Cut a length of 1/2-inch-wide twill tape or seam tape that measures 1/2 inch longer than the upper edge of the cuff.

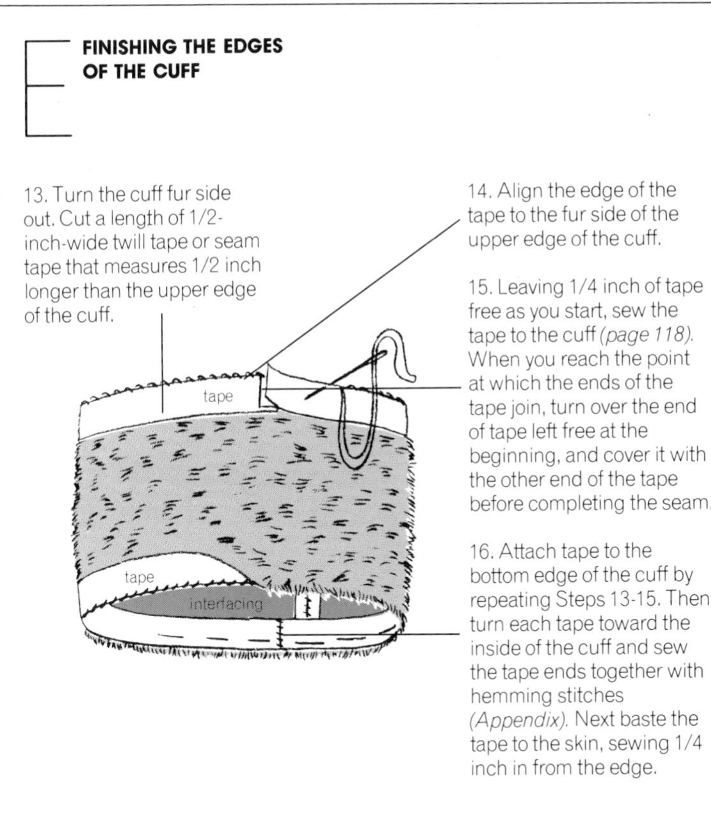

14. Align the edge of the tape to the fur side of the upper edge of the cuff.

15. Leaving 1/4 inch of tape free as you start, sew the tape to the cuff *(page 118).* When you reach the point at which the ends of the tape join, turn over the end of tape left free at the beginning, and cover it with the other end of the tape before completing the seam.

16. Attach tape to the bottom edge of the cuff by repeating Steps 13-15. Then turn each tape toward the inside of the cuff and sew the tape ends together with hemming stitches *(Appendix).* Next baste the tape to the skin, sewing 1/4 inch in from the edge.

F MAKING THE LINING

17. Fold the lining fabric in half, wrong sides out, and pin the cuff pattern to the lining. Draw an outline of the cuff, adding 1/2 inch on all sides. Then cut out the lining pieces.

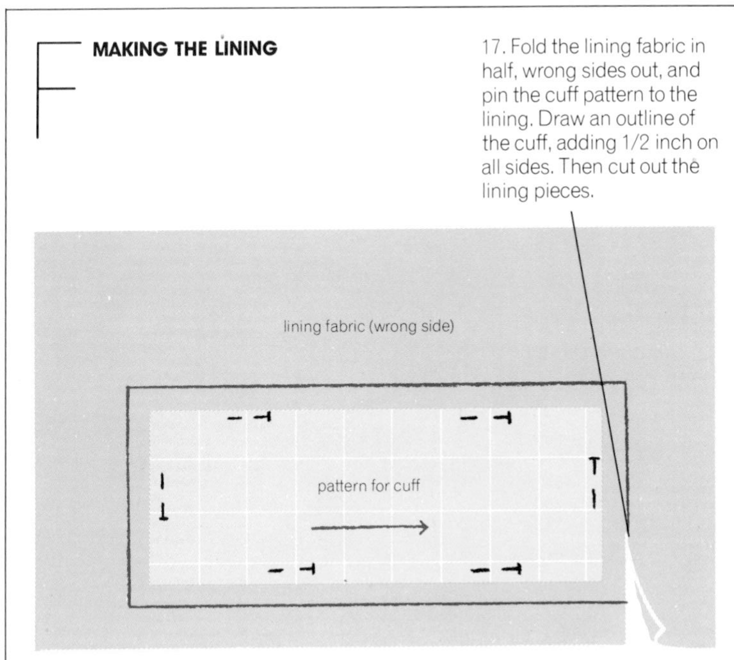

lining (wrong side)

18. Fold one lining piece in half, wrong side out. Align the ends and pin them together. Machine stitch 1/2 inch in from the edge, removing the pins as you sew. Press the seam open.

19. Turn under the top and bottom edges 1/2 inch, and press them flat.

continued

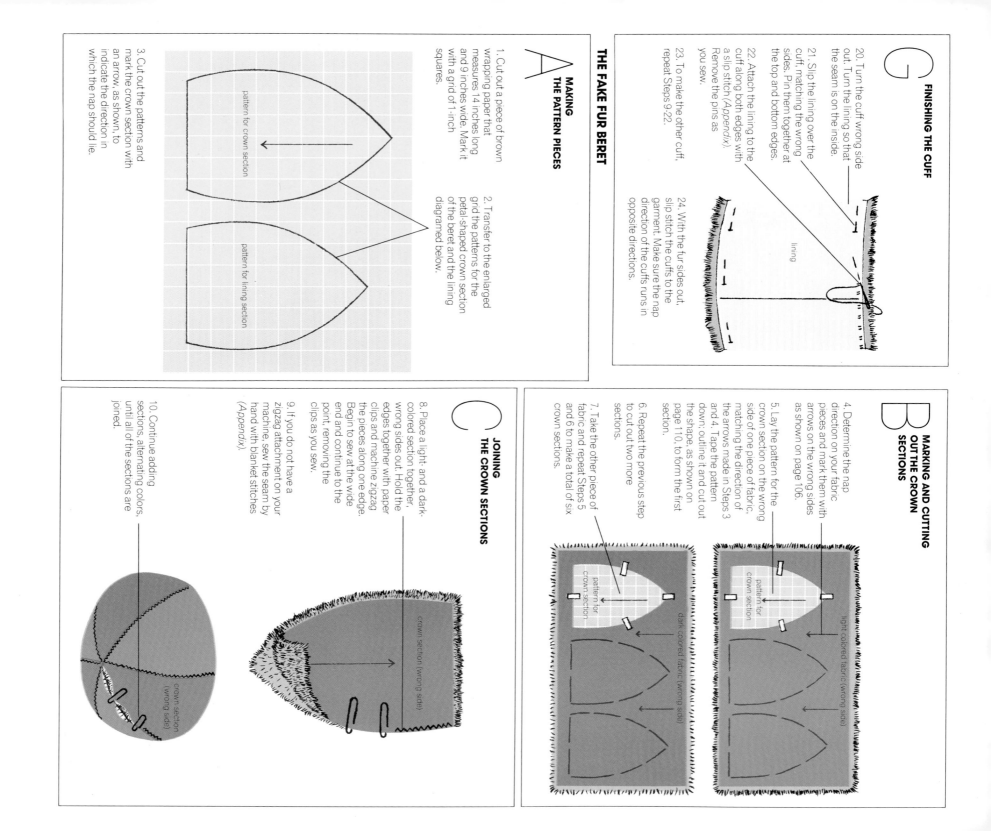

G FINISHING THE CUFF

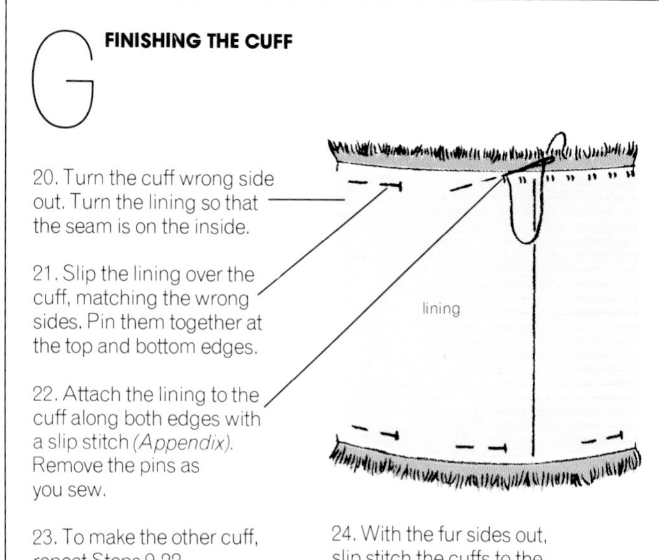

20. Turn the cuff wrong side out. Turn the lining so that the seam is on the inside.

21. Slip the lining over the cuff, matching the wrong sides. Pin them together at the top and bottom edges.

22. Attach the lining to the cuff along both edges with a slip stitch *(Appendix)*. Remove the pins as you sew.

23. To make the other cuff, repeat Steps 9-22.

24. With the fur sides out, slip stitch the cuffs to the garment. Make sure the nap direction of the cuffs runs in opposite directions.

THE FAKE FUR BERET

A MAKING THE PATTERN PIECES

1. Cut out a piece of brown wrapping paper that measures 14 inches long and 9 inches wide. Mark it with a grid of 1-inch squares.

2. Transfer to the enlarged grid the patterns for the petal-shaped crown section of the beret and the lining diagramed below.

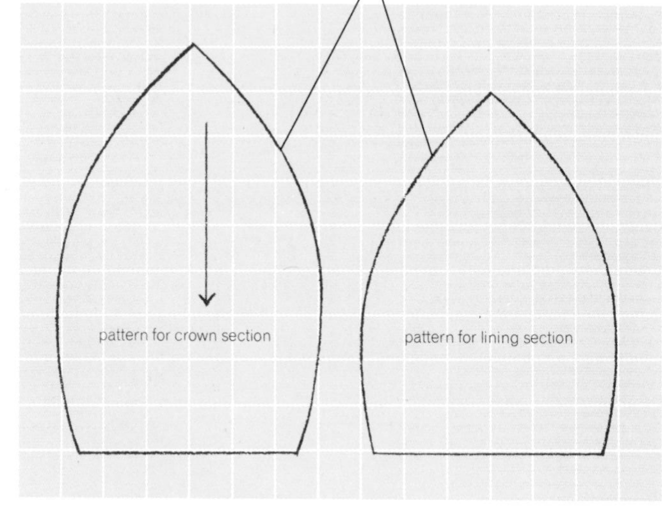

3. Cut out the patterns and mark the crown section with an arrow, as shown, to indicate the direction in which the nap should lie.

B MARKING AND CUTTING OUT THE CROWN SECTIONS

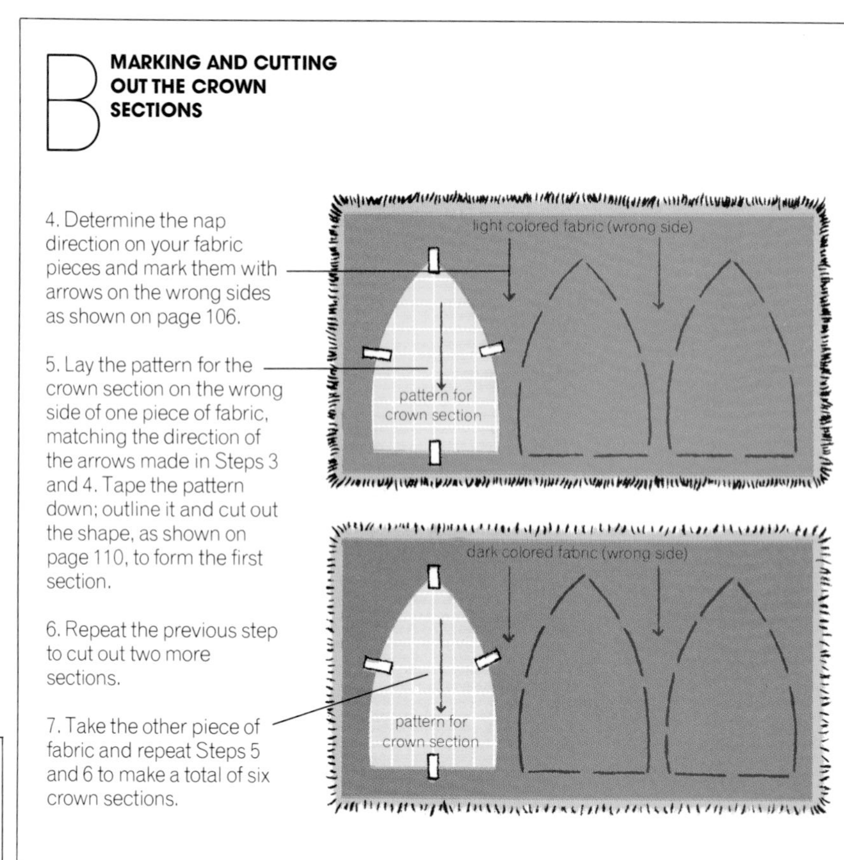

4. Determine the nap direction on your fabric pieces and mark them with arrows on the wrong sides as shown on page 106.

5. Lay the pattern for the crown section on the wrong side of one piece of fabric, matching the direction of the arrows made in Steps 3 and 4. Tape the pattern down; outline it and cut out the shape, as shown on page 110, to form the first section.

6. Repeat the previous step to cut out two more sections.

7. Take the other piece of fabric and repeat Steps 5 and 6 to make a total of six crown sections.

C JOINING THE CROWN SECTIONS

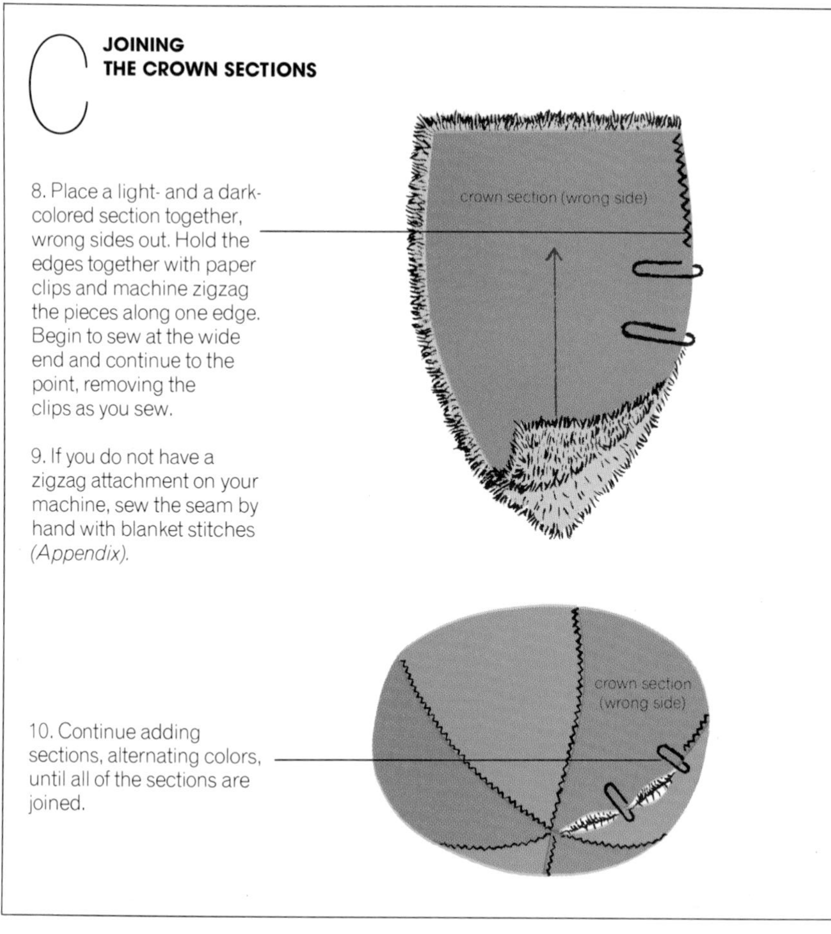

8. Place a light- and a dark-colored section together, wrong sides out. Hold the edges together with paper clips and machine zigzag the pieces along one edge. Begin to sew at the wide end and continue to the point, removing the clips as you sew.

9. If you do not have a zigzag attachment on your machine, sew the seam by hand with blanket stitches *(Appendix)*.

10. Continue adding sections, alternating colors, until all of the sections are joined.

D MAKING THE LINING

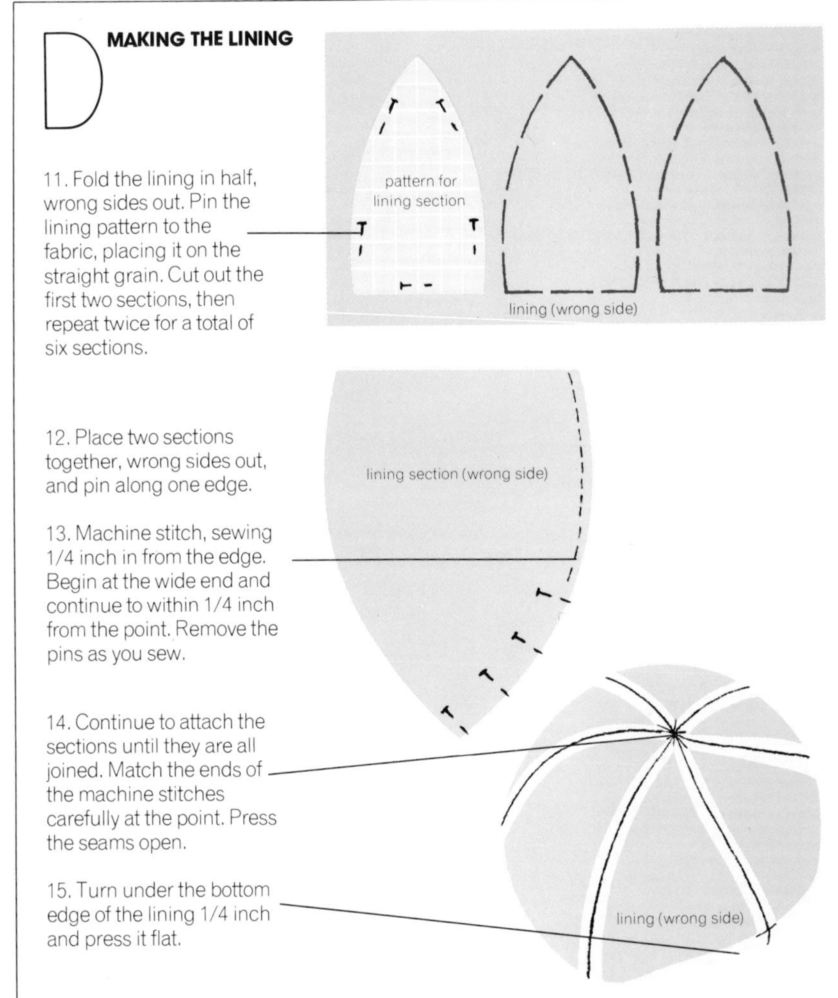

11. Fold the lining in half, wrong sides out. Pin the lining pattern to the fabric, placing it on the straight grain. Cut out the first two sections, then repeat twice for a total of six sections.

12. Place two sections together, wrong sides out, and pin along one edge.

13. Machine stitch, sewing 1/4 inch in from the edge. Begin at the wide end and continue to within 1/4 inch from the point. Remove the pins as you sew.

14. Continue to attach the sections until they are all joined. Match the ends of the machine stitches carefully at the point. Press the seams open.

15. Turn under the bottom edge of the lining 1/4 inch and press it flat.

E ATTACHING THE LINING TO THE BERET

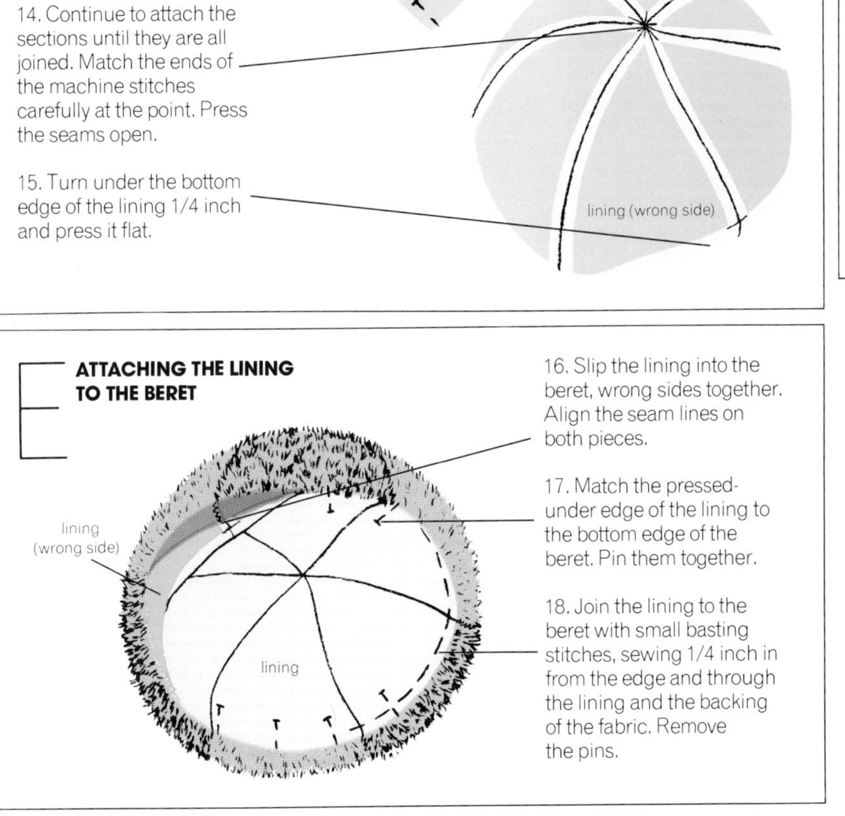

16. Slip the lining into the beret, wrong sides together. Align the seam lines on both pieces.

17. Match the pressed-under edge of the lining to the bottom edge of the beret. Pin them together.

18. Join the lining to the beret with small basting stitches, sewing 1/4 inch in from the edge and through the lining and the backing of the fabric. Remove the pins.

F PREPARING THE ELASTIC

19. Cut a strip of 3/4-inch-wide elastic that measures approximately 24 inches long. Place the strip around your head, and pull the elastic until it fits snugly but is not so tight that it is uncomfortable.

20. Add approximately 1 inch beyond the point you determined in the previous step and cut off the excess.

21. Overlap the ends of the elastic 1 inch and pin them together. Machine stitch a rectangle at the overlap, pivoting at the corners *(Appendix)*. Remove the pin.

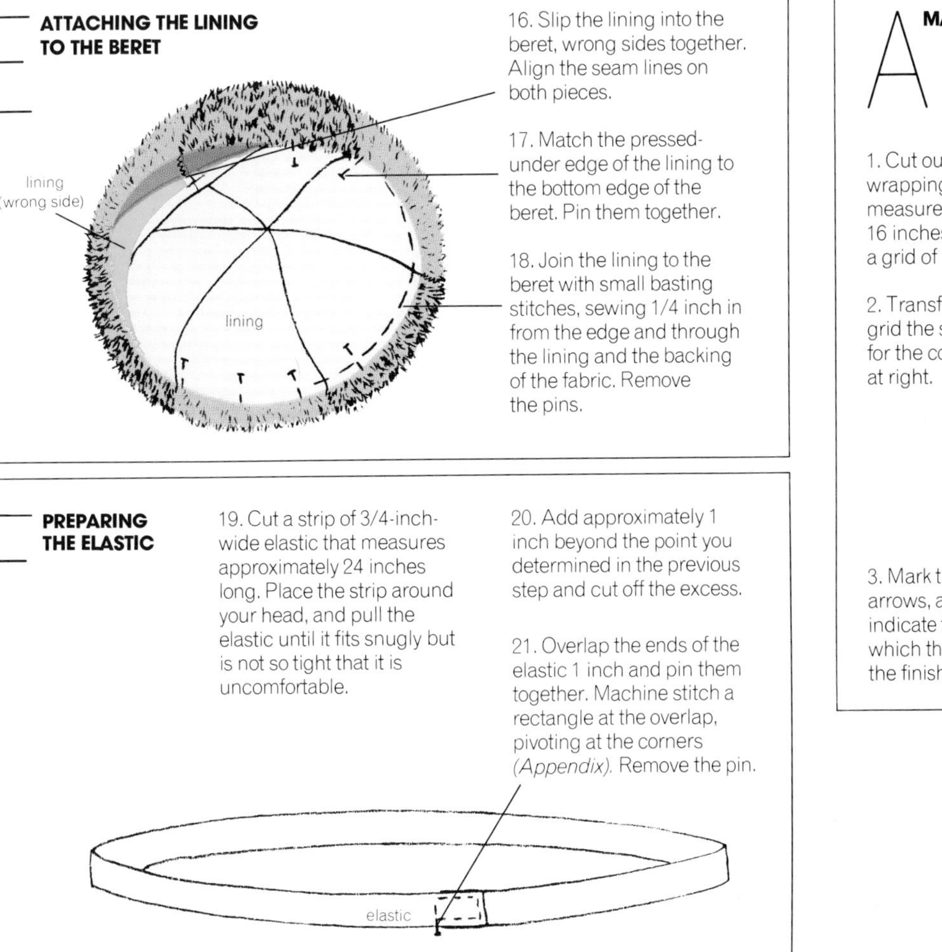

G FINISHING THE BERET

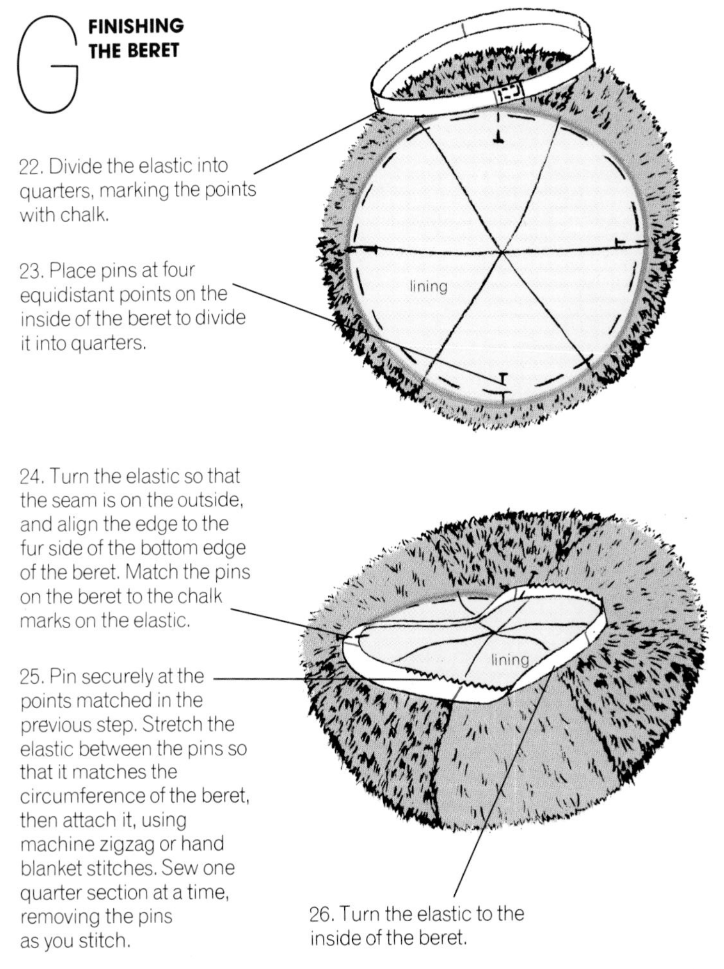

22. Divide the elastic into quarters, marking the points with chalk.

23. Place pins at four equidistant points on the inside of the beret to divide it into quarters.

24. Turn the elastic so that the seam is on the outside, and align the edge to the fur side of the bottom edge of the beret. Match the pins on the beret to the chalk marks on the elastic.

25. Pin securely at the points matched in the previous step. Stretch the elastic between the pins so that it matches the circumference of the beret, then attach it, using machine zigzag or hand blanket stitches. Sew one quarter section at a time, removing the pins as you stitch.

26. Turn the elastic to the inside of the beret.

THE FAKE FUR SHAWL COLLAR

A MAKING THE PATTERN

1. Cut out a piece of brown wrapping paper that measures 19 inches long by 16 inches wide. Mark it with a grid of 1-inch squares.

2. Transfer to the enlarged grid the shape of the pattern for the collar diagramed at right.

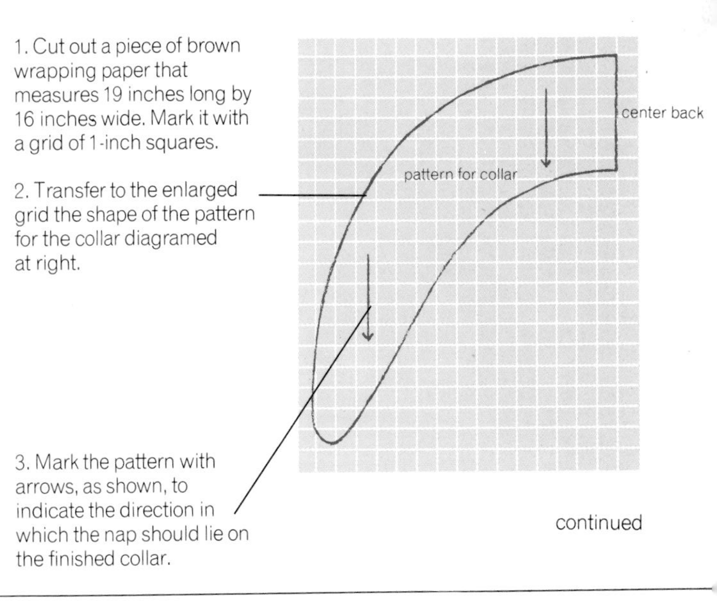

3. Mark the pattern with arrows, as shown, to indicate the direction in which the nap should lie on the finished collar.

continued

B MARKING AND CUTTING OUT THE COLLAR

4. Determine the nap direction on your fabric and mark the backing with arrows *(page 106)*.

5. Lay the pattern on the fabric as shown, matching the direction of the arrows made in Steps 3 and 4.

6. Tape the pattern down and outline it on the fabric.

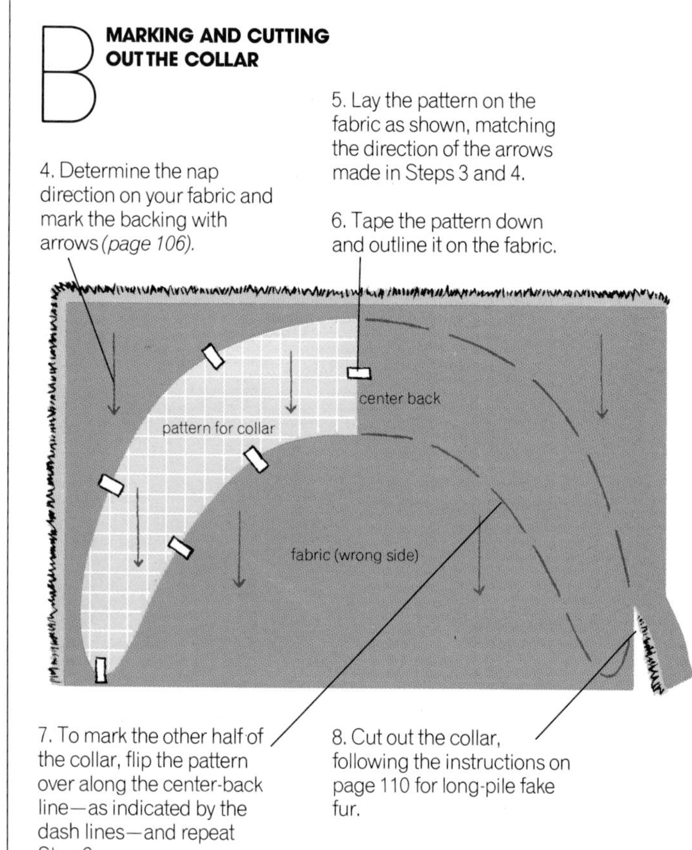

7. To mark the other half of the collar, flip the pattern over along the center-back line—as indicated by the dash lines—and repeat Step 6.

8. Cut out the collar, following the instructions on page 110 for long-pile fake fur.

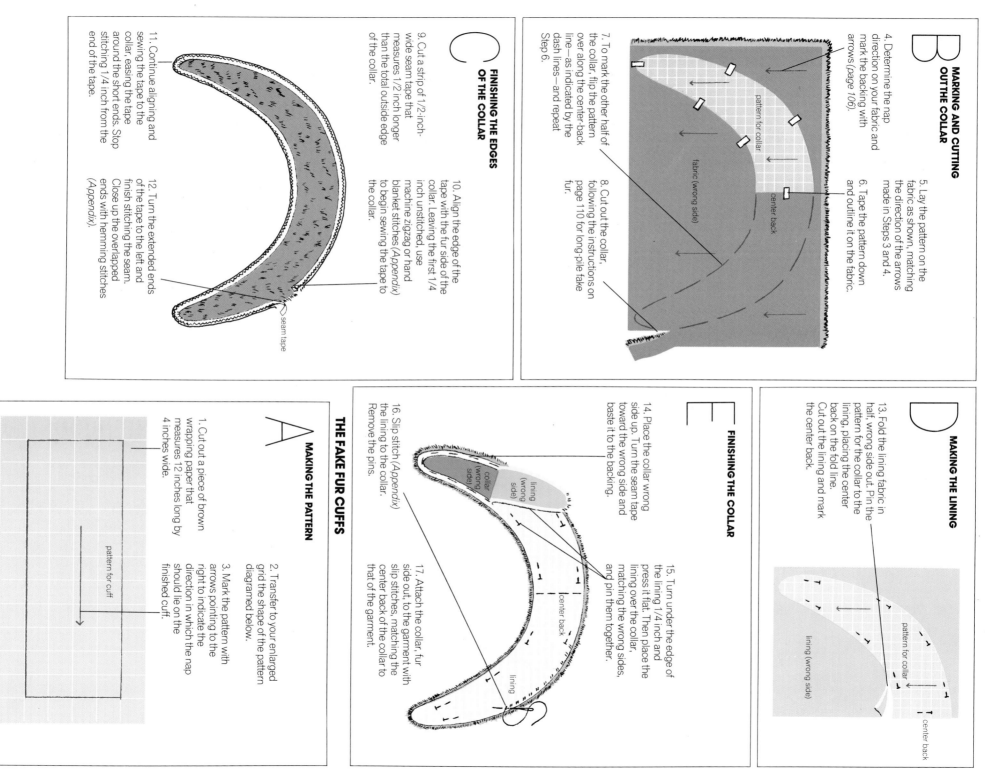

C FINISHING THE EDGES OF THE COLLAR

9. Cut a strip of 1/2-inch-wide seam tape that measures 1/2 inch longer than the total outside edge of the collar.

10. Align the edge of the tape with the fur side of the collar. Leaving the first 1/4 inch unstitched, use machine zigzag or hand blanket stitches *(Appendix)* to begin sewing the tape to the collar.

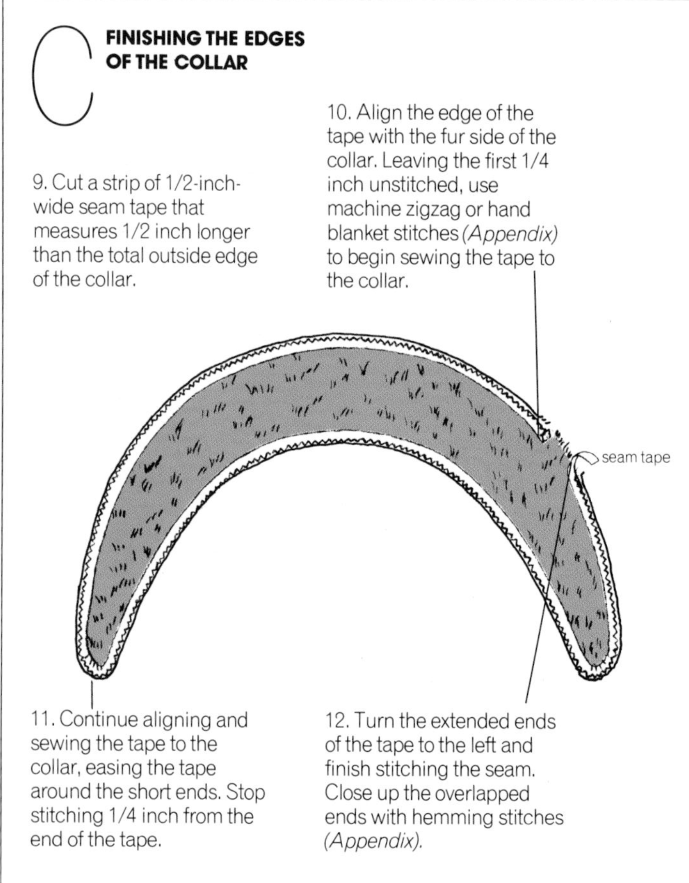

11. Continue aligning and sewing the tape to the collar, easing the tape around the short ends. Stop stitching 1/4 inch from the end of the tape.

12. Turn the extended ends of the tape to the left and finish stitching the seam. Close up the overlapped ends with hemming stitches *(Appendix)*.

D MAKING THE LINING

13. Fold the lining fabric in half, wrong side out. Pin the pattern for the collar to the lining, placing the center back on the fold line. Cut out the lining and mark the center back.

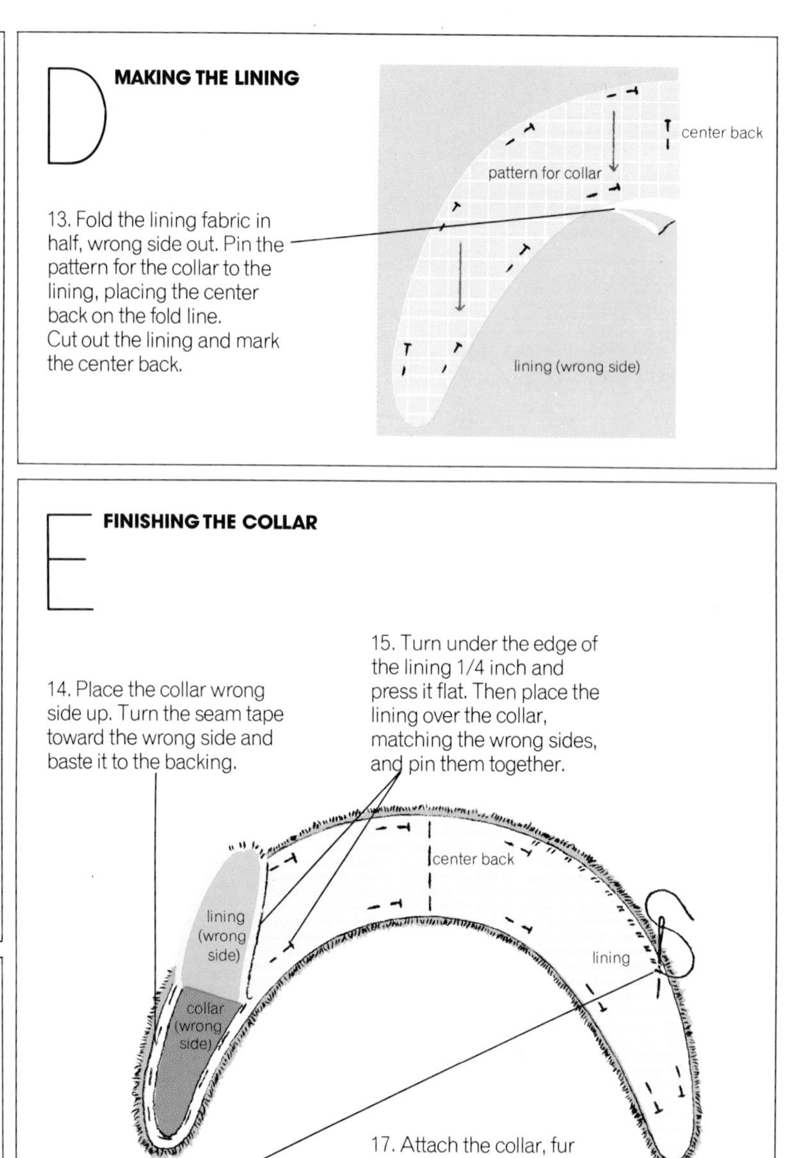

E FINISHING THE COLLAR

14. Place the collar wrong side up. Turn the seam tape toward the wrong side and baste it to the backing.

15. Turn under the edge of the lining 1/4 inch and press it flat. Then place the lining over the collar, matching the wrong sides, and pin them together.

16. Slip stitch *(Appendix)* the lining to the collar. Remove the pins.

17. Attach the collar, fur side out, to the garment with slip stitches, matching the center back of the collar to that of the garment.

THE FAKE FUR CUFFS

A MAKING THE PATTERN

1. Cut out a piece of brown wrapping paper that measures 12 inches long by 4 inches wide.

2. Transfer to your enlarged grid the shape of the pattern diagramed below.

3. Mark the pattern with arrows pointing to the right to indicate the direction in which the nap should lie on the finished cuff.

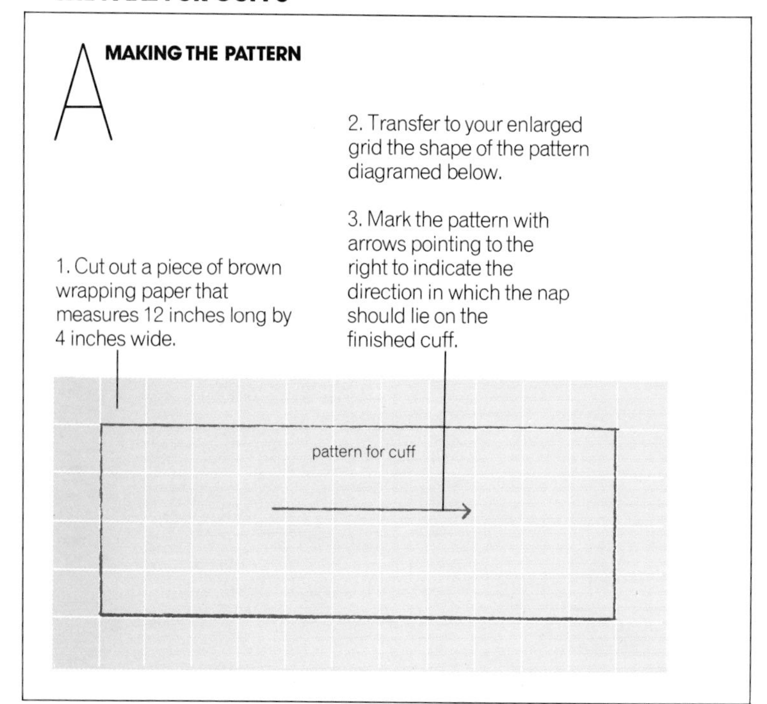

B MARKING AND CUTTING OUT THE CUFFS

4. Determine the nap direction on your fabric and mark the backing with arrows *(page 106)*.

5. Turn the fabric so that the arrows point to the right. Lay the pattern on the fabric as shown, matching the direction of the arrows made in Steps 3 and 4.

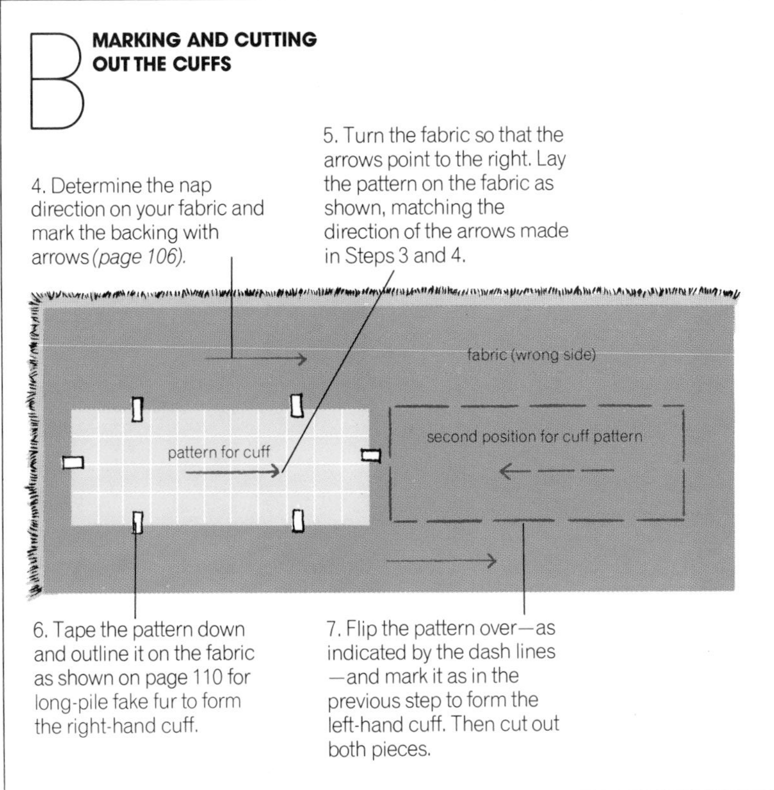

6. Tape the pattern down and outline it on the fabric as shown on page 110 for long-pile fake fur to form the right-hand cuff.

7. Flip the pattern over—as indicated by the dash lines—and mark it as in the previous step to form the left-hand cuff. Then cut out both pieces.

C JOINING THE CUFF ENDS

8. Fold one of the cuffs in half, wrong sides out, and match the ends. Paper-clip the edges together. Stitch the ends, using machine zigzag stitches or hand blanket stitches *(Appendix)*. Remove the clips as you sew.

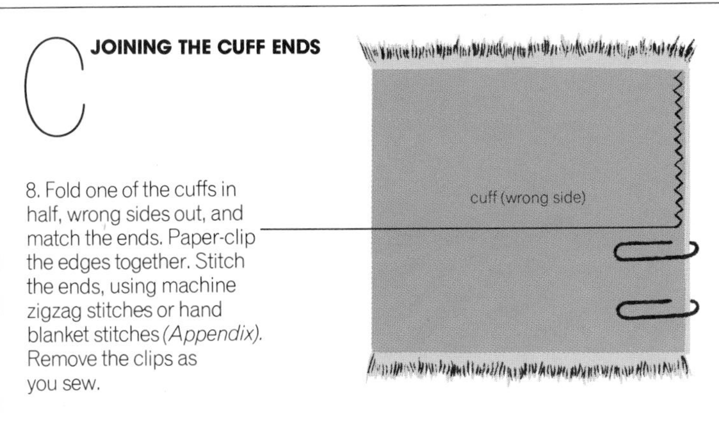

D FINISHING THE EDGES OF THE CUFF

9. Cut two strips of 1/2-inch-wide seam tape that measure 1/2 inch longer than the edges of the cuff. Leaving 1/4 inch extending at both ends, attach the pieces of tape to the top and bottom edges of the cuff with machine zigzag stitches or hand blanket stitches.

10. Turn the extended ends of the tape to the left, and finish the seam.

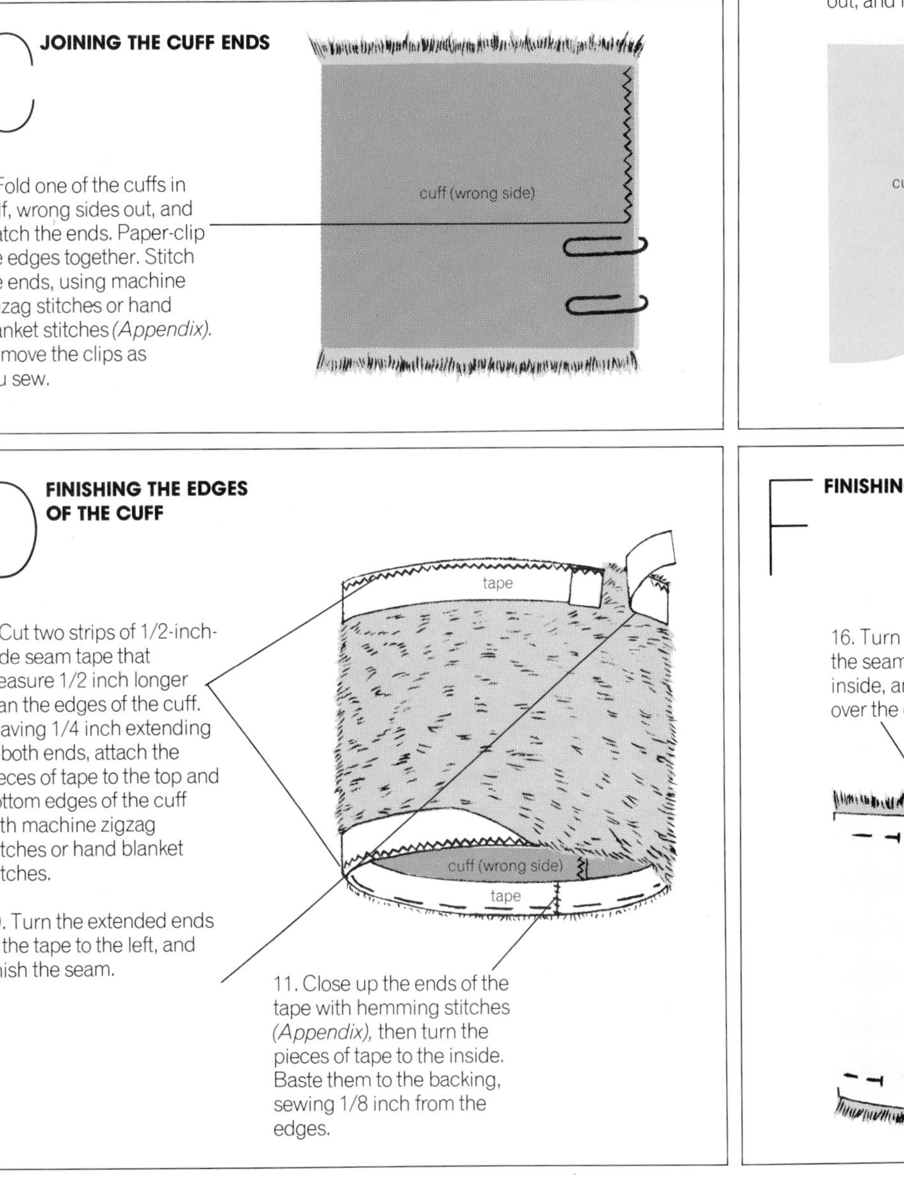

11. Close up the ends of the tape with hemming stitches *(Appendix)*, then turn the pieces of tape to the inside. Baste them to the backing, sewing 1/8 inch from the edges.

E MAKING THE LINING

12. Fold the lining fabric in half, wrong side out. Pin the cuff pattern to the lining. Cut out the two sections along the edge of the pattern.

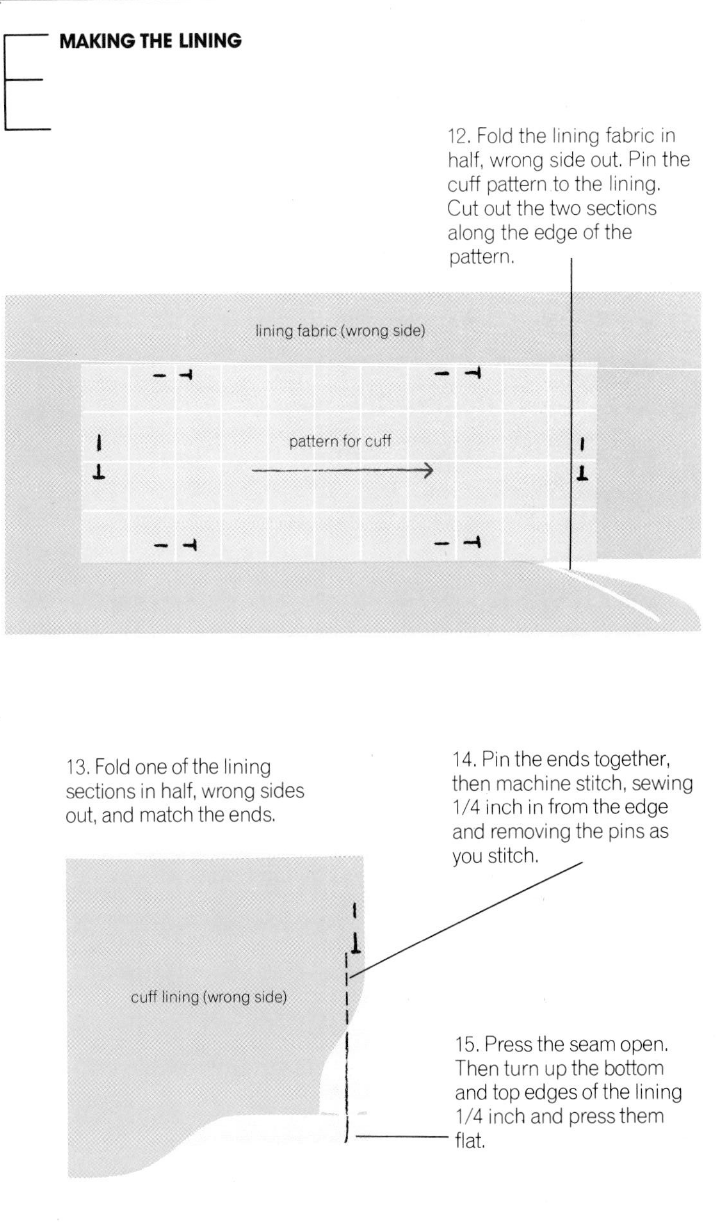

13. Fold one of the lining sections in half, wrong sides out, and match the ends.

14. Pin the ends together, then machine stitch, sewing 1/4 inch in from the edge and removing the pins as you stitch.

15. Press the seam open. Then turn up the bottom and top edges of the lining 1/4 inch and press them flat.

F FINISHING THE CUFF

16. Turn the lining so that the seam faces toward the inside, and slip the lining over the cuff.

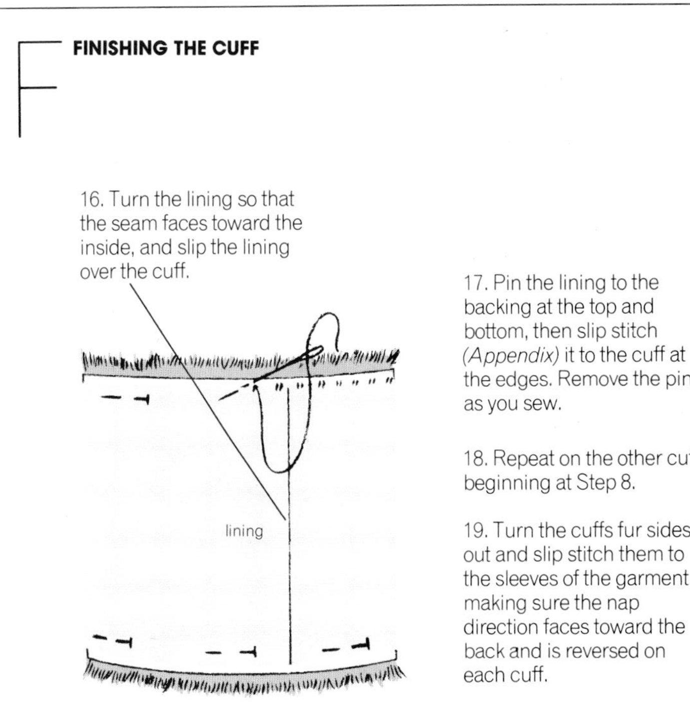

17. Pin the lining to the backing at the top and bottom, then slip stitch *(Appendix)* it to the cuff at the edges. Remove the pins as you sew.

18. Repeat on the other cuff, beginning at Step 8.

19. Turn the cuffs fur sides out and slip stitch them to the sleeves of the garment, making sure the nap direction faces toward the back and is reversed on each cuff.

4
TEST-TUBE TEXTILES

PLASTICS—FROM COLLARS TO THE COSMOS

During a scene from the 1967 movie *The Graduate,* an eager-beaver businessman corners the hero, Benjamin, at his graduation party and whispers portentously, "I just want to say one word to you, just one word. Are you listening? PLASTICS." Benjamin can only blink his eyes and ask, "Exactly how do you mean?" The reply is like a command from the burning bush: "There's quite a great future in plastics. Will you think about it? Will you think about it?"

Benjamin never did get into plastics, but he could have been given worse advice. The plastic business is currently a multibillion-dollar bonanza in the United States. And the clothing industry accounts for a tidy share of that windfall, with dresses, shoes, boots, handbags and earrings in mad geometric patterns and blazing colors making the very word plastics synonymous with the new, far out and futuristic in fashion.

The first articles of plastic clothing ever to appear were anything but far out—or sexy. They were the homely celluloid collars, dickeys and cuffs wom by heads of families, waiters and vaudevillians of the 19th Century. Their one advantage over the tonier standard linen, for which they were designed as substitutes, was that they never had to be laundered. Instead, a quick wipe with a damp cloth made them spick-and-span. The first major breakthrough in plastic textiles came in 1912 with the introduction of rayon hosiery. Soon rayon lingerie and outerwear began to challenge silk. Then, in 1938, Du Pont brought forth nylon, which drove silk literally to the back of the closet.

The nylon age is still very much with us. But since the end of the war, other new manmade fibers have spun out like the endless gossamer threads of Charlotte's Web: Arnel, Orlon, Dacron, Fortrel, Kodel, Lycra, Cantrece. These plastics are made by being extruded as filament, then woven like cloth. Thus, while their substance is novel, their structure—and ultimately their look—is completely conventional.

Until the 1960s the arbiters of style scorned plastics. Then, a few pioneers began to make high-fashion items from thin films of nonwoven plastic, whose outer surface of vinyl, they discovered, could be bonded to a knitted backing for strength. In 1964, the daring young Paris designer André Courrèges and several of his colleagues realized that the plastic wet look had modish potentialities after all. They applied the hottest colors ever used in clothing to vinyl, and they splashed them into designs that would have looked absurd on conventional fabrics.

In their hands, the nonwoven plastics bloomed. The stuff had practical virtues too. In times past, a smashing white Courrèges ball gown would have become a disaster area if food or wine were spilled on it. But now, being vinyl, it can be sponged clean in a moment. Recently other Paris couturiers have introduced phosphorescent plastic dresses that glow in darkened rooms, when the wearer herself is nearly invisible; battery-powered pants that light up like neon signs; garments cast, buttons and all, from a single mold and impregnated with seductive, longlasting perfumes.

With all its seemingly limitless possibilities for novelty, vinyl suffers from one major drawback. The nonporous property that makes it waterproof and cleanable with the swipe of a sponge also makes it uncomfortably hot for summer wear; the famous wet look all too often spreads from the wearer's dress to her body. Nonplastic substances such as silicone and fluorochemicals offer a partial solution. Applied to porous fabrics, they provide water repellancy without changing the fabric's basic characteristics. But the finishes are temporary, and not fully stain resistant. Another nonwoven plastic—urethane—solves these problems and others. A coating of urethane is applied to nylon or cotton backing in layers as thin as 3/1000 of an inch. Unlike vinyl, urethane is permeable and therefore breathes. Bikinis made with urethane can be stuffed into air-mail envelopes. Yet it is tough enough to be used for footwear. Furthermore, urethane has none of the stiff, somewhat bulky texture that plagued some vinyls; nor is it limited to vinyl's wet look. It takes readily to other finishes, including those as disparate as suede and patent leather.

But in the fast-moving space age, even urethane does not appear to be the ultimate in plastic fabric. Already a range of futuristic plastic materials is casting its shadow across the garment field. Appropriately, the products of the era have come out of NASA's space program. The suits in which the astronauts explored the moon's surface were lined with multiple layers of miracle plastics with insulating properties that sustain life in a furnace or a deep freeze.

For example, one of the new fabrics, Kevlar, is three times as strong as its cousin nylon, but with only one third the weight of Fiberglas. Teflon, which first appeared as a lining for frying pans, has come out of the kitchen as an impregnable coating for cosmic clothing. Beta cloth can be tossed onto a blazing fire, with no damage. Yet, as the photographs on these pages show, each one of these incredible materials—along with such partner fabrics as Nomex, Durette and Fluorel—can be cut, pinned and sewed. And the day may not be far off when these far-out plastics appear in wondrous designs dreamed up by the Courrègeses and Saint Laurents of the future.

The latest in $100,000 plastic space suits—worn on a moonwalk by astronaut Buzz Aldrin *(far right)*—was put together in a Delaware factory not unlike a large dressmaking shop. The suit consists of 21 layers of nylon, various aluminized plastics, Kevlar, and teflon-coated Beta cloth. Accessories to the suit include a plastic helmet, plastic boots and gloves made—for perfect fit—from plaster casts of the astronaut's hands.

1. Patterns made to measurements are taped to plastic materials.

2. A seamstress stitches together layers of aluminized plastic.

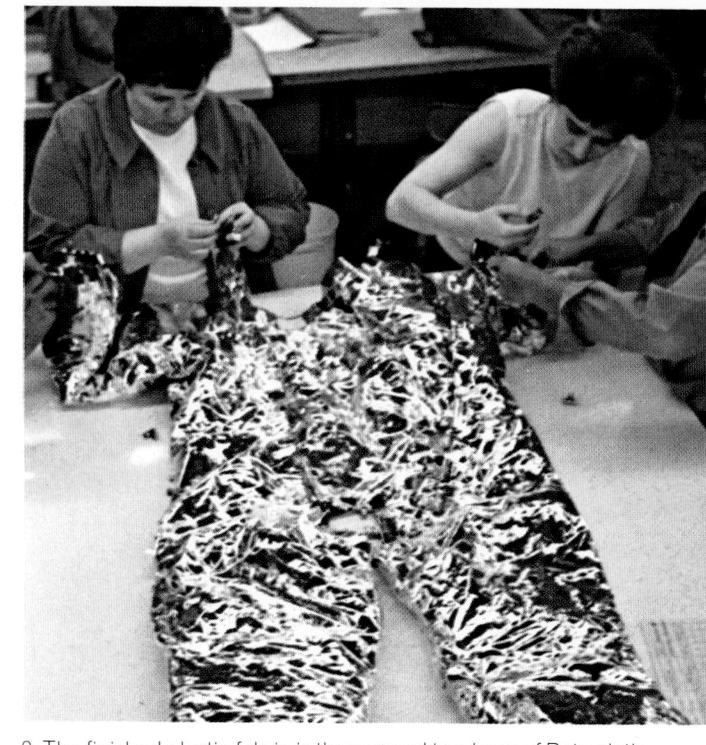
3. The finished plastic fabric is then sewed to a layer of Beta cloth.

4. Inspectors check pieces of the suit.

5. Rivets reinforce seams.

New tricks with old cloth

Coated fabrics are used primarily for rainwear. With a little imagination, however, they can be turned into as many fashions as there are materials in this kaleidoscope. Counterclockwise from left are: blue urethane-coated nylon tricot for a shirt; tan cotton and polyester bonded with rubber, a trench coat; yellow print vinylized cotton, seat covers; yellow urethane-lacquered nylon, babies' pants; striped nylon with silicone finish, a smashing cocktail skirt; and silicone-finished green nylon and cotton, tailored pants.

A guide to choosing coated fabrics

The most popular and versatile of coated fabrics are those treated with finishes so delicate that they do not close the pores of the cloth. Because these coatings allow the cloth to breathe, garments made from them are comfortable. These treated fabrics can be sewed much like their original uncoated cloth bases—if you allow for exceptional circumstances that are summarized in the chart shown at right and detailed in the pages that follow.

Porous coatings can be either visible or invisible. The visible variety is urethane, a tough, flexible plastic that repels water but admits air when the coating is thin enough. The invisible finishes are silicone and fluorochemical. They both make cloth water resistant without changing its appearance. The fluorochemicals make it oil resistant as well.

Though nonporous coated fabrics may be hot to wear, they are fully waterproof. The most common are produced with vinyl or—more recently—with urethane spread in such a thick layer that it loses its porosity. The most unusual nonporous coated fabrics are made by bonding rubber in a sort of sandwich between two layers of cloth. Special sewing and maintenance requirements for bonded and heavy plastic-coated fabrics also appear in the chart and the pages that follow.

TYPE OF FABRIC	CHARACTERISTICS
URETHANE-COATED FABRICS	This flexible plastic coating is available in a wide range of finishes, from glossy to dull, with either a smooth or a crinkly texture. In thin films it is relatively porous, but in thick applications a urethane coating becomes impermeable and will not "breathe." Urethane, which may be clear or solid-colored or printed in a pattern, comes on a wide variety of synthetic and natural, woven and knit fabrics—cotton, rayon, nylon as well as blends. Fabrics that have been coated with urethane can be used to make anything from sportswear to raincoats, depending on the thickness of the original fabric and the coating.
VINYL-COATED FABRICS	This nonporous plastic coating has a dull to lustrous finish and a slick texture. Vinyl is available in clear form as well as in solid colors, and can be printed or embossed with patterns after it has been applied to any one of a wide variety of synthetic and natural, woven and knit fabrics—cotton, rayon, nylon, Dacron, blends. The coating is resistant to water, oils, foods and most common chemicals—but should be kept away from chlorinated solvents, nail polish and nail polish remover. Aside from rainwear, the coated fabric is best used for such projects as table or chair covers and pillows.
RUBBER-BONDED FABRICS	The natural or synthetic rubber bonding in this type of coated fabric is a thin layer fused between two pieces of tightly woven natural or synthetic cloth. The rubber bonding is nonporous and waterproof; the fabrics are porous and are treated with a water repellent so that they shed drops of water. The finished material may be used for sportswear and jackets as well as for raincoats, hats and capes.
SILICONE-COATED FABRICS	This coating—identified by trade names such as Cravenette or Unisec—is invisible, although it does tend to soften the texture of the fabric to which it is applied. The coating resists both water and waterborne stains. It comes in a wide variety of synthetic and natural fabrics that may be selected for any kind of garment—from smocks and hats to raincoats and capes.
FLUOROCHEMICALLY COATED FABRICS	This liquid coating, identified by trade names such as Zepel and Scotchgard, is invisible and has no noticeable effect on the texture of the fabric to which it is applied. The treatment, which resists both water and oil stains, coats a wide variety of synthetic and natural fabrics that may be used for outdoor or indoor wear.

MARKING AND CUTTING	SEWING	PRESSING AND CLEANING
If the finish is slippery, lay out the material wrong side down. Attach the pattern to the fabric with silk pins inserted in the seam allowance. Mark the wrong side of the fabric with a smooth-edged tracing wheel and dressmaker's carbon. Cut with dressmaker's shears.	Sew by machine, using a Size 14 to 16 needle and polyester or mercerized cotton thread. Set the machine for 10 to 12 stitches to the inch. To prevent the fabric from sticking to your machine's throat plate or presser foot, use a roller presser foot or a Teflon foot on the machine, or apply sewing-machine or baby oil to the coated face of the fabric, or insert tracing paper between the foot and the fabric.	Urethane breaks down under heat, changing color or even cracking. It should not be pressed. Straighten out wrinkles before cutting by rolling the fabric over an empty cardboard wrapping tube. If wrinkles persist, arrange the paper pattern pieces in such a way that wrinkles fall in inconspicuous places. Dry clean, or wash gently with a damp sponge and mild soap or detergent.
To prevent the fabric from slipping, lay it out wrong side down. Attach the pattern to the fabric with silk pins inserted in the seam allowance. Mark the wrong side of the fabric with a smooth-edged tracing wheel and dressmaker's carbon. Cut with dressmaker's shears.	Sew by machine, using a Size 14 to 16 needle and polyester or mercerized cotton thread. Set the machine for 10 to 12 stitches to the inch. Pin and baste within the seam allowance. To prevent the fabric from sticking as it is sewed, use a roller presser foot or a Teflon foot, or apply sewing-machine or baby oil to the coated face of the fabric, or insert tracing paper between the foot and the fabric. To keep seams and hems flat, topstitch at 6 to 8 stitches to the inch. Finish the edges with bias tape.	The coating will soften and degrade at a temperature of about 130°; the fabric can only be pressed on the wrong (cloth) side with a cool dry iron. If wrinkles persist, arrange the paper pattern pieces in such a way that wrinkles fall in inconspicuous places. Wipe the fabric clean with a damp sponge and, if necessary, warm soapy water. Do not dry clean.
Attach the pattern to the fabric with silk pins inserted in the seam allowance. Mark the fabric with a smooth-edged tracing wheel and dressmaker's carbon.	Sew by machine, using a Size 14 needle and setting the machine for 10 to 12 stitches to the inch, or by hand with a Size 7 to 10 Sharp needle. Pin and baste within the seam allowance. Choose polyester or mercerized cotton thread. To keep seams and hems flat, topstitch at 6 to 8 stitches to the inch.	Because the rubber layer is covered by cloth, this material is not so sensitive to heat as other coated fabrics. Press with a warm, dry iron, using a pressing cloth and heavy pressure. Dry clean only.
Lay out, mark and cut most silicone-coated fabrics in the conventional manner, using the sorts of equipment and techniques recommended for the basic fabric itself. Test a pin in a scrap of fabric. If it leaves visible holes, pin only in the seam allowance and use a smooth-edged tracing wheel to mark the wrong side of the fabric. If the fabric is a glazed or ciré-finished type, cut it with the wrong side down, to prevent slippage.	Sew the fabric in the conventional manner, using the sorts of needles and threads, stitches and machine settings that are recommended for the fabric when it is not coated. If pin holes show, pin and baste within the seam allowance. Some silicone-coated fabrics may require topstitching to keep seams and hems flat.	Press with a warm, dry iron, using a pressing cloth and light pressure to prevent the fabric from scorching. Dry clean or wash gently with mild soap or detergent and lukewarm water, then rinse thoroughly. Repeated cleanings or washings will leave a residue on the coating that diminishes its water repellency. At this stage the fabric can be re-treated at home with a water-repellent spray-can product, or it can be refinished professionally by a dry cleaner.
Lay out, mark and cut most fluorochemically coated fabrics in the conventional manner, using the sorts of equipment and techniques recommended for the basic fabric itself. Test a pin in a scrap of fabric. If it leaves visible holes, pin only in the seam allowance and mark the wrong side with a smooth-edged tracing wheel. If the fabric is a glazed or ciré-finished type, cut it with the wrong side down to prevent slippage.	Sew the fabric in the conventional manner, using the sorts of needles and threads, stitches and machine settings that are recommended for the fabric when it is not coated. If pins leave visible holes, pin and baste within the seam allowance. Topstitching may be required to keep seams and hems flat on some fluorochemically coated fabrics.	Press with a warm dry iron, using a pressing cloth and light pressure to prevent scorching. If the fabric is a glazed or ciré-finished type, press on the wrong side of the fabric with a cool dry iron and a pressing cloth. Dry clean or wash by machine or by hand, depending on the nature of the fabric; rinse thoroughly to avoid leaving a residue of soap or detergent. If the fabric loses some repellency, it can be re-treated at home with a spray-can product, or refinished by a dry cleaner.

Techniques for sewing with plastics

Working with coated fabrics is a challenge to the home seamstress. All such materials require special handling, which may involve equipment that is not found in an ordinary sewing bag—like the cardboard tube and eyelet punch shown in the background of these pages. Such tools, and an understanding of the characteristics of each fabric, are keys to success with these materials.

The first thing to do with your coated fabric is to thoroughly test a sample. Find out whether the fabric can be pressed without discoloring or cracking. Puncture it with a pin, to determine whether such marking will show. Dab glue on the backing to see if it will show through. Test the fabric on the sewing machine to see if it slips around or sticks in the machine.

If the coated fabric presents any of these problems, try the solutions detailed in this section. For example, rolling wrinkled fabric on a tube is a gentle substitute for pressing. Topstitching the seams will work where glue will not; and tracing paper, oil or talcum will ease the problems of sticking and slippage during machine stitching.

PREPARING COATED FABRIC THAT CANNOT BE PRESSED

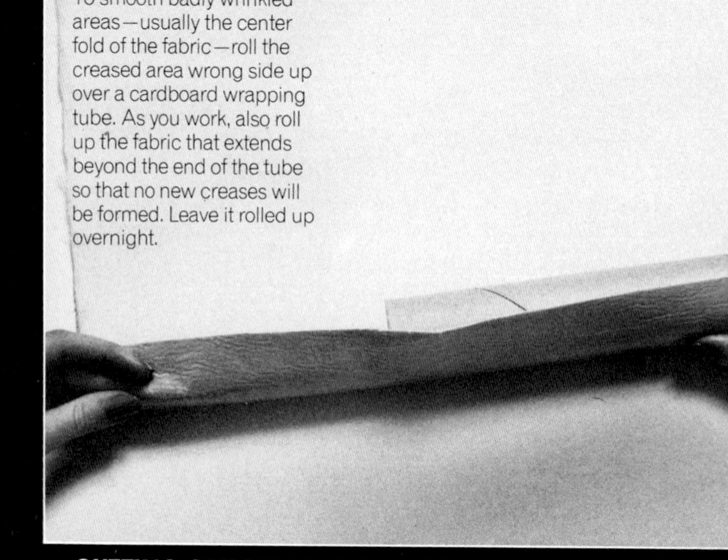

To smooth badly wrinkled areas—usually the center fold of the fabric—roll the creased area wrong side up over a cardboard wrapping tube. As you work, also roll up the fabric that extends beyond the end of the tube so that no new creases will be formed. Leave it rolled up overnight.

CUTTING OUT SLIPPERY COATED FABRIC

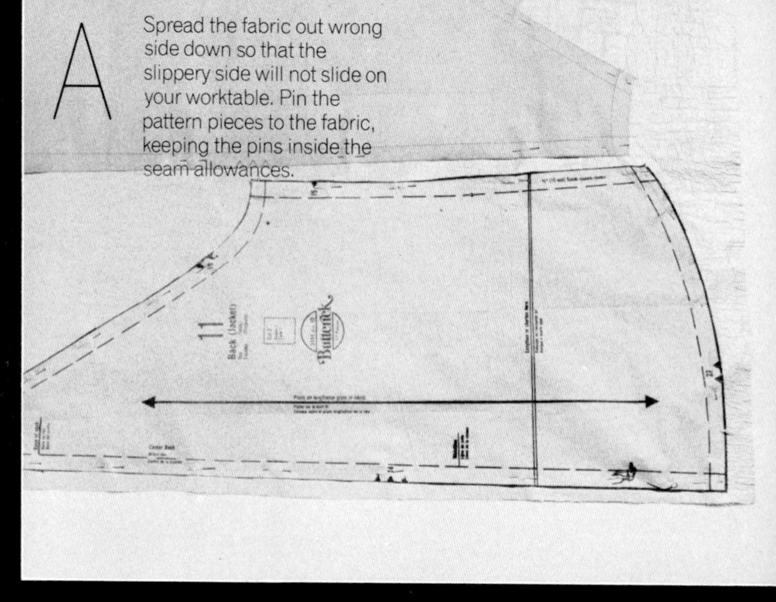

A Spread the fabric out wrong side down so that the slippery side will not slide on your worktable. Pin the pattern pieces to the fabric, keeping the pins inside the seam allowances.

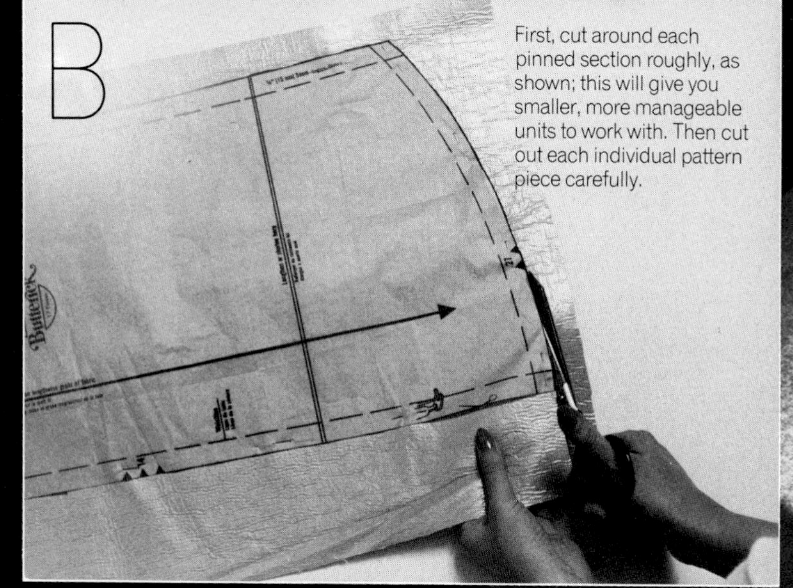

B First, cut around each pinned section roughly, as shown; this will give you smaller, more manageable units to work with. Then cut out each individual pattern piece carefully.

STITCHING PLAIN SEAMS ON SLIPPERY COATED FABRICS

A Lay one garment section, wrong side down, on a flat surface. Place a piece of tracing paper on top of it, as shown. Then lay the other garment section on the paper, wrong side up, and align the seam lines.

B Pin together the garment sections and sandwiched paper, placing the pins inside the seam allowance. Stitch and remove the pins.

C Tear the paper away from the stitched seam, working from one side at a time. Pick out any remaining shreds of paper with your fingers.

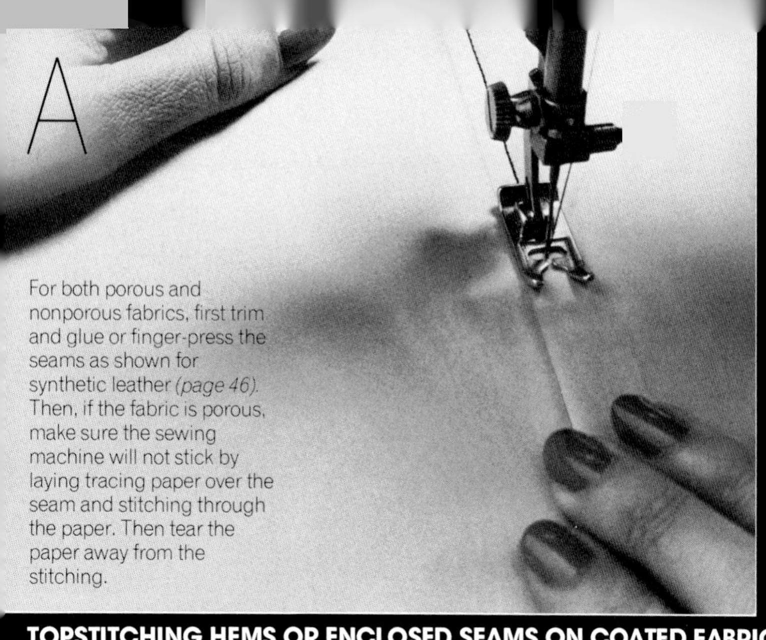

A

For both porous and nonporous fabrics, first trim and glue or finger-press the seams as shown for synthetic leather *(page 46)*. Then, if the fabric is porous, make sure the sewing machine will not stick by laying tracing paper over the seam and stitching through the paper. Then tear the paper away from the stitching.

B

If the fabric is nonporous, apply baby or sewing-machine oil with a cotton ball in front of the presser foot as you stitch to prevent the machine from sticking. Alternatively use talcum powder.

TOPSTITCHING HEMS OR ENCLOSED SEAMS ON COATED FABRICS THAT STICK

A

For porous fabrics, first sandwich the garment section to be topstitched between two pieces of tracing paper to avoid having the fabric stick to the machine.

B

Then position a strip of black adhesive tape on the throat plate of your machine to serve as a stitching guide that can be seen through the layers of tracing paper.

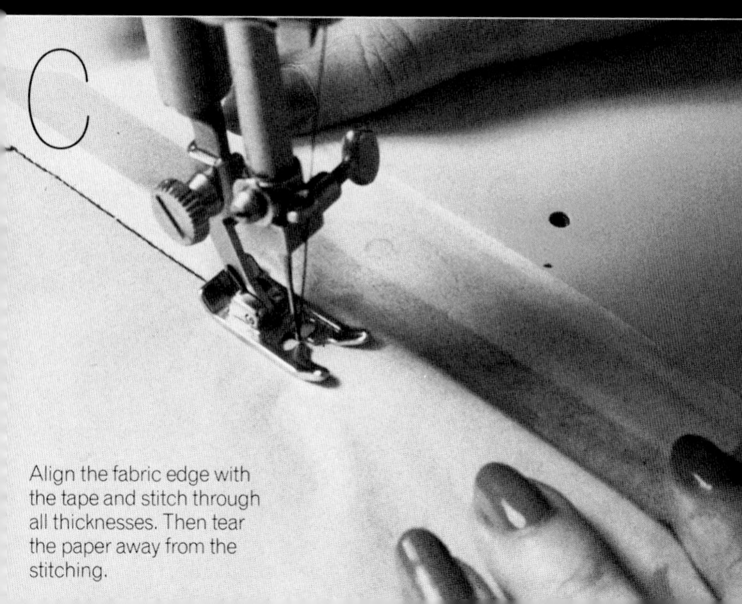

C

Align the fabric edge with the tape and stitch through all thicknesses. Then tear the paper away from the stitching.

D

For nonporous fabrics, place tracing paper under the garment section only and apply oil or talcum on top to prevent the machine from sticking.

MAKING VENTILATION HOLES

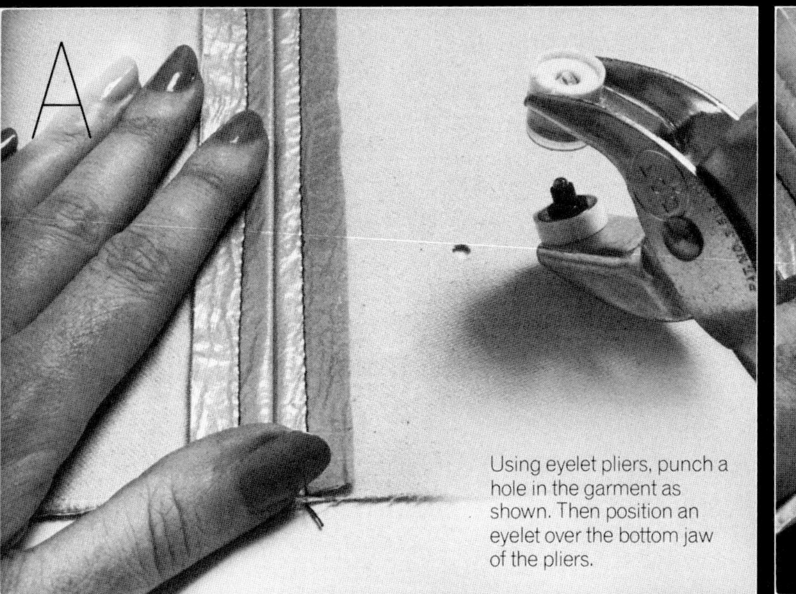

Using eyelet pliers, punch a hole in the garment as shown. Then position an eyelet over the bottom jaw of the pliers.

Place the garment, wrong side up, between the jaws of the pliers. Push the eyelet through the hole and squeeze the pliers to fasten the eyelet in position.

BINDING SEAMS AND RAW EDGES

Unfold one side of a strip of bias tape and pin it to the wrong side of the raw seam edge. Then stitch the tape to the seam 1/4 inch in from the edge, using the fold line in the tape as your guide. Remove the pins as you stitch.

Wrap the folded edge of the tape over the raw edge of the seam allowance and stitch 1/8 inch in from the edge; keep wrapping the tape over the edge as you stitch.

HEMMING COATED FABRICS THAT CANNOT BE PRESSED OR PINNED

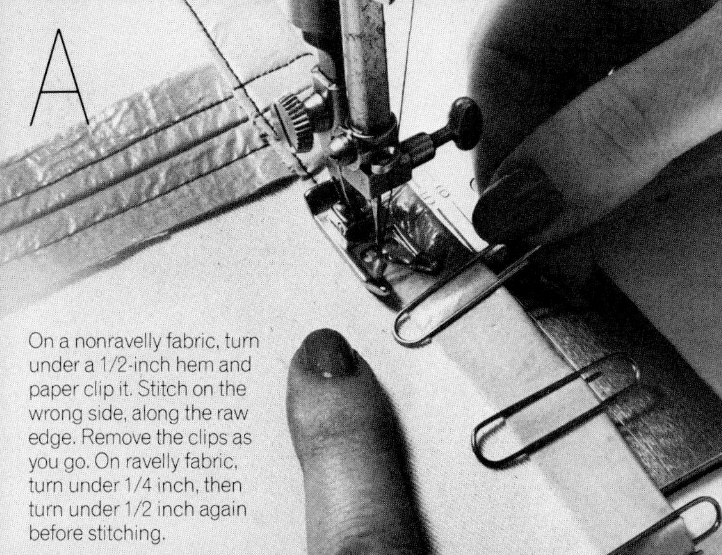

On a nonravelly fabric, turn under a 1/2-inch hem and paper clip it. Stitch on the wrong side, along the raw edge. Remove the clips as you go. On ravelly fabric, turn under 1/4 inch, then turn under 1/2 inch again before stitching.

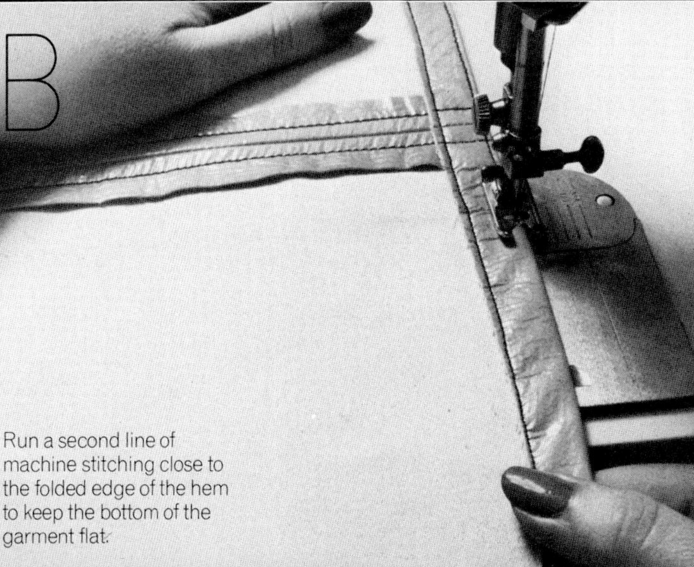

Run a second line of machine stitching close to the folded edge of the hem to keep the bottom of the garment flat.

Swinging in the rain

This yellow cotton raincoat incorporates the new technology of water-resistant coating with the dashing lines of a 19th Century coachman's cloak. And it can be turned out simply and easily—without even resorting to a pattern. Cut the cloth into six basic pieces according to the instructions on the following pages. The result will be a billowing cape with an elbow-covering capelet that is right out of a Dickens novel.

Sewing the flared rain cape

The sweeping, wide-bottomed cape shown on the preceding pages can easily be made without a commercial pattern. Rather, a homemade pattern for the back panel of the cape should be created to the wearer's measurements. Then this piece is used as a module, as shown on the following pages, for drawing the patterns of the two flared front panels and the three-piece short overcape. The two curved collar pieces are cut from another basic pattern piece.

Next, determine the yardage required for these eight pieces, using the string box method shown on page 166. Then you can begin assembling the cape. This is a simple matter of attaching a 24-inch separating zipper to the fronts, joining all the pieces at the shoulders and along the side seams and topstitching all seams and hems. A hook and eye at the collar ensures a neat, stand-up fit—and good protection from the weather.

The raincape was fashioned from a medium-weight, medium-gloss coated nylon and cotton twill known as Beaver Nylon Plus. But other water-repellant fabrics with similar soft, draping characteristics can be substituted. Because the wearer's arms are covered by a loose-fitting cape —rather than being enclosed in sleeves—no provisions for ventilation are needed.

MAKING THE PATTERNS

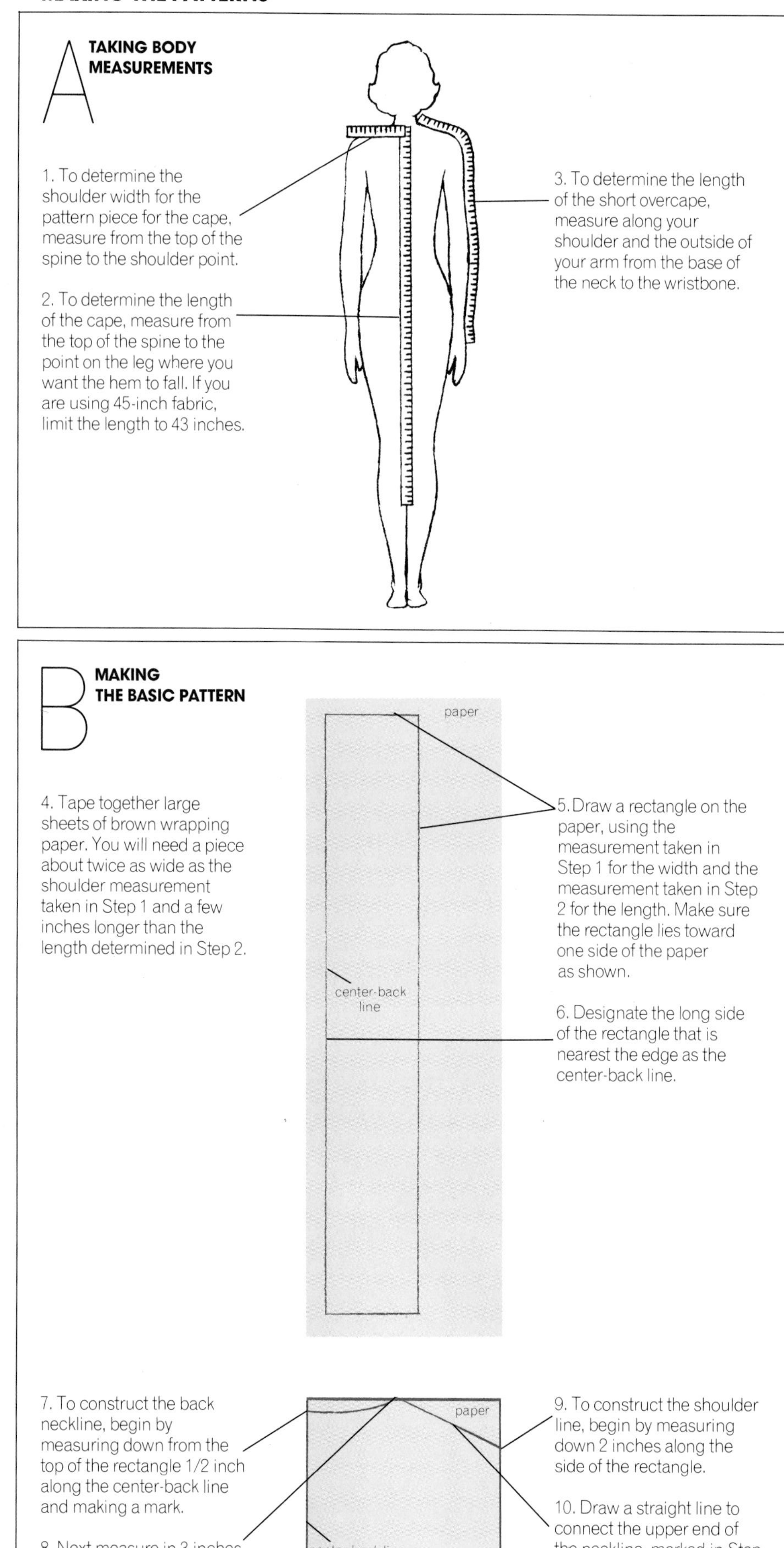

A TAKING BODY MEASUREMENTS

1. To determine the shoulder width for the pattern piece for the cape, measure from the top of the spine to the shoulder point.

2. To determine the length of the cape, measure from the top of the spine to the point on the leg where you want the hem to fall. If you are using 45-inch fabric, limit the length to 43 inches.

3. To determine the length of the short overcape, measure along your shoulder and the outside of your arm from the base of the neck to the wristbone.

B MAKING THE BASIC PATTERN

4. Tape together large sheets of brown wrapping paper. You will need a piece about twice as wide as the shoulder measurement taken in Step 1 and a few inches longer than the length determined in Step 2.

5. Draw a rectangle on the paper, using the measurement taken in Step 1 for the width and the measurement taken in Step 2 for the length. Make sure the rectangle lies toward one side of the paper as shown.

6. Designate the long side of the rectangle that is nearest the edge as the center-back line.

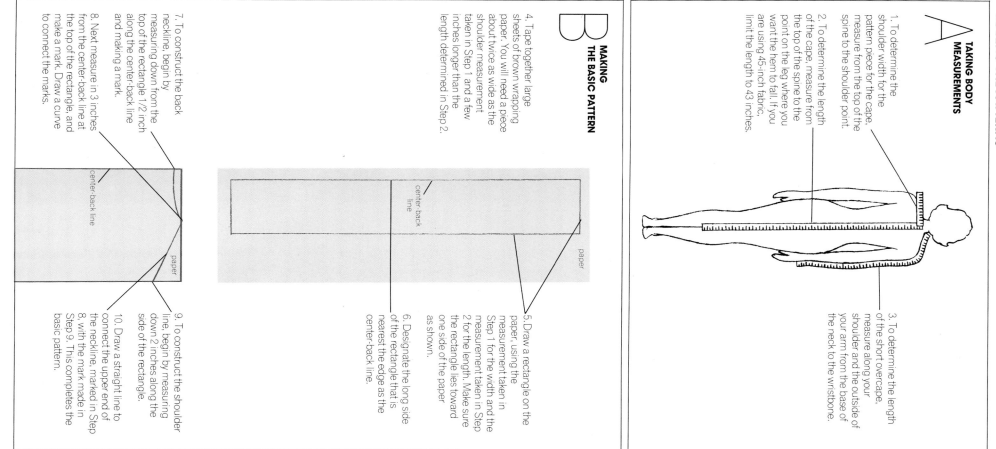

7. To construct the back neckline, begin by measuring down from the top of the rectangle 1/2 inch along the center-back line and making a mark.

8. Next measure in 3 inches from the center-back line at the top of the rectangle, and make a mark. Draw a curve to connect the marks.

9. To construct the shoulder line, begin by measuring down 2 inches along the side of the rectangle.

10. Draw a straight line to connect the upper end of the neckline, marked in Step 8, with the mark made in Step 9. This completes the basic pattern.

5 WHIMSICAL KNIT AND CROCHET

QUIRKY TURNS IN THE ART OF NEEDLECRAFT

When I work, I like to feel I'm part of what I'm doing. That's why I work in three dimensions. I like working with my materials because I can move with rope and sisal and straw; they take shape in my hands; I mold them, twist them, almost like a potter touching clay. What comes out is an extension of me, another arm, another body. I can stand apart and look at a work, and at the same time feel I'm looking at myself. What I do is what I am." Thus Hiromi Oda, a Japanese-born artist, describes her very personal feelings about her crochet.

Her CROCHET?

Yes, crochet. The once fusty craft that lately has become the medium of sexy, slinky fashions is also turning up in art galleries and museums as the high-spirited stuff of a new group of iconoclastic artists. Many of them, like Susanna Lewis of Brooklyn and Virginian Lannie Hart, whose vest and marionette are shown overleaf, combine their crochet stitches with beads, feathers, unwoven fleece, old jewelry, leather and even kitchen hardware.

Crochet, the freest of all the textile crafts, is a natural medium for this kind of far-out expressionism. A crochet stitch is formed with nothing but a hook and a length of yarn; the yarn can be a spider-thin filament of silk or a hank of manila rope as thick as a hawser. Each stitch exists separately, with only the most casual connections to its neighbors, allowing fluid changes from texture to texture. Thus the artist can work in any direction or sequence, be it in ever-enlarging circles, in squares, in undulating hills and valleys, or in dangling tubes and tendrils. And the crocheter can weave in all those novelties mentioned above, just by looping the yarn through or around them.

By crocheting in this uninhibited manner, ideas can begin to take shape almost as fast as they are conceived. Unlike most other visual arts, no preliminary steps intervene: there is no canvas to prepare, no marble or wood to rough out, rarely even a sketch to draw. Nor are there any precious materials to spoil if the idea goes sour; one can simply unravel back to the starting point and find all the parts intact. Such simplicity and flexibility are an invitation to the artist to test out an infinity of new ideas.

Many of these experimental crocheters speak of their medium in mystical terms, describing a kind of organic inner life that the fibers themselves bring to the work. Nicki Hitz Edson, a New York artist, sees her wool as being alive, and marvels at the tactile closeness she feels to a work as it progresses. Along with many of her fellow artists, she did not come upon crocheting until she had explored more conventional avenues of expression—in her case photography. Edson began her professional life with a camera in hand, but photography left her with a sense of distance from her subjects.

As a leisure-time antidote, Nicki first took to crocheting what she terms "straight stuff"—hats and vests. It was not until she saw an exhibition at New York's Museum of Modern Art that she turned to crochet's larger possibilities. A crocheted wall hanging by Walter Nottingham entitled *Celibacy,* an eight-foot-long three-dimensional cascade of red-dyed spirals, convinced her that something far more satisfying than "straight stuff" was just waiting to be created.

She tried crocheting miniature houses, then toys, then eccentric helmets and masks. Eventually she began to concentrate on a very personal kind of fantasy clothing —elaborately colored and stitched coats and capes and footgear. It was, in effect, wearable sculpture that could accompany its owner to a party, travel down the street, then come home to hang as wall tapestry.

Edson's evolution as an artist—and her recent interest in crocheted sculpture—is paralleled by that of other interpretive crocheters. Arlene Stimmel, co-author with Edson of a book entitled *Creative Crochet,* began as a painter, but found that she missed dimension in her work. She eventually found her solution in needlework.

She takes extra pleasure in work that isn't instantly recognized as crochet. "One of the reactions I like best is 'Wow, is that really crochet?'" In her search for new textures and forms she frequently combines natural fibers with metallics or rayon ribbon or swatches of machine knitting.

Artist Mark Dittrick, something of a classicist among crocheters, transforms the fibers themselves into something quite uncrochet-like. He uses a Size 0 steel hook, heavy wool yarn, a single crochet stitch, and a great deal of strength to produce his tightly crocheted, seemingly bullet-proof clothing. (He has in the process developed calluses on his fingers; but he comforts novices with the assurance that Band-Aids on the fingers and tape on the hook will serve as protection during apprenticeship.)

Because crochet is so portable, some crocheters make a point of working at their craft in sociable circumstances, like a sewing bee. Edson and Stimmel meet informally with other artist-crocheters nearly every week to show their work in progress and to swap ideas on stitches and techniques.

Many of them also teach crocheting. Nicki Edson says of her class at New York's New School, "It's not so much about crochet as it is about liberation—teaching people to get rid of bad learning habits, to set themselves free from conventional thinking." One of her favorite shock techniques is to send a new class home with the startling assignment, "Crochet a sandwich."

A marionette, in a glittering crochet costume that includes metallic thread, beads and bells, presides over a gallery of crocheted *objets d'art.* From top: a jangling vest incorporating metal symbols made for New York telephone poles and joined together here by crochet stitches; a double-crochet purse in the form of a fish; and a waggish dog mask with stitched picot teeth, a single-crocheted tongue and a double-crocheted snout.

Everything—including the kitchen sink

For the daring home seamstress, even a piece of hardware from the kitchen sink can become glamorous. The stainless-steel disks that emblazon this evening skirt are, indeed, kitchen sink drainers. Enmeshed in whorls of silver metallic crochet and applied to the overlap and hem, they turn a plain wrap skirt into a campy. but tasteful conversation piece. Directions for crocheting the disks start on page 181.

Instructions for the knit and crochet projects

The following directions are for knitting the fake-fur jacket and crocheting the strainer screen disks pictured on the preceding pages. The instructions describe each step fully in simple terms. Most books, magazines and patterns use a shorthand of standard abbreviations. The ones translated here are terms you will find in most other instructions for knit or crochet projects.

KNITTING ABBREVIATIONS

K—knit	**REP**—repeat
P—purl	**PAT**—pattern
ST—stitch	**SL**—slip stitch
YO—yarn over	**PSSO**—pass slipped stitch over
INC—increase	**BEG**—beginning
DEC—decrease	**MC**—main color

—starting point for a repeated sequence of steps: when instructions tell you to "rep from," read back to find the point (*) where you must begin to repeat.

CROCHETING ABBREVIATIONS

SC—single crochet	**HDC**—half double crochet
CH—chain	**DC**—double crochet
HK—hook	**TRC**—triple crochet
ST—stitch	**DTRC**—double triple crochet
SL ST—slip stitch	**SK**—skip
REP—repeat	**LP**—loop
PAT—pattern	**SP**—space

—starting point for a repeated sequence of steps: when instructions tell you to "rep from," read back to find the point (*) where you must begin to repeat.

CHECKING THE GAUGE

All knit and crochet instructions are preceded by a stitch gauge, a specification of the number of stitches to the inch (and often how many rows to the inch) you must have if your project is to come out the proper size.

To check the gauge, that is to make sure your needle or hook and yarn provide the desired number of stitches to the inch, knit or crochet a sample swatch before beginning your project. It should measure at least 4 by 4 inches and be made with the yarn and needles or hook recommended in the pattern. If two sizes of needles or hook are required—a smaller one for a ribbed edging and a larger one for the main part of the garment—the gauge is measured using the larger needles or hook.

Remove the swatch from the needles or hook without binding off. Lay it on a flat surface and count the stitches to the inch, measuring with a ruler, not a tape measure. If the gauge calls for more stitches to the inch, change to smaller needles or a smaller hook. If the gauge calls for fewer stitches to the inch, use a larger hook or needles. This change of needle size will also adjust the row-to-the-inch gauge.

KNITTING THE BATTLE JACKET

The following directions are written for a small size (8-10); changes for a medium size (12-14) follow in parentheses. You will need 9 (11) four-ounce skeins of bulky yarn in the main color (medium brown in the picture on pages 176-177); 3 (4) skeins each of colors A (deep brown) and B (dark brown), and 2 skeins each of colors C (white), D (light gray) and E (medium gray). The yarn may be any bulky yarn that will give a gauge of 3 pattern stitches to 1 inch as described below. You will also need straight knitting needles, Sizes 7 and 10; an aluminum crochet hook, Size J; a tapestry needle; 7 buttons; and 1 snap fastener.

Using the Size 10 needles, knit a sample swatch in the pattern stitch described below to check the gauge, which is 3 stitches to the inch.

Pattern stitch: The following 4-row sequence should be made whenever a pattern stitch is called for in the instructions below: Purl across 3 rows. Then, on row 4, which must appear on the outside of the finished work, bring the yarn over, slip 1 stitch, knit 1 stitch, and pass the slipped stitch over the knitted stitch. Repeat this sequence across the row.

The back: With Size 7 needles, cast on 48 (54) stitches. Knit 1, purl 1 to make a 9-inch ribbed border. Change to Size 10 needles and purl for 2 inches. On the last purl row, decrease 4 stitches evenly spaced across the row. On the next row, work the fourth row of the pattern stitch *(described above)*. Then make the 4-row pattern sequence on 44 (50) stitches until 4 rows of spaces—which occur on each row 4 of the pattern—have been completed. Purl 1 row.

The armholes: Maintaining the pattern, bind off 3 stitches at the beginning of each of the next 2 rows. Work row 4 of the pattern, then decrease 1 stitch at the beginning and end of each of the next 3 purl rows. Continue to work the pattern now on 32 (38) stitches until 7 (8) rows of spaces have been completed, ending with row 4 of the pattern.

The shoulders: Bind off 5 (6) stitches at the beginning of each of the next 4 rows. Bind off loosely the remaining 12 (14) stitches for the back of the neck.

The left front: With Size 7 needles, cast on 29 (33) stitches. Knit 1, purl 1 to make a 9-inch ribbed border. Purl 5 stitches; then slip these stitches onto a safety pin or stitch holder to be worked later for the front band. Change to Size 10 needles and purl across the remaining 24 (28) stitches. Working on these stitches only, now purl for 2 inches. At the beginning and end of the last purl row, decrease 1 stitch. Starting with row 4, work the 4-row pattern on 22 (26) stitches until the left front piece measures the same as the back did at the start of the armhole shaping; end at the side edge.

The armholes: Maintaining the pattern, bind off 3 stitches at the side edge of the next row. Then work through row 4 of the pattern, and decrease 1 stitch at the side edge of each of the next 3 purl rows. Work the pattern on 16 (20) stitches until 5 (6) rows of spaces have been completed, ending with row 4 of the pattern at the front edge.

The neck: Bind off 4 (6) stitches at the beginning of the next row, then decrease 1 stitch at this same edge every row twice more. Work the pattern now on 10 (12) stitches until the piece measures the same as the back did at the shoulder; end at the side edge.

The shoulder: Bind off 5 (6) stitches twice.

The right front: Work the same as you did on the left front, but reverse the armhole and neck shaping. Make 3 buttonholes evenly spaced on the 9-inch ribbed border of the jacket. Place the first buttonhole 1 1/2 inches up from the bottom; place the top buttonhole 1 inch below the end of the ribbed border. To make the buttonholes, start at the front edge of the right front and work in the knit 1, purl 1 ribbing sequence across the first 2 stitches. Bind off the next stitch; then continue making the ribbing to the end of the row. On the return row, cast on 1 stitch directly above the one you bound off on the previous row.

The sleeves: With Size 7 needles, cast on 30 (34) stitches. Knit 1, purl 1 stitch to make a 2 1/2 inch ribbed border. At the beginning and end of the next row, increase 1 stitch. Repeat this increase every 2 inches twice more. Continue to work in the ribbing sequence on 36 (40) stitches until the ribbed border measures 7 inches in all. Change to Size 10 needles and purl for 2 inches. At the beginning and end of the last purl row decrease 1 stitch. Starting with row 4, work the 4-row pattern on the 34 (38) stitches until 7 rows of spaces have been completed.

The sleeve cap: Continuing to maintain the 4-row pattern, bind off 3 stitches at the beginning of each of the next 2 rows; then decrease 1 stitch at the beginning and end of every other purl row until 7 rows of spaces have been completed. Bind off the remaining stitches.

The front and neck ribbed borders: Sew the shoulder seams together. With Size 7 needles, pick up the 5 stitches for the left front ribbed border from the pin or stitch holder and work in the knit 1, purl 1 ribbing sequence until the strip measures the same as the left front did at the start of the neck shaping. Again, slip these 5 stitches onto a pin. Work the right front stitches for the ribbed border in the same manner, making 4 buttonholes evenly spaced on this portion of the ribbed border. Place the last buttonhole 1 inch below the start of the neck shaping. End the last row of the right front ribbed border at the front edge, then work back across the 5 stitches. Pick up and knit all the stitches around the neck edge until you reach the 5 stitches on the left front that are being held on the pin. Work in the knit 1, purl 1 ribbing sequence across these 5 stitches. Work in the knit 1, purl 1 ribbing sequence on all stitches around the neck edge for 1 inch; bind off loosely in the ribbing stitches. Finish the edge of the left and right front bands with 1 row of single crochet stitches.

The fringe: Cut several strands of the main color and colors A, B, C, D and E yarn, each measuring 9 inches. Knot the fringe, as described below, in each horizontal and each vertical bar formed by the spaces in the pattern rows on the back, fronts and sleeves. In each horizontal bar, knot 4 strands—1 of the main color, 1 of A color, 1 of color B, and 1 strand of any of the lighter colors. In each of the vertical bars, knot 3 strands—2 strands of any of the deeper colors and 1 of any of the lighter colors. When placing the fringes, leave 2 spaces unfringed at the side edges above the armholes on the jacket back, fronts, and sleeve caps.

The finishing touches: Sew the side and sleeve seams. Sew the front ribbed borders in place, then sew in the sleeves. Sew on the buttons to correspond to the buttonholes, and sew the snap fastener in place on the edge of the neck opening. Block the ribbed borders on the jacket body and sleeves, and brush the fringes so that they lie in place as desired.

CROCHETING THE STRAINER SCREEN DISKS

You will need 2 75-yard spools of 3-ply silver lamé yarn to make 3 strainer screen disks. For each disk, you will also need a silver-colored sink strainer 2 3/4 inches in diameter with large holes. Make sure each strainer has exactly 18 holes around its outer edge. Use an aluminum crochet hook, Size J. All stitches needed are described in the Appendix, except for the double triple crochet stitch, which is shown on page 182. Use double strands of yarn throughout. Crochet a sample swatch in single crochet to check the gauge, which is 4 stitches to the inch.

Round 1: For this round, treat the holes around the outer edge of the strainer as if they were the stitches in a foundation chain. Start by tying the yarn to the hook as described in Steps 1-2 for the chain stitch *(Appendix)*. Then, make 1 single crochet stitch in any outside hole on the strainer. Chain 1 and make 1 single crochet stitch in each of the next 5 holes, chaining 1 between each stitch. Chain 1, and make 1 single crochet stitch and then 1 half double crochet stitch in the next hole. Make 1 half double crochet stitch and then 1 double crochet stitch in the next hole; and 1 double crochet stitch and 1 triple crochet stitch in the hole after that. Make 1 triple crochet stitch and 1 double triple crochet stitch in the next hole. Then in each of the next four holes, make 2 double triple crochet stitches. Continue by making 1 double triple crochet stitch and 1 triple crochet stitch in the next hole; and 2 triple crochet stitches in the hole after that. Then make 1 triple crochet stitch and 1 double crochet stitch in the next-to-last hole. In the last hole, make 1 double crochet stitch and 1 half double crochet stitch. Complete this round by making a slip stitch in the first single crochet stitch of the round.

Round 2: Chain 1, then make a slip stitch into the next 6 chain-1 spaces, chaining 1 between each slip stitch. Make 1 single crochet stitch in the next stitch and 1 half double crochet stitch in the stitch after that. Chain 1; make 1 double crochet stitch in the next stitch. Chain 1; make 1 triple crochet stitch in the next stitch. Chain 1; make 2 triple crochet stitches in the next space, with a chain 1 between them. Chain 1; make 2 double triple crochet stitches—with a chain 1 between them—in each of the next 10 stitches. Chain 1; make 2 triple crochet stitches in the next stitch with a chain 1 between them. Chain 1; make 1 triple crochet stitch and 1 double crochet stitch in the next stitch with a chain 1 between them. Chain 1 and make a double crochet stitch and a half double crochet stitch—with a chain 1 between them—in the next stitch. Chain 1 and make a half double crochet stitch in the next stitch. Chain 1 and make a single crochet stitch in the next stitch. Chain 1 in each of the last 3 stitches of the previous round, making a slip stitch with a chain 1 between each stitch.

Round 3: Chain 1 after each stitch that you make in this round. Start by repeating this sequence 8 times—make a single crochet stitch in the back loop of the next stitch and skip a stitch. Then make 1 single crochet stitch in the next space, 1 half double crochet stitch in the next space; and 1 double crochet stitch in the space after that. Make 1 triple crochet in each one of the next 28 spaces. Continue by making 1 double crochet stitch in the next space; 1 half double crochet stitch in the next space; and 1 single crochet stitch in the space after that. Then repeat the following sequence—slip stitch in the back loop of the next stitch and skip 1 stitch—10 times. Finish by making 1 slip stitch in each of the next 4 spaces. Then fasten off.

THE DOUBLE TRIPLE CROCHET STITCH

To make the first row after a foundation chain *(Appendix)*, start by chaining 5. Then bring the yarn over the hook from back to front 3 times. Insert the hook into the fifth chain stitch from the hook *(drawing 1)*. Bring the yarn over the hook once, and draw it through the loop closest to the tip *(drawing 2)*. There are now 5 loops on the hook.

Bring the yarn over the hook again and draw it through the 2 loops that are closest to the tip *(drawing 3)*. Bring the yarn over the hook again and draw it through the next 2 loops closest to the tip *(drawing 4)*. Again, bring the yarn over the hook and draw it through the 2 loops closest to the tip *(drawing 5)*. Bring the yarn over the hook once more and draw it through the remaining 2 loops *(drawing 6)*. These steps form 1 double triple crochet stitch. Repeat these steps in each succeeding chain across the row. At the end of the row, chain 4 and turn.

For the next and each successive row, bring the yarn over the hook 3 times, then insert the hook in the first stitch of the row. Continue as instructed in the preceding steps. At the end of the row, chain 5 and turn.

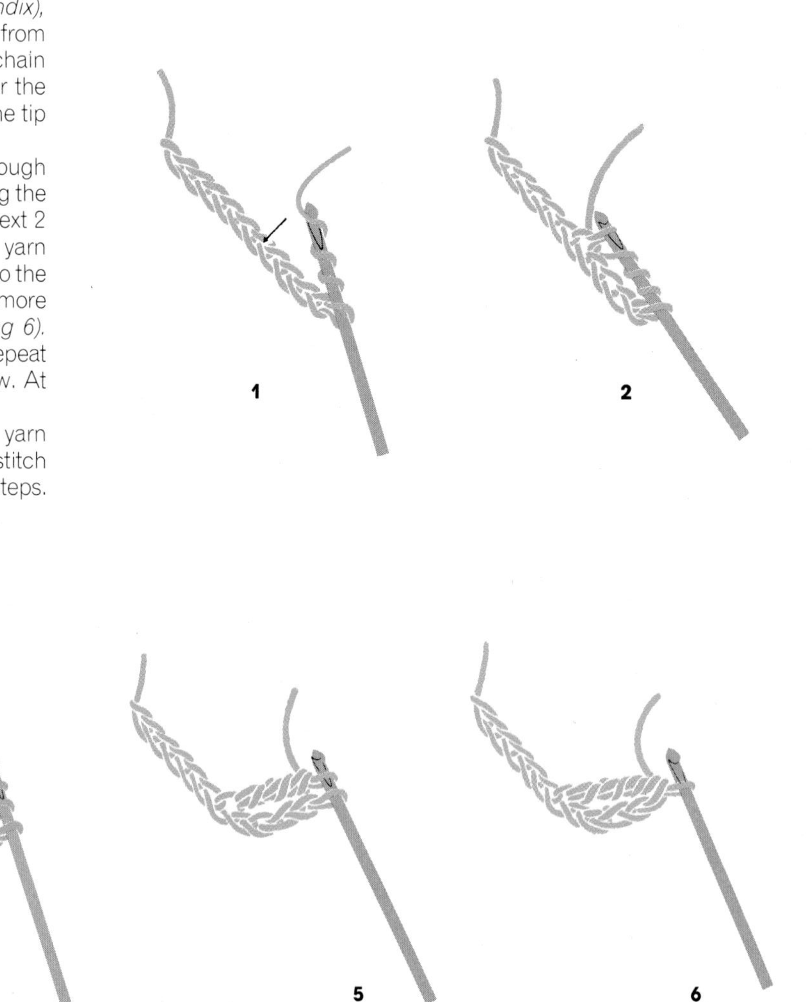

GLOSSARY

BACKSTITCH: To reinforce the beginning or end of a seam by making several machine stitches back over the seam line.

BASTE: To stitch together pieces of fabric temporarily, or to indicate pattern markings on both sides of a piece of fabric.

BIAS: A line running diagonally to the threads in a woven fabric. A 45° bias is called a true bias.

BIAS TAPE: A folded strip of nylon, rayon or cotton, cut diagonally to the fabric threads, i.e., on the bias, so that the strip will stretch smoothly to cover curved and straight edges of a garment piece. It can be used in place of furrier's tape to reinforce the seams of fur garments. Double-fold bias tape is called bias binding; commonly made of cotton or a cotton-synthetic blend, it is used to bind raw edges.

BONDING TAPE: An adhesive tape used to attach interfacings and to reinforce areas of wear. The heat of an iron fuses the tape to fabrics without the need for sewing.

DART: A stitched fold, tapering to a point at one or both ends, used to shape fabric around curves.

EYELET: A small round hole made in fabric for a cord tie or for ventilation. Also, the metal ring that reinforces such a hole.

FACING: A piece of fabric that is sewed along the raw edge of an opening such as a neckline and then turned to the inside to give the edge a smooth finish. Facings are usually cut from the same cloth as the garment itself.

FASTENING STITCH: A stitch used to anchor a thread by making three or four stitches, one over the other, in the same place.

FELT: A nonwoven fabric made from fibers that are matted together. Because its bulk and stiffness are similar to those of leather and suede, it is especially suitable for making prototypes for styling and fitting garments that are to be made of those materials.

FLAT-FELLED SEAM: A double-stitched seam used on synthetic leathers to create the look of a lapped seam. One seam allowance is trimmed so that the opposite seam allowance can be turned and stitched on top of it to give a finished effect on both sides of the garment.

FOOT: See PRESSER FOOT

FURRIER'S COLD TAPE: A special tape, sticky on one side and silky on the other, applied as reinforcement to edges or dart areas of fur before seams are sewed.

FUSING TAPE: See BONDING TAPE

GLOVER'S NEEDLE: A three-sided, wedgelike needle used for stitching leather and fur.

GRAIN: In woven fabrics, the grain is the direction of the threads: the warp (the threads running from one cut end to the other) forms the lengthwise grain; the woof, or weft (the threads running across the lengthwise grain from one finished edge to the other) forms the crosswise grain. In leather, the grain is the direction of the most give or stretch. In paper, the grain is the direction in which the paper rolls more easily.

GRAIN-LINE ARROW: The double-ended arrow printed on a pattern piece indicating how the piece should be aligned with the grains of the fabric.

INTERFACING: A fabric sewed between two layers of garment fabric to stiffen and strengthen the support parts of the garment.

LAPPED SEAM: For leather, a seam made by aligning the trimmed seam line of one piece of leather over the seam allowance and along the seam line of another piece and then topstitching 1/8 inch in from the trimmed edge. A second row of topstitches is then made 1/4 inch from the first line of stitching.

LINING: A fabric covering the inside of part or all of a garment.

MENDING TAPE: See BONDING TAPE

NAP: The short fibers on the surface of a fabric that are pulled and brushed in one direction. Also, the direction of the hair on fur or the rough surface on suede.

NAP LAYOUT: A cutting direction on patterns to indicate how the pattern is to be aligned with fabrics that, because of their surface, nap, or printed design, change in appearance with the direction in which they are set. When such fabrics are used, all pattern pieces must be laid out and cut in one direction—with the nap.

NOTCH: A V- or diamond-shaped marking made on the edge of a garment piece as an alignment guide; intended to be matched with a similar notch or group of notches on another piece. Also a triangular cut made in the seam allowance of a curved seam to help it lie flat.

PILE: A surface of upright fibers found on fabrics such as velvet, terry cloth, real fur and fake fur. The pile of a fabric tends to lie in a particular direction, so the way the fabric is positioned during sewing affects the appearance of the finished garment.

PIVOT: A technique for machine stitching around angular corners that involves stopping the machine, with the needle down, at the apex of a corner, raising the presser foot, pivoting the fabric and then lowering the presser foot before continuing to stitch.

PLAIN SEAM: The joining of two pieces of fabric by placing the right sides together and stitching along the seam-line marking; the seam allowances are then usually pressed open.

PRESSER FOOT: The part of a sewing machine that holds down fabric while it is being advanced under the needle. An all-purpose, or general purpose, foot has two prongs of equal length and is used for most stitching. A roller presser foot has two rollers with grids to prevent bulky or sheer fabric from sticking or slipping while stitching. A straight-stitch foot has one long and one short prong and can be used for straight stitching and stitching fabrics of varying thicknesses. A zipper foot has only one prong and is used to stitch zippers and cording.

PRESSING CLOTH: A piece of fabric, preferably cotton drill cloth, that is placed between the iron and the garment when pressing.

ROLLER PRESSER FOOT: See PRESSER FOOT

SEAM TAPE: A flat tape of finishing fabric—rayon or nylon with a woven edge, or nylon or polyester stretch lace—usually 1/2 to 5/8 inch wide, that is sewed over a seam to reinforce it or is used to finish hems.

SKIVING: The technique of shaving leather, with a safety bevel or skiving tool, to make it less bulky, usually along edges to be seamed.

TAILOR'S CHALK: Flat squares of wax, stone or clay, used to transfer pattern markings or adjustments onto fabric.

TAILOR'S HAM: A firm, ham-shaped cushion used for pressing areas that require special shaping.

TENSION: The degree of tightness of the two threads forming machine stitches.

THROAT PLATE: A flat metal piece with a hole through which a sewing-machine needle passes as it stitches. Most throat plates have guidelines marked on both the left and the right sides to help keep seams straight.

TOPSTITCHING: A line of machine stitching on the visible side of the garment, parallel to a seam.

TWILL TAPE: A thin, extra-strong tape of twilled linen or cotton fabric that may be used to reinforce the seams of fur garments.

ZIGZAG STITCH: A serrated line of machine stitching.

BASIC STITCHES

The diagrams below and on the following pages demonstrate how to make the elementary hand-sewing, knitting and crocheting stitches referred to in this volume.

THE SLIP STITCH

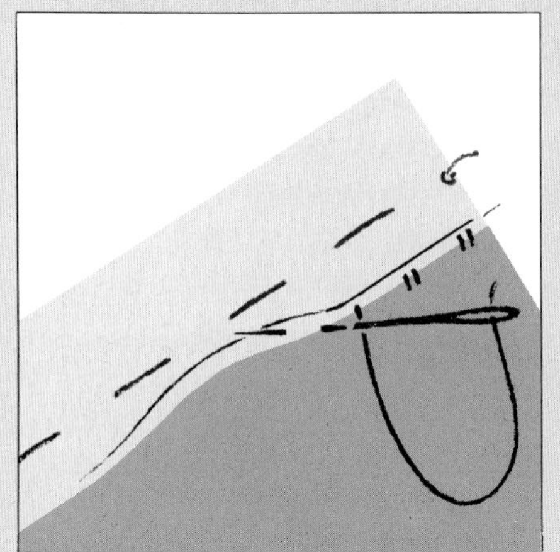

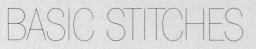

Fold under the hem edge and anchor the first stitch with a knot inside the fold. Point the needle to the left. Pick up one or two threads of the garment fabric close to the hem edge, directly below the first stitch, and slide the needle horizontally through the folded edge of the hem 1/8 inch to the left of the previous stitch. End with a fastening stitch *(Glossary).*

THE HEMMING STITCH

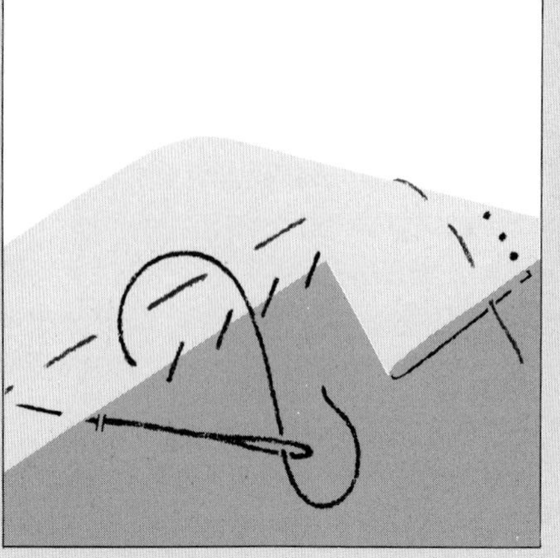

Anchor the first stitch with a knot inside the hem; then, pointing the needle up and to the left, pick up one or two threads of the garment fabric close to the hem. Push the needle up through the hem 1/8 inch above the edge; pull the thread through. Continue picking up one or two threads and making 1/8-inch stitches in the hem at intervals of 1/4 inch. End with a fastening stitch *(Glossary).*

THE OVERCAST STITCH

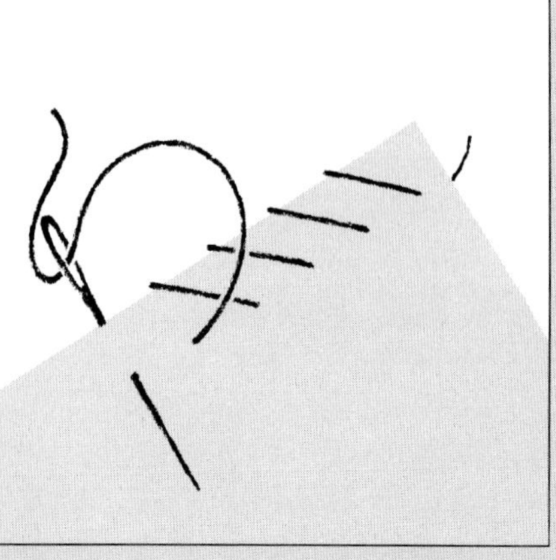

Draw the needle, with knotted thread, through from the wrong side of the fabric 1/8 to 1/4 inch down from the top edge. With the thread to the right, insert the needle under the fabric from the wrong side 1/8 to 1/4 inch to the left of the first stitch. Continue to make evenly spaced stitches over the fabric edge and end with a fastening stitch *(Glossary).*

THE BLANKET STITCH

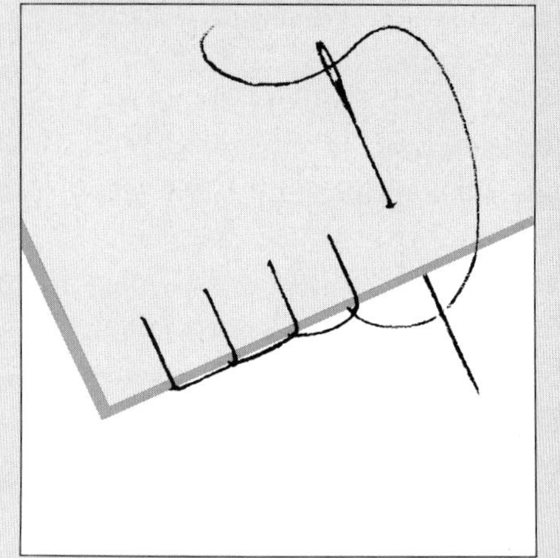

Using a knotted thread, bring the needle up from the bottom piece of fabric 1/4 inch from the edge at the left side of the fabric. Pull it through. To make the first stitch, hold the thread down with your left thumb, and insert the needle just to the right of the point from which the thread emerged. Make sure the needle is at a right angle to the edge and goes over the thread before you draw the thread taut. For each succeeding stitch, repeat these steps but insert the needle into the fabric 1/4 inch to the right of the preceding stitch. End with a fastening stitch *(Glossary).*

THE WHIPSTITCH

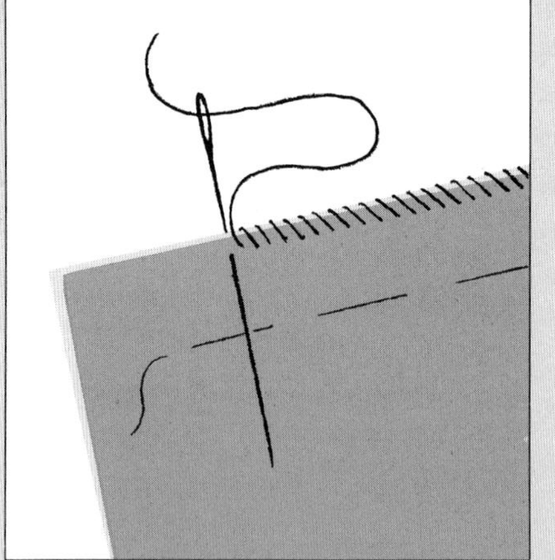

Using a knotted thread, draw the needle up from the bottom layer of fabric about 1/16 inch from the edge. Reinsert the needle—again from the bottom layer of fabric—about 1/16 inch to the left of the point from which the thread emerged, making sure the needle is at a right angle to the edge. Continue to make tiny, slanted, even stitches over the fabric edge. End with a fastening stitch *(Glossary).*

THE HAND ZIGZAG STITCH

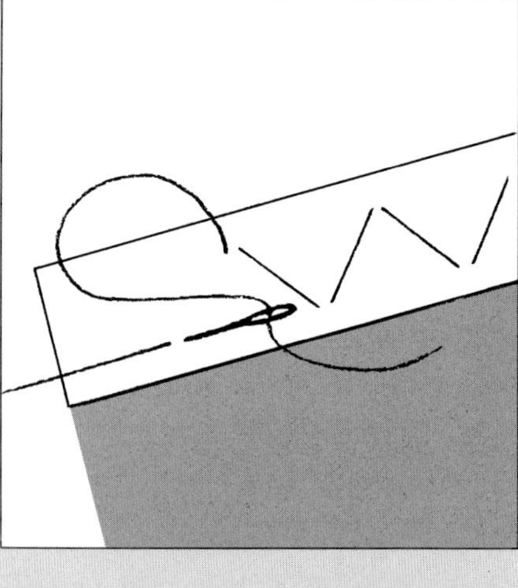

To attach tape to a piece of fabric, use knotted thread and make tiny, even, horizontal stitches going through the tape and picking up only a few threads of the fabric. Make the first stitch 1/8 inch from one edge of the tape and the next stitch 1/8 inch from the other edge, so that the thread stretches diagonally across the tape between the stitches. Continue alternating from one edge to the other, keeping the stitches at least 1/4 inch apart, depending on the width of the tape. End with a fastening stitch *(Glossary).*

KNITTING / CASTING ON STITCHES

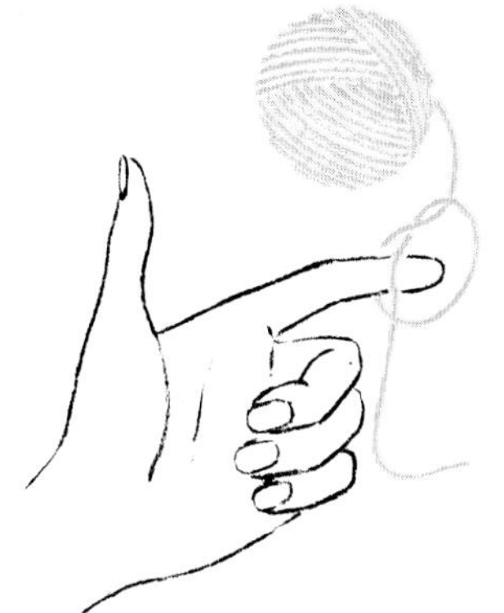

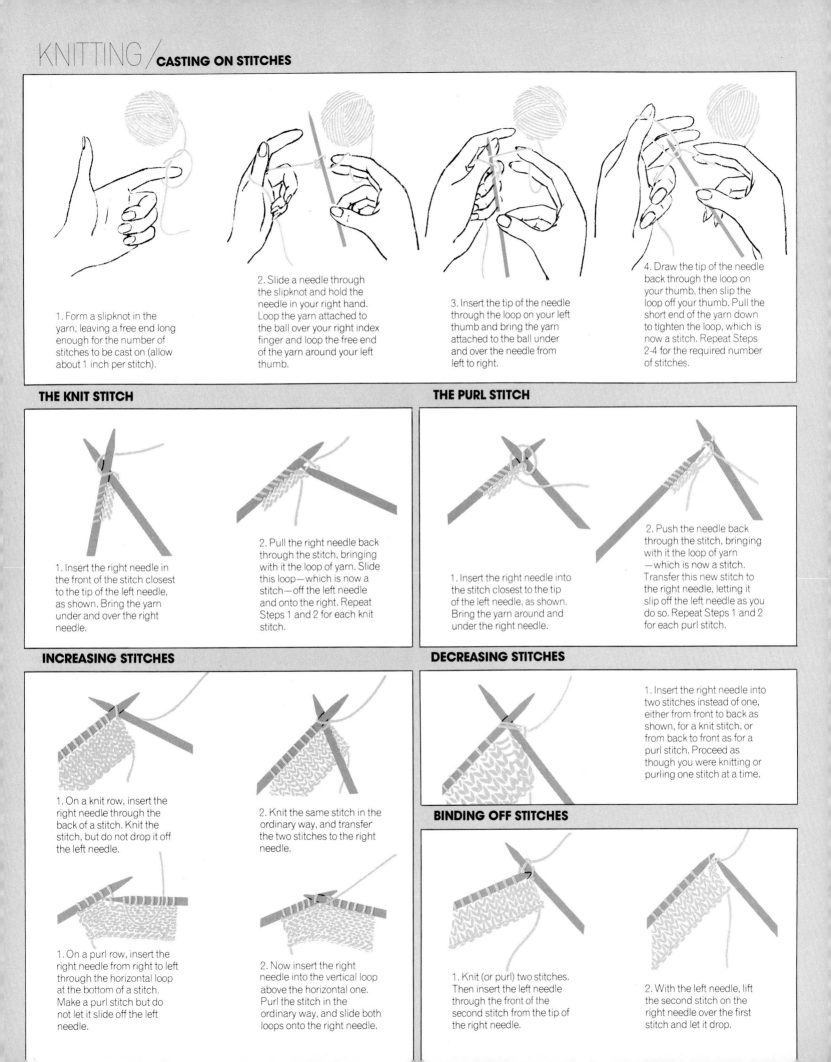

1. Form a slipknot in the yarn, leaving a free end long enough for the number of stitches to be cast on (allow about 1 inch per stitch).

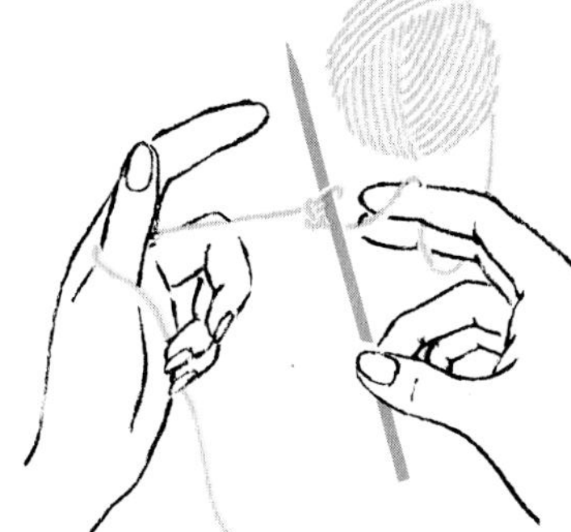

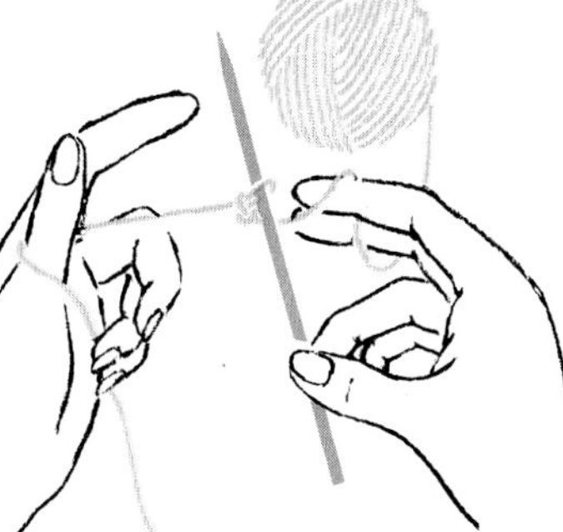

2. Slide a needle through the slipknot and hold the needle in your right hand. Loop the yarn attached to the ball over your right index finger and loop the free end of the yarn around your left thumb.

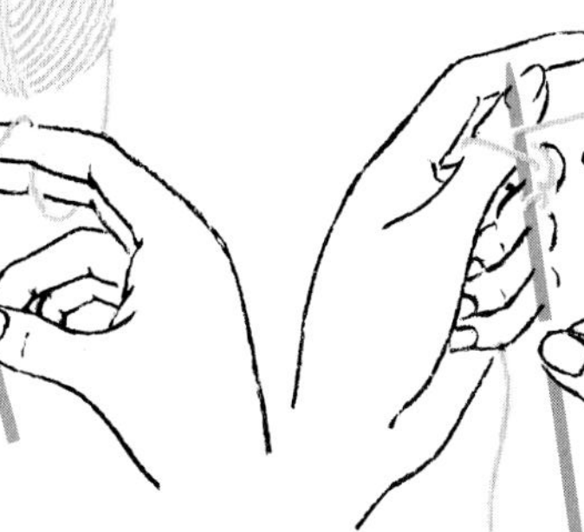

3. Insert the tip of the needle through the loop on your left thumb and bring the yarn attached to the ball under and over the needle from left to right.

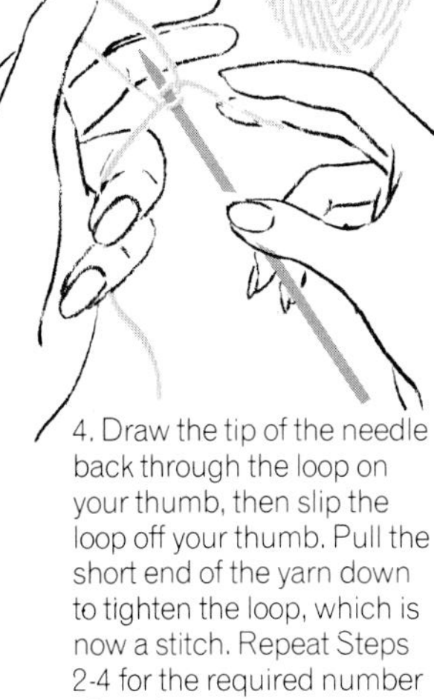

4. Draw the tip of the needle back through the loop on your thumb, then slip the loop off your thumb. Pull the short end of the yarn down to tighten the loop, which is now a stitch. Repeat Steps 2-4 for the required number of stitches.

THE KNIT STITCH

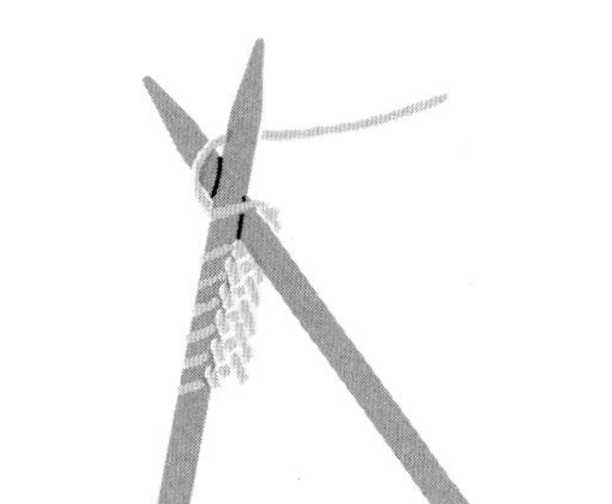

1. Insert the right needle in the front of the stitch closest to the tip of the left needle, as shown. Bring the yarn under and over the right needle.

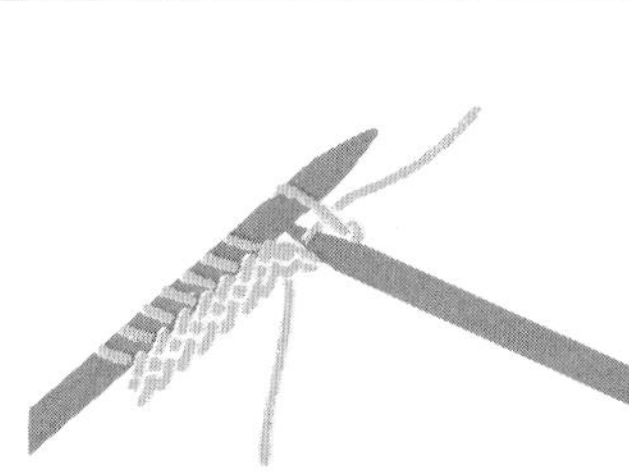

2. Pull the right needle back through the stitch, bringing with it the loop of yarn. Slide this loop—which is now a stitch—off the left needle and onto the right. Repeat Steps 1 and 2 for each knit stitch.

THE PURL STITCH

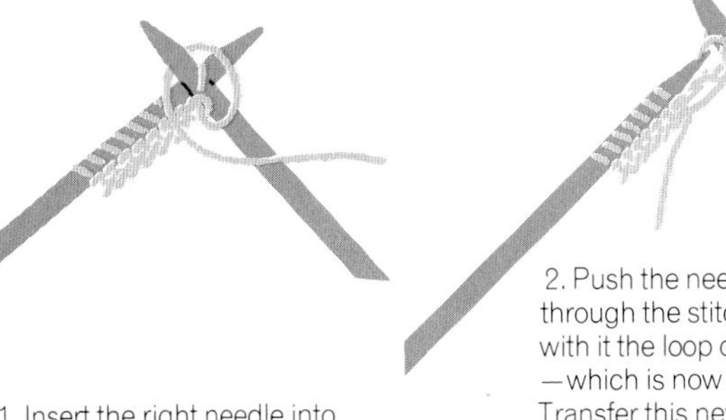

1. Insert the right needle into the stitch closest to the tip of the left needle, as shown. Bring the yarn around and under the right needle.

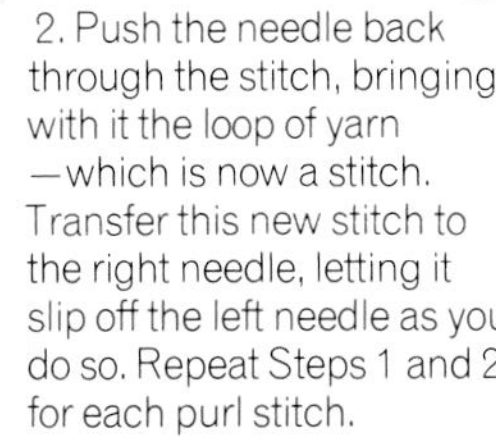

2. Push the needle back through the stitch, bringing with it the loop of yarn —which is now a stitch. Transfer this new stitch to the right needle, letting it slip off the left needle as you do so. Repeat Steps 1 and 2 for each purl stitch.

INCREASING STITCHES

1. On a knit row, insert the right needle through the back of a stitch. Knit the stitch, but do not drop it off the left needle.

2. Knit the same stitch in the ordinary way, and transfer the two stitches to the right needle.

1. On a purl row, insert the right needle from right to left through the horizontal loop at the bottom of a stitch. Make a purl stitch but do not let it slide off the left needle.

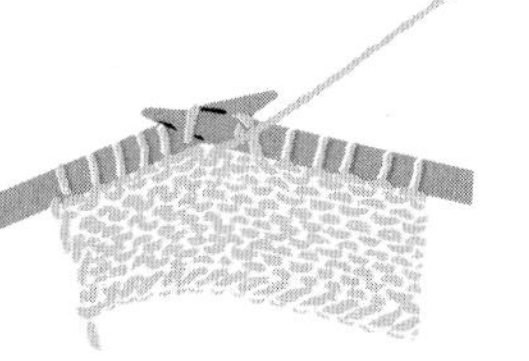

2. Now insert the right needle into the vertical loop above the horizontal one. Purl the stitch in the ordinary way, and slide both loops onto the right needle.

DECREASING STITCHES

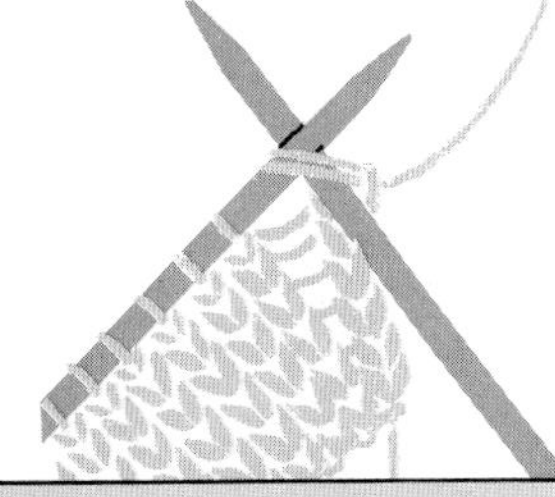

1. Insert the right needle into two stitches instead of one, either from front to back as shown, for a knit stitch, or from back to front as for a purl stitch. Proceed as though you were knitting or purling one stitch at a time.

BINDING OFF STITCHES

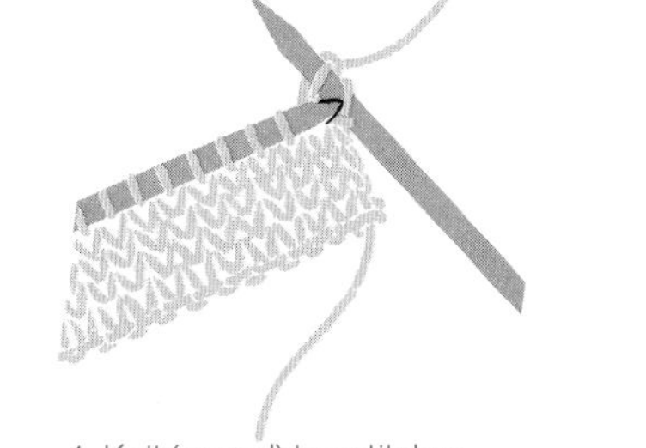

1. Knit (or purl) two stitches. Then insert the left needle through the front of the second stitch from the tip of the right needle.

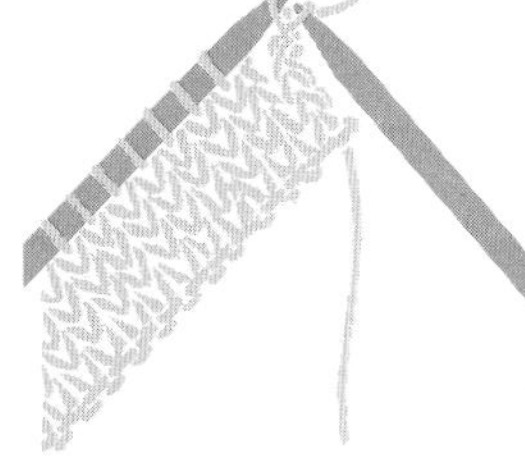

2. With the left needle, lift the second stitch on the right needle over the first stitch and let it drop.

CROCHETING / THE CHAIN STITCH

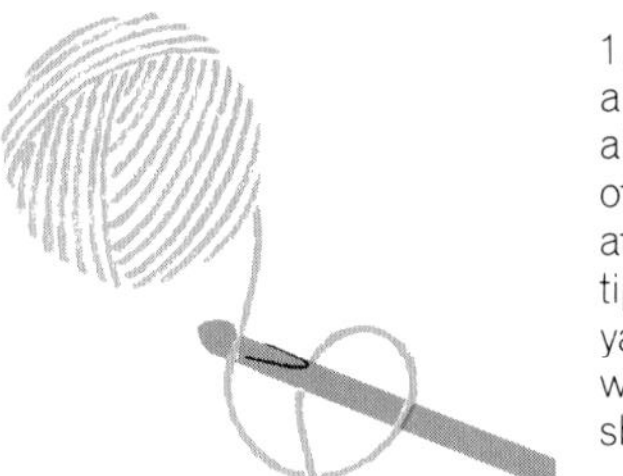

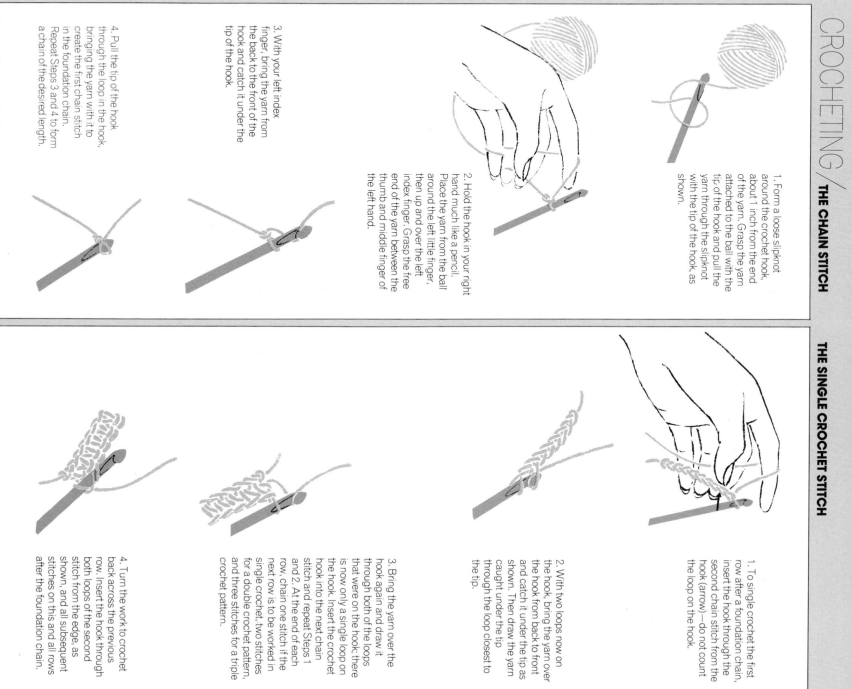

1. Form a loose slipknot around the crochet hook, about 1 inch from the end of the yarn. Grasp the yarn attached to the ball with the tip of the hook and pull the yarn through the slipknot with the tip of the hook, as shown.

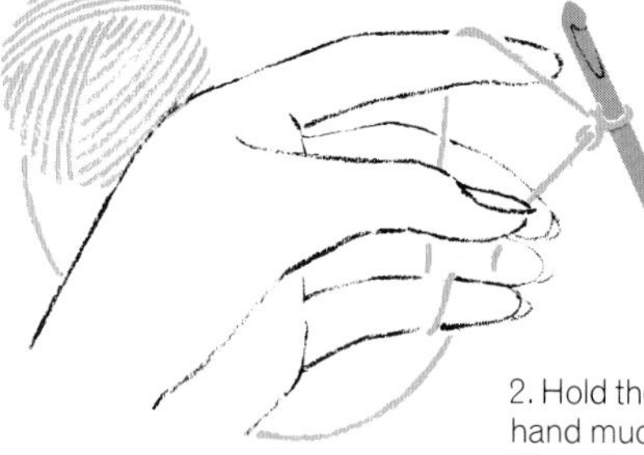

2. Hold the hook in your right hand much like a pencil. Place the yarn from the ball around the left little finger, then up and over the left index finger. Grasp the free end of the yarn between the thumb and middle finger of the left hand.

3. With your left index finger, bring the yarn from the back to the front of the hook and catch it under the tip of the hook.

4. Pull the tip of the hook through the loop in the hook, bringing the yarn with it to create the first chain stitch in the foundation chain. Repeat Steps 3 and 4 to form a chain of the desired length.

THE SINGLE CROCHET STITCH

1. To single crochet the first row after a foundation chain, insert the hook through the second chain stitch from the hook (arrow)—do not count the loop on the hook.

2. With two loops now on the hook, bring the yarn over the hook from back to front and catch it under the tip as shown. Then draw the yarn caught under the tip through the loop closest to the tip.

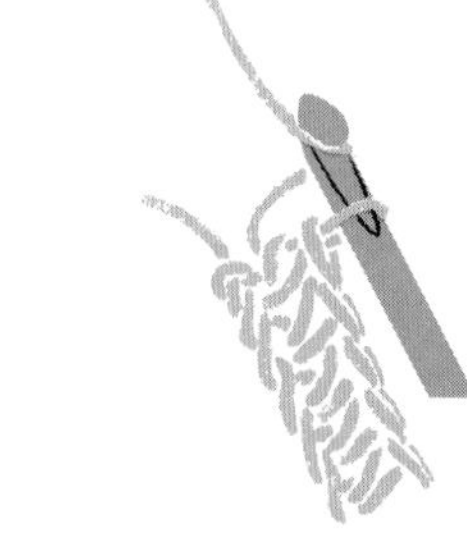

3. Bring the yarn over the hook again and draw it through both of the loops that were on the hook; there is now only a single loop on the hook. Insert the crochet hook into the next chain stitch and repeat Steps 1 and 2. At the end of each row, chain one stitch if the next row is to be worked in single crochet, two stitches for a double crochet pattern, and three stitches for a triple crochet pattern.

4. Turn the work to crochet back across the previous row. Insert the hook through both loops of the second stitch from the edge, as shown, and all subsequent stitches on this and all rows after the foundation chain.

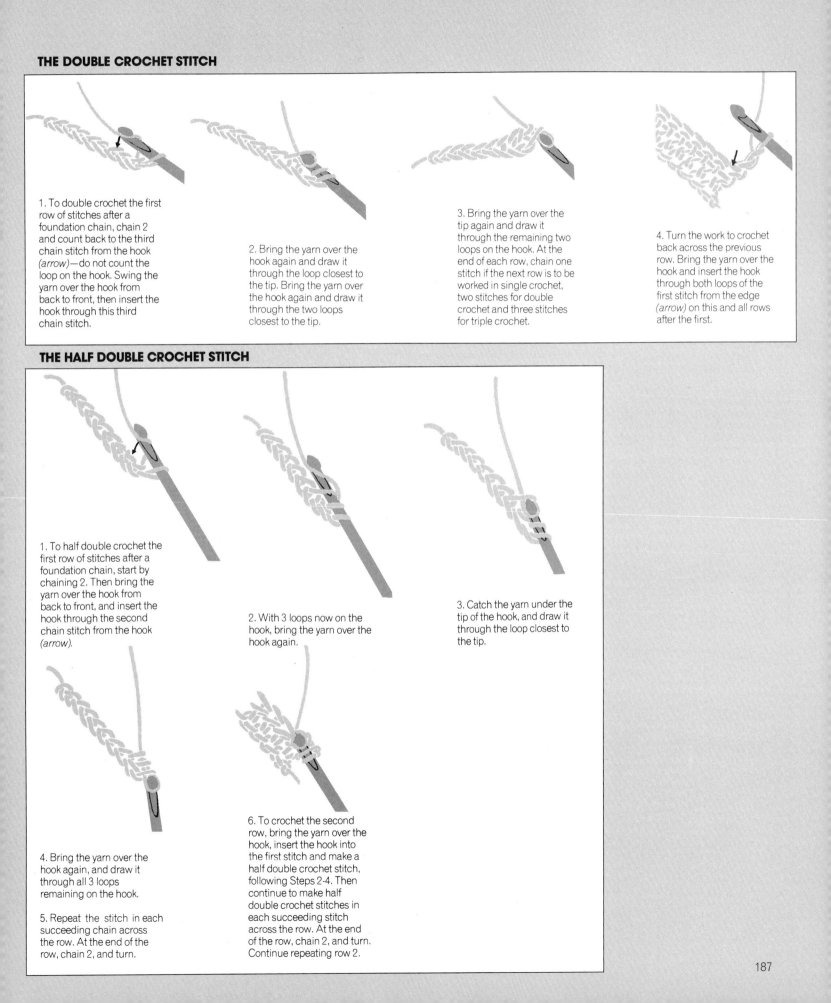

THE DOUBLE CROCHET STITCH

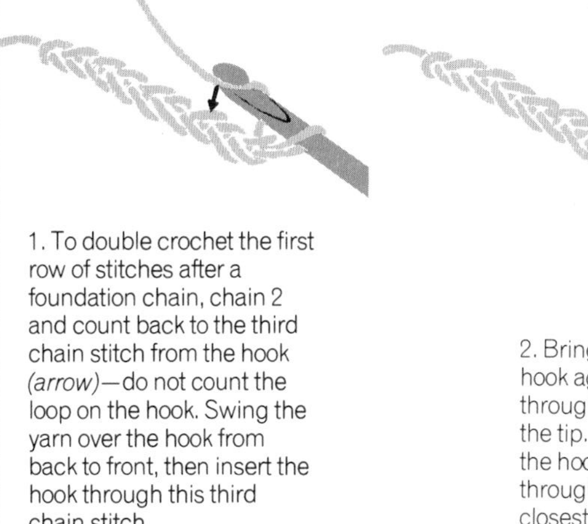

1. To double crochet the first row of stitches after a foundation chain, chain 2 and count back to the third chain stitch from the hook *(arrow)*—do not count the loop on the hook. Swing the yarn over the hook from back to front, then insert the hook through this third chain stitch.

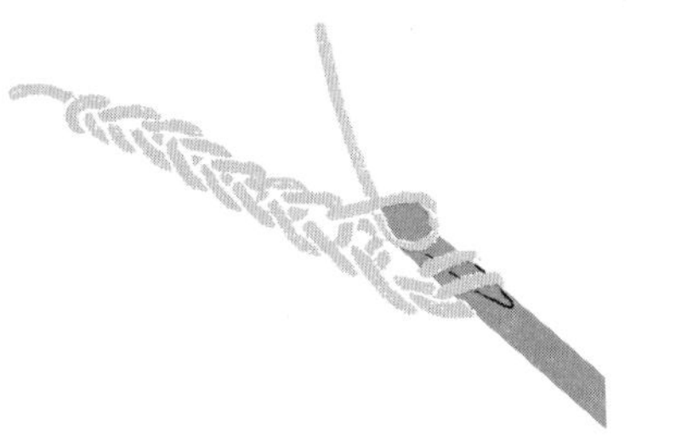

2. Bring the yarn over the hook again and draw it through the loop closest to the tip. Bring the yarn over the hook again and draw it through the two loops closest to the tip.

3. Bring the yarn over the tip again and draw it through the remaining two loops on the hook. At the end of each row, chain one stitch if the next row is to be worked in single crochet, two stitches for double crochet and three stitches for triple crochet.

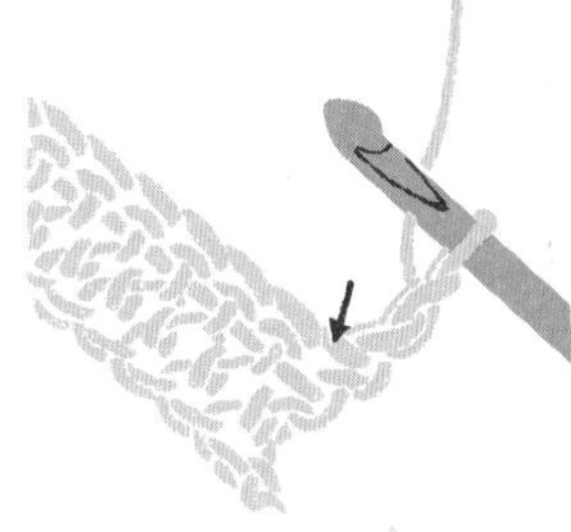

4. Turn the work to crochet back across the previous row. Bring the yarn over the hook and insert the hook through both loops of the first stitch from the edge *(arrow)* on this and all rows after the first.

THE HALF DOUBLE CROCHET STITCH

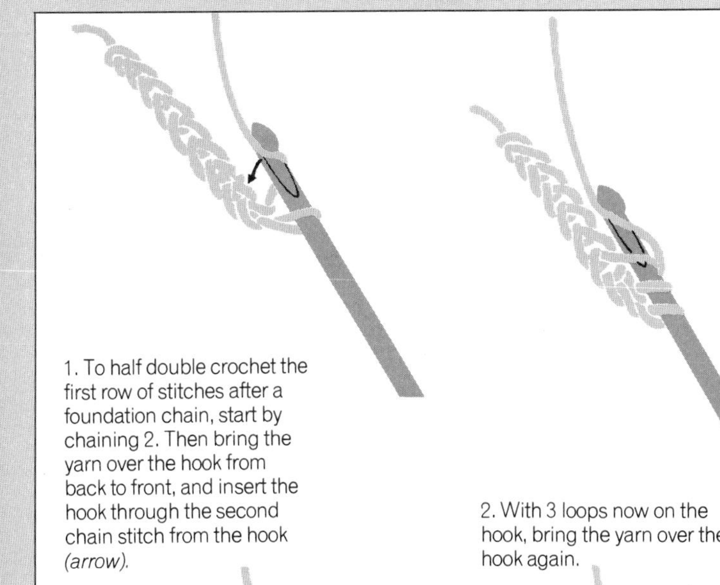

1. To half double crochet the first row of stitches after a foundation chain, start by chaining 2. Then bring the yarn over the hook from back to front, and insert the hook through the second chain stitch from the hook *(arrow)*.

2. With 3 loops now on the hook, bring the yarn over the hook again.

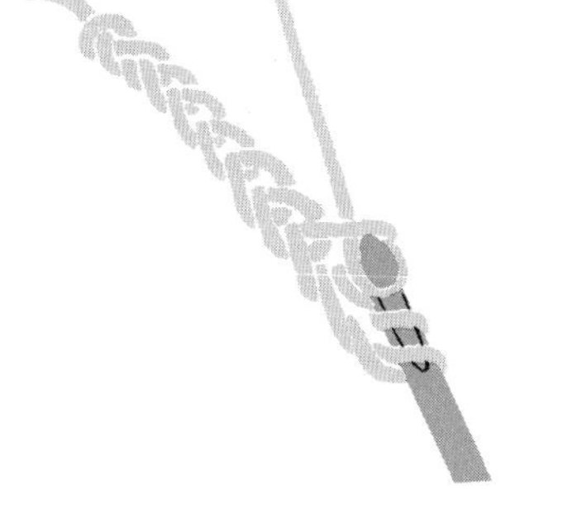

3. Catch the yarn under the tip of the hook, and draw it through the loop closest to the tip.

4. Bring the yarn over the hook again, and draw it through all 3 loops remaining on the hook.

5. Repeat the stitch in each succeeding chain across the row. At the end of the row, chain 2, and turn.

6. To crochet the second row, bring the yarn over the hook, insert the hook into the first stitch and make a half double crochet stitch, following Steps 2-4. Then continue to make half double crochet stitches in each succeeding stitch across the row. At the end of the row, chain 2, and turn. Continue repeating row 2.

THE TRIPLE CROCHET STITCH

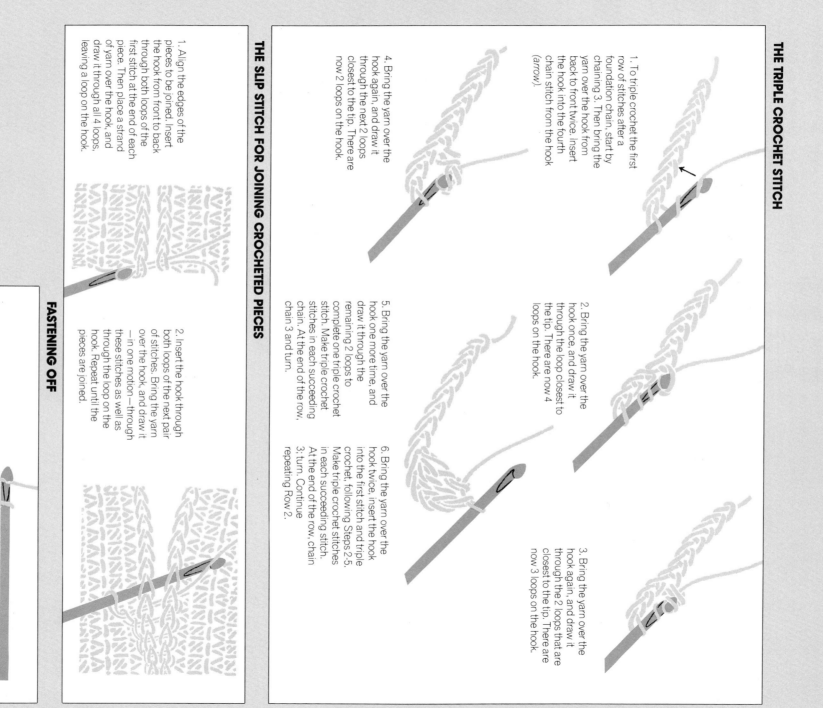

1. To triple crochet the first row of stitches after a foundation chain, start by chaining 3. Then bring the yarn over the hook from back to front twice. Insert the hook into the fourth chain stitch from the hook *(arrow).*

2. Bring the yarn over the hook once, and draw it through the loop closest to the tip. There are now 4 loops on the hook.

3. Bring the yarn over the hook again, and draw it through the 2 loops that are closest to the tip. There are now 3 loops on the hook.

4. Bring the yarn over the hook again, and draw it through the next 2 loops closest to the tip. There are now 2 loops on the hook.

5. Bring the yarn over the hook one more time, and draw it through the remaining 2 loops to complete one triple crochet stitch. Make triple crochet stitches in each succeeding chain. At the end of the row, chain 3 and turn.

6. Bring the yarn over the hook twice, insert the hook into the first stitch and triple crochet, following Steps 2-5. Make triple crochet stitches in each succeeding stitch. At the end of the row, chain 3; turn. Continue repeating Row 2.

THE SLIP STITCH FOR JOINING CROCHETED PIECES

1. Align the edges of the pieces to be joined. Insert the hook from front to back through both loops of the first stitch at the end of each piece. Then place a strand of yarn over the hook, and draw it through all 4 loops, leaving a loop on the hook.

2. Insert the hook through both loops of the next pair of stitches. Bring the yarn over the hook, and draw it —in one motion—through these stitches as well as through the loop on the hook. Repeat until the pieces are joined.

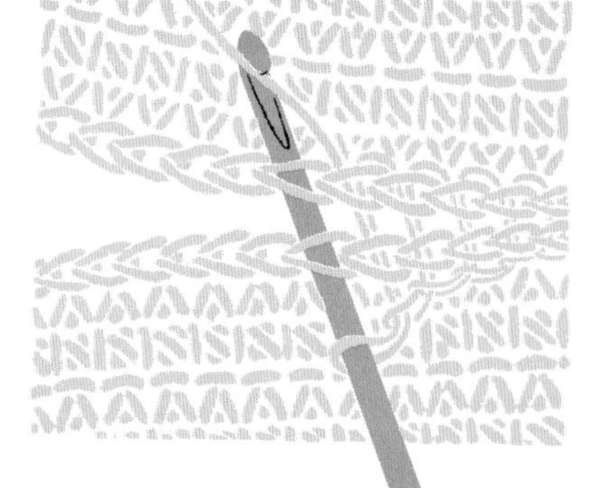

FASTENING OFF

Cut the yarn from the ball, leaving a 2-inch-long end. Pull this end through the loop on the hook to secure it and weave it through one or two nearby stitches.

CREDITS

Sources for the illustrations in this book are shown below. Credits from left to right are separated by semicolons, from top to bottom by dashes.

6,7—Dan Budnik. 11—Michael Avedon, TIME-LIFE Picture Agency; Drive Fotostudio (Zurich), courtesy Paco Rabanne; courtesy Paco Rabanne. 12 through 17—Dan Budnik. 18,19—Tasso Vendikos. 23—The Bettmann Archive; Al Freni; The Bettmann Archive; courtesy Bonnie Cashin Designs. 24 through 27—Ryszard Horowitz. 30,31—Al Freni. 32,33—Drawings by John Sagan. 34 through 37—Drawings by Carolyn Mazzello. 38 through 59—Ken Kay. 60,61—Al Freni. 62 through 69—Drawings by Raymond Skibinski. 70,71—Richard Jeffery. 72 through 83—Drawings by Raymond Skibinski. 84,85—Richard Jeffery. 86 through 93—Drawings by John Sagan. 94,95—Tasso Vendikos. 98 through 101—Ryszard Horowitz. 104 through 123—Ken Kay. 124,125—Tasso Vendikos. 126 through 131—Drawings by Carolyn Mazzello. 132,133—Tasso Vendikos. 134 through 143—Drawings by John Sagan. 144,145—Al Freni. 148,149—Ralph Morse; except extreme right, NASA. 150,151—Al Freni. 154 through 157—Ken Kay. 158,159—Alen MacWeeney. 160 through 169—Drawings by John Sagan. 170,171—Richard Jeffery. 174,175—Photographs by Ken Kay, vest, crochet by Susanna Lewis—fish and wolf mask, crochet by Nicki Hitz Edson; doll, courtesy Barry Williams, crochet by Lannie Hart. 176,177—Ryszard Horowitz. 178,179—Tasso Vendikos. 181—Drawings by John Sagan. 184—Drawings by John Sagan—Drawings by Raymond Skibinski. 185 through 188—Drawing by John Sagan.

ACKNOWLEDGMENTS

For their help in the preparation of this book the editors would like to thank the following individuals: Victor Carmona, Reeves Brothers; Susan Costello; Nicki Hitz Edson; Christina Galante, Film Coordinator for the City of New York; Harold Garry, Superb Gloves; Irving Glass, President, The Tanner's Council of America, Inc.; Cynthia Gold; Lannie Hart; Ben Keller; Susanna Lewis; Marie Martin; Jill Mason; Henry Moscow; Fred Nash; Richard Oulahan; Charles H. Picard; Samuel Robers; Julie Schafler, Artisans' Gallery; Inge Steppan; Lee K-Thorpe, Thorpe Furs; Morey Weisman, Comark Plastics Division, United Merchants and Manufacturers, Inc.; Barry Williams.

The editors would also like to thank the following: Ameritex Division, Cohn Hall Marx; Avila Group, Inc., Converters of Synthetic Fabrics; Blassport, Inc.; Earl-Glo Fabrics; David Evins, Shoes; Fe-Ro Fabrics, Inc.; Glenoit Mills, Inc.; Henri Bendel, Inc.; Kenneth Jay Lane, Inc.; Hernando, Ltd.; Les-Lee Leather Company; Loewengart & Co.; Marbella Textiles; Minerva Leather Co., Inc.; New York City Police Department; Springs Mills, Inc.; Sommers-Artcraft; Ben Thylan Furs Corp.; E. F. Timme & Son, Inc.; A Touch of Whimsy; Weller Fabrics, Inc.; Harry Winston, Inc.; The Yarn Center.

INDEX

Numerals in italics indicate an illustration of the subject mentioned.

Accessory(ies). *See* Belt(s); Glove(s); Handbag(s)
Acryline, 26
Adjustment(s) to pattern(s), for leather, 32, *34-37;* to add yokes, 32, *34, 36-37;* to allow for creases, 32; to avoid blemishes, 32; to curve corners, *35;* to divide pants legs, 32, *35, 36;* to eliminate darts, 32, *34, 35;* enlarging, *33;* lengthening, *32;* reducing, *33;* shortening, *33;* to utilize small pieces, 32
Alligatorskin, simulated, 30, *31*
Aluminum, in clothing, 9; pop-top rings, 10-*11;* in space suits, 148
Arnel, 147

Backstitching, 46
Beaver: fake, *chart* 102-103, *104-105;* real, *chart* 102-103
Beaver, nylon plus, *158-159,* 160
Beeswax, *chart* 102-103
Belt(s), *60-69;* buckles for, *60-61,* 62; of crocheted disks, *16;* instructions for, *62-69;* interfacings for, 62; leather, *60-61, 62-65;* linings for, 62; materials for, *60-61,* 62; pattern for two-buckled, *63;* of pseudo suede, *60-61, 68-69;* sash, *60-61, 68-69;* of whip snake and kidskin, *60-61, 65-67*
Beret, fake fur, 132, *133,* 134, *140-141;* instructions for, *140-141;* materials needed for, 134; nap direction in, 134, 140; pattern for, *140*
Beta cloth, 11, 148
Binding off (knitting), instructions for, *185*
Blanket stitch (hand sewing), *114;* instructions for, *184*
Boa constrictor: fake, *26-27;* real, *24-25, chart* 28-29
Bonded rubber fabric(s), *150-151, chart* 152-153
Borg, George W., 97
Borg Textiles, 10
Broadtail: coat lining of fake, *124,* 125; fake, *100-101, chart* 102-103; real, *chart* 102-103
Buckle(s), *60-61,* 62
Button loop(s), *124, 131;* instructions for, *131*
Buttonhole(s), instructions for: by binding technique, 54; in leather, 54, *58;* in synthetic leather and pseudo suede, 54, *59*

Cabretta, *14,* 72, 85
Calf fur, 97
Calfskin: fake, 18, *19;* real, *25*
Cantrece, 147
Canvas, 106
Cape, *158-159;* cutting, *166;* fabrics for, 160; inserting zipper in, *167;* instructions for, *160-169;* marking, *166;* pattern for, *160-165;* yardage requirements for, 160, 166
Cashin, Bonnie, 23
Casting on (knitting), instructions for, *185*
Chain, 86; on handbag, *93*
Chain stitch (crochet), instructions for, *186*
Cheetah, fake, 10, 97
Chinchilla: fake, *chart* 102-103; real, *98-99, chart* 102-103
Chromel R, 11
Ciré, 12, *13, 150-151, chart* 152-153
Cleaning: bonded fabrics, *chart* 152-153; coated fabrics, *chart* 152-153; fake fur, *chart* 102-103; real fur, *chart* 102-103; real leather, *chart* 28-29; synthetic leather, *chart* 28-29
Cloche, fur, *132, 134-137;* instructions for, *134-137;* materials for, 134; nap direction in, 134; pattern for, *134*
Coat lining(s), fake fur, detachable, *124-131;* accessories for, 126; attaching to coat, *131;* of broadtail, *124,* 125; button loops for, *131;* choosing coat for, 126; constructing, *130;* cutting, *129;* furs for, *124-125.* 126; grip fasteners for, *131;* making patterns for, *126-129;* man's, *124-125;* marking, *129;* of stone marten, *124-125;* thickness of, 126; woman's, *124,* 125; yardage needed for, 126
Coated fabric(s): for belts, 62; Beta cloth, 11, *148;* binding seams and edges of, *157;* bonded with rubber, *150-151, chart* 152-153; cape of, *158-159;* characteristics of, 147-148, *chart* 152-153, 154; ciré-finished, 12, *13, 150-151, chart* 152-153; cleaning, *chart* 152-153; clothing of, 12-*13,* 146-147, *158-159;* Cravanette, *chart* 152-153; cutting, *chart* 152-153, *154;* Durette, 148; Fluorel, 148; fluorochemical, 147, *chart* 152-153; handling, 154; hemming, *157;* with invisible coating, 152; Kevlar, 148; with knitted backing, 147; marking, *chart* 152-153; Nomex, 148; nonporous, 152, *chart* 152-153, 156; perfumed, 147; phosphorescent, 147; plain seams on, *155;* porous, 152, *chart* 152-153, 156; pressing, *chart* 152-153, 154; problems with, 154; for rainwear, 151, *158-159;* rolling, on tube, *154;* rubber-bonded, *150-151, chart* 152-153; Scotchgard, *chart* 152-153; sewing, *chart* 152-153, 154, *155;* silicone, 147, 152-153; slippery, *154, 155;* in space suits, 148; sticky, 154, *156;* Teflon, 148; testing, 154; tools for, 154; topstitching, *156;* Unisec, *chart* 152-153; urethane, 147, *150-151, chart* 152-153; uses of, 62, 146-148, 151, *chart* 152-153; ventilation holes in, *157;* vinyl, 147, *150-151, chart* 152-153; with visible coating, 152; wet look of, 147; Zepel, *chart* 152-153
Cobra, *chart* 28-29
Cody, Buffalo Bill, 21, *23*
Cold tape, furrier's, 106, *111*
Collar(s): of fake fur, 132, *133,* 134, *141-142;* furs for, 134; instructions for, *137-138, 141-142;* of leather, *51-52;* materials needed for, 134; nap direction on, 138, 142; from old fur, 120, *132;* patterns for, *137, 141;* Peter Pan, *132,* 134, *137-138;* pointed, *51-52;* of real fur, *16-17,* 99, *132,* 134, *137-138;* shawl, 132, *133,* 134, *141-142;* from swatches of fur, 99, pointed, curving, *35*
Cotton, vinylized, *150-151*
Cowhide: with alligator finish, 30, *31;* with aniline finish, *24,* 25; antiqued, *24,* 25, 30, *31;* characteristics of, *chart* 28-29; cleaning, *chart* 28-29; cutting, *chart* 28-29; fake, *18-19, 26, 27;* imitations made from, *chart* 28-29, *30-31;* with lizard finish, *18,* 30, 31; marking, *chart* 28-29; with ostrich finish, 30, *31;* pressing, *chart* 28-29; reversed, *24,* 25; sewing, *chart* 28-29; with silver lamé finish, *30;* with tooled motif, *30;* with tweed finish, *30;* uses of, *chart* 28-29, 30
Cravanette. *See* Silicone
Crochet stitch(es): abbreviations for, 180; chain, *186;* double, *174, 187;* double triple, *182;* fastening off, *188;* half double, *187;* instructions for, *182, 186-188;* for joining crocheted pieces, *188;* picot, *174;* single, *174, 186;* slip, *188;* triple, *188.* *See also* Crocheting
Crocheting: as art form, 172-174, *174-175;* belt of, *16;* combined with novel decorations, *16, 174-175, 178-179;* gauge for, 180; novelty, 172-174, *174-175;* with disks, *16, 178-179,* 181-182. *See also* Crochet stitch(es)
Cuff(s), fur, 132-133; of fake fur, 132, *133,* 134, *142-143;* furs for, 134; instructions for, *138-140, 142-143;* materials for, 134; nap direction on, 134, 139, 143; from old fur, *132;* pattern for, *138;* of real fur, *132,* 134, *138-140;* from swatches of fur, 99
Cutting: bonded fabrics, *chart* 152-153; coated fabrics, *chart* 152-153; furs, *chart* 102-103, 106, *109, 110;* leathers, *42-45, chart* 28-29; tools for, *42-43,* 106

Dacron, 147
Dart(s): eliminating from pattern, 32, *34, 35;* on leather, *50;* on long-pile fake fur, *117;* on pseudo suede, *51;* on real fur, *116;* on short-pile fake fur, *117;* on synthetic leather, *50*
Decreasing (knitting), instructions for, *185*
Deerskin, 21
Denim, *14*
Denis, Michaela, 97
Disks, metal: in belt, *16;* instructions for crocheting, 181-182; as trim for skirt, *178-179*
Dittrick, Mark, 174
Double crochet stitch (crochet), *174;* instructions for, *187*
Double triple crochet stitch (crochet), instructions for, *182*
Durette, 148

Edson, Nicki Hitz, 173, 174
Ermine, 97
Eyelet punching pliers, 62, 154, *155, 157*

Fabric(s), coated. *See* Coated fabric(s)
Fake fur(s). *See* Fur(s), fake
Fastening off (crochet), instructions for, *188*
Felt, 106, 134
Fitch: fake, *100-101, chart* 102-103; real, *chart* 102-103
Fluorel, 148
Fluorochemical finish, 147, *chart* 152-153
Fortrel, 147
Fox: fake, 97, *100-101, chart* 102-

103; real, *16-17, 94,* 96, *chart* 102-103; red, *94,* 97, *98-99, 100-101;* white, *98-99*
Fringe, on knitted jacket, *176-177;* instructions for, 181
Fun fur(s), 10
Fur(s), fake: accessories of, 132, *133,* 134; advantages of, 100, 125, 126; beaver, *chart* 102-103, *104-105;* beret of, 132, *133,* 134, *140-141;* by Borg, 10, 97; broadtail, *100-101, chart* 102-103, *124,* 125; characteristics of, 100, *chart* 102-103, 125, 126; cheetah, 10, 97; chinchilla, 97, *chart* 102-103; cleaning, *chart* 102-103; coat lining of, *124-131;* collar of, 132, *133,* 134, *141-142;* cost of, 10, 97, 100; cuffs of, 132, *133,* 134, *142-143;* cutting, *chart* 102-103, 106, *110;* darts on, *117;* for detachable coat linings, *124-125,* 126; dyed, *104-105;* edges on, finishing, *118;* edges on, flattening, *119;* European polecat, *100-101;* fitch, *100-101, chart* 102-103; fox, 97, *100-101, chart* 102-103; hat of, 132, *133,* 134, *140-141;* hems on, finishing, *118;* implements for sewing, 112; jaguar, 97; knitted, 97; knitted fringed jacket as, *176-177;* leopard, 10, 97; lining of, *124-131;* long-pile, *110,* 111, *114, 117,* 126, *133,* 134; lynx, 97, *chart* 102-103; marking, *chart* 102-103, 106, *110;* mink, *94-95,* 97, *100-101, chart* 102-103; monkey, *95, chart* 102-103, *104;* nap direction of, *106,* 134; needles for, *chart* 102-103; ocelot, 97, *100-101, chart* 102-103; otter, 97; patterns for, 106; Persian lamb, *chart* 102-103; polecat, European, *100-101;* preparing patterns for, *110;* pressing, *chart* 102-103; rabbit, *100-101, chart* 102-103, 104, *105;* realism of, 97; reinforcing seams of, *111;* seam allowances on, finishing, *115;* sewing, *chart* 102-103, 106, *114, 115;* sheep, *chart* 102-103, 104, *105;* short-pile, *chart* 102-103, *110,* 111, *115, 117,* 126; stone marten, *124-125,* 132, *133;* taping seams of, *111;* tiger, *100-101, chart* 102-103; as trim, 132, *133;* uses of, 97, 100, *124-125,* 126, 132, *133;* zebra *chart* 102-103
Fur(s), real: accessories of, 99, *132,* 134; as badge of social class, 96-97; beaver, 9, *chart* 102-103; broadtail, *chart* 102-103; calf, 97; cat, 97; characteristics of, *chart* 102-103; chinchilla, *98-99, chart* 102-103; in classic styles, *12-13;* cleaning, *chart* 102-103, 120, 121; cloche of, *132, 134-137;* collars of, *16-17,* 99, *132,* 134, *137-138;* cuffs of, 99, *132,* 134, *138-140;* cutting, *chart* 102-103, 106, *109;* darts on, *116;* disadvantages of, 125, 126; dyed, 10; edges on, finishing, *118;* edges on, flattening, 119; of endangered species, 97; ermine, 97; examining, *121;* fitch, *chart* 102-103; flattening edges of, *119;* fox, *16-17, 94,* 96, *98-99, chart* 102-103; freshening, 120, *121;* fun, 9-10; grooming, 120, *121;* hamster, 10; hats of, 99, *132, 134-137;* hems on, finishing, *118;* history of, 96-97; implements for sewing, 112; inspection of, 120, *121;* jackets of, 12, *13, 14;* jaguar, 98; kangaroo, 97; by Kaplan, 10; lamb, 97; leopard, 97; long-haired, *chart* 102-103; lynx, *chart* 102-103; Manchurian weasel, 10; marking, *chart* 102-103, 106, *108-109;* marten, 97; mending, 120, *122-123;* miniver, 97; mink, 10, 97, *98-99, chart* 102-103; monkey, *14,* 97, *chart* 102-103; moth infestation of, 120, *121;* nap direction of, *106,* 134; needle for, *chart* 102-103, *112-113,* 134; novel uses of, 9-10, 12, *13;* old, restoring, 120; by Partos, 10; patching, 120, *122-123;* patterns for, 106; Persian lamb, *chart* 102-103; plates of, 97, 102; preparing pattern for, *107;* pressing, *chart* 102-103; preservationist view of, 97; rabbit, *14,* 97, *98-99, chart* 102-103; rabbit, sheared, *chart* 102-103; raccoon, 97, *98-99, chart* 102-103; reinforcing seams of, *111;* repairing, 120; restoring, 106, 120; sable, 96, 97, *98-99, chart* 102-103; sewing, *chart* 102-103, 106, *112-113;* sheep, unsheared, *chart* 102-103; short-haired, *chart* 102-103, *132,* 134; squirrel, *132;* stone marten, *chart* 102-103; taping seams of, *111;* testing skins of, *120;* thread for, 112, 134; tiger, 97; trim of, 99, *132;* uses of, 9-10, 12, *13,* 99, *132-133;* wildebeest, 10; weasel, 10, 97; wolf, 10
Furrier's cold tape, 106, *111*
Fusing tape, 46

Glover's needle, *chart* 102-103, *112-113*
Glove(s), *70-83;* flare, adding to, *76;* instructions for, 70, *72-83;* materials for, 72; needle for, 72; patterns for, *72-74;* stitches for, *70-71, 79;* stretching leather for, 72, *75,* 76, 77, 78; thread for, 79, 83; vent opening of, *77, 83*
Grip fastener(s), *131*

Half double crochet stitch (crochet), instructions for, *187*
Hand sewing stitch(es): blanket, *114, 184;* hemming, *115, 184;* instructions for, *184;* locking, *113;* overcast, *115, 184;* whipstitch, *70-71, 112-113, 116, 118, 184;* slip, *184;* zigzag, *111, 116, 184*
Handbag(s), *84-93;* attaching chain to, *93;* attaching snap to, *89, 92;* clutch, *84-85;* crocheted, *174;* cutting out, *87;* instructions for, *86-93;* of lamb suede and whip snake, *84-85;* lining of, *90-92;* materials for, 85, 86; pattern for, *86;* shoulder bag, *84-85;* of whip snake and lamb suede, *84-85*
Hat(s), 99, 120, *132-133. See also* Beret; Cloche
Hem(s): on coated fabrics, *157;* on furs, *118;* on leather, *53;* on pseudo suede, *53;* on synthetic leather, 53
Hemming stitch (hand sewing), *115;* instructions for, *184*

Increasing (knitting), instructions for, *185*
Indians, American, 21, 22

Jacket, knitted, *176-177;* instructions for, 180-181
Jaguar, fake, 97

Kangaroo, 97
Kevlar, 148
Kidskin, *23,* 60, *61,* 72
Knit stitch (knitting), instructions for, *185*
Knitting: gauge for, 180; jacket of, *176-177,* 180-181
Knitting stitch(es): abbreviations for, 180; binding off, *185;* casting on, *185;* decreasing, *185;* increasing, *185;* instructions for, *185;* knit, *185;* purl, *185. See also* Knitting
Kodel, 147

Lamb, 97
Lamb, Persian, *chart* 102-103
Lambskin, *chart* 28-29, 85; suede, *84-85,* 86; sueded false, *26*
Leather, real: accessories of, *60-61, 70-71, 84-85;* adjusting patterns for, *32-37;* antiqued, 30, *31;* belt of, *60-61, 62-65;* buttonholes in, 54, *58;* cabretta, *14,* 72, 85; calculating yardage requirements for, 28; calfskin, *25;* centered zipper on, *54-55;* characteristics of, 22, *chart* 28-29, 42; cleaning, *chart* 28-29; clothing of, 21-22, *23;* collar, pointed, *51-52;* cowboys' use of, 22; cutting, *chart* 28-29, *42;* darts in, *50;* dampening, *75;* direction of maximum stretch of, 38, 72, 75; dyed, *12,* 20, *24-25;* flattening seam allowances on, *47;* frog, 10; gloves of, *70-83;* handbags of, *84-93;* heavy, *45,* 48, 52, 58; hem on, *53;* history of, 10, 21-22, 23; Indians' use of, 21, 22; inserting zipper in lapped seam of, 54, *57;* inspection of, *38;* interfacing for, 46; kid, 72; kidskin, *23, 60-61;* lambskin, *chart* 28-29, 85; lapped seam on, *48-49;* lapped zipper on, 54, *56-57;* lightweight, *45,* 48, 58; lining jacket of, *53;* marking, *chart* 28-29, 42, 45; medium-weight, 48; napa, 72; needles for, *chart* 28-29, 72; novel uses of, 10; pigskin, *25, chart* 28-29, 72; pioneers' use of, 21-22; placement of pattern pieces on, 38, *42;* plain seams on, *46;* pointed collar on, *51-52;* preparation of, *38-40;* pressing, *chart* 28-29; reinforcing weak spots in, *38;* seams for, *46, 48-49;* sewing, *chart* 28-29, *46;* skirt of, *14;* skiving, *46;* stretch of, direction of maximum, 38, 72, 75; stretching, for gloves, 72, *75,* 76, 77, 78; topstitched seams on, *48;* uses of, 10, 20-21, *chart* 28-29; wallaby, 10; Western fashions of, *23;* yardage requirements for, calculating, 28; zippers, inserting on, *54-57. See also* Adjustment(s) to pattern(s), for leather; Cowhide; Snakeskin; Suede